Eroticism

With contributions from distinguished scholars and clinicians who view human erotic desire from modern developmental, relational, societal, and cross-cultural perspectives, *Eroticism: Developmental, Cultural, and Clinical Realms* offers a multifaceted and up-to-date glimpse into what we find sexually attractive and why. While psychoanalysis has unshackled itself from the narrow confines of instinct theory to include ego psychology, object relations theory, self psychology, and the contemporary relational paradigm, such heuristic and clinical advance is sorely needed to further our grasp of human eroticism and love. Accommodation also needs to be made for the cultural changes that have occurred over the last five or six decades. These include the feminist corrective to the phallocentrism of 'classical' psychoanalysis, the new insights into human subjectivity and personality development provided by the gay and lesbian movement, the contemporary de-centering of the essentialist and binary gender formulations, and the post-colonial voices of the non-Western people. By providing theoretically anchored clinical guidelines, *Eroticism* provides not only an update on the early analytic understanding of human eroticism but advances clinical praxis as well.

Salman Akhtar is Professor of Psychiatry at Jefferson Medical College and a Training and Supervising Analyst at the Psychoanalytic Center of Philadelphia. He has 97 books to his credit and received the prestigious Sigourney Award in 2012.

Rajiv Gulati is Training and Supervising Psychoanalyst at the Psychoanalytic Association of New York, which is affiliated with NYU Langone Medical Center in New York.

This much-needed new volume edited by Salman Akhtar and Rajiv Gulati, brings freshness and vitality to the topic of embodied sexuality. The multitude of issues taken up within the book's developmental, cultural, and clinical sections broadens psychoanalytic discourse about the sexual, while the diversity of contributors helps open the discussion to all. One of the oldest topics in psychoanalysis is made new again just when we need it most.

Charles Fisher, MD, Training and Supervising Analyst,
San Francisco Center for Psychoanalysis

This exquisite collection of essays on the topic of eroticism, will fascinate, challenge, and indeed, mesmerize its readers. It gives us new insights into areas that have been explored before, and takes up, boldly, beautifully, and incisively, certain aspects of eroticism that have not been written about enough. Akhtar and Gulati have edited a masterpiece, the readers of which can look forward to a wonderful feast of learning about the erotic world in our minds.

Aisha Abbasi, MD, Training and Supervising
Analyst at the Michigan Psychoanalytic Institute

Eroticism

Developmental, Cultural, and Clinical Realms

Edited by
Salman Akhtar and Rajiv Gulati

Routledge
Taylor & Francis Group

LONDON AND NEW YORK

First published 2020
by Routledge
2 Park Square, Milton Park, Abingdon, Oxon OX14 4RN

and by Routledge
52 Vanderbilt Avenue, New York, NY 10017

Routledge is an imprint of the Taylor & Francis Group, an informa business

British Library Cataloguing-in-Publication Data
A catalogue record for this book is available from the British Library

Library of Congress Cataloging-in-Publication Data
A catalog record for this book has been requested

ISBN: 978-0-367-35516-6 (hbk)
ISBN: 978-0-367-35514-2 (pbk)
ISBN: 978-0-429-33190-9 (ebk)

Typeset in Times New Roman
by Apex CoVantage, LLC

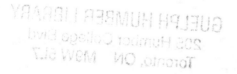

To
Muge Alkan SA
Sonia Pauley-Gulati RG

Contents

Acknowledgments

Twelve distinguished colleagues devoted much time and effort to writing original works for inclusion in this book and responded to our editorial suggestions with the utmost grace. One other colleague, namely Dr. Andrea Celenza, graciously permitted us to include a chapter from her fine book, *Erotic Revelations: Clinical Applications and Perverse Scenarios* (Routledge, 2014). Drs. Muge Alkan, Peter Hoffer, and Shelley Orgel, as well as David Pauley, helped us in subtle and not-so-subtle ways in the preparation of this book. Russell George and Elliott Morsia of Routledge Books, London, shepherded this project through various stages of publication. Jan Wright prepared the manuscript of this book with her characteristic diligence and good humor. To all the individuals mentioned here, our sincere thanks indeed.

About the editors and contributors

Salman Akhtar, MD, is Professor of Psychiatry at Jefferson Medical College and a Training and Supervising Analyst at the Psychoanalytic Center of Philadelphia. He has served on the editorial boards of the *International Journal of Psychoanalysis*, the *Journal of the American Psychoanalytic Association*, and the *Psychoanalytic Quarterly*. His more than 300 publications include 82 books, of which the following 18 are solo authored: *Broken Structures* (1992), *Quest for Answers (1995)*, *Inner Torment* (1999), *Immigration and Identity* (1999), *New Clinical Realms* (2003), *Objects of Our Desire* (2005), *Regarding Others* (2007), *Turning Points in Dynamic Psychotherapy* (2009), *The Damaged Core* (2009), *Comprehensive Dictionary of Psychoanalysis* (2009), *Immigration and Acculturation* (2011), *Matters of Life and Death* (2011), *The Book of Emotions* (2012), *Psychoanalytic Listening* (2013), *Good Stuff* (2013), *Sources of Suffering* (2014), *No Holds Barred* (2016), and *A Web of Sorrow* (2017). Dr. Akhtar has delivered many prestigious invited lectures, including a Plenary Address at the Second International Congress of the International Society for the Study of Personality Disorders in Oslo, Norway (1991), an Invited Plenary Paper at the Second International Margaret S. Mahler Symposium in Cologne, Germany (1993), an Invited Plenary Paper at the Rencontre Franco-Americaine de Psychanalyse meeting in Paris, France (1994), a Keynote Address at the 43rd IPA Congress in Rio de Janiero, Brazil (2005), the Plenary Address at the 150th Freud Birthday Celebration sponsored by the Dutch Psychoanalytic Society and the Embassy of Austria in Leiden, Holland (2006), and the Inaugural Address at the first IPA-Asia Congress in Beijing, China (2010). Dr. Akhtar is the recipient of numerous awards, including the American Psychoanalytic Association's Edith Sabshin Award (2000), Columbia University's Robert Liebert Award for Distinguished Contributions to Applied Psychoanalysis (2004), the American Psychiatric Association's Kun Po Soo Award (2004), and the Irma Bland Award for being the Outstanding Teacher of Psychiatric Residents in the country (2005). He received the highly prestigious Sigourney Award (2012) for distinguished contributions to psychoanalysis. In 2013, he gave the Commencement Address at graduation ceremonies of the Smith College School of Social Work in Northampton, Massachusetts. Dr. Akhtar's books have been translated into many languages, including German, Italian, Korean, Romanian, Serbian, Spanish, and Turkish. A true Renaissance man, Dr. Akhtar has served as the Film Review Editor for the *International Journal of Psychoanalysis*, and is currently serving as the Book Review Editor for the *International Journal of Applied Psychoanalytic Studies*. He has published nine collections of poetry and serves as a Scholar-in-Residence at the Inter-Act Theatre Company in Philadelphia.

Kathryn Baselice, MD, graduated from the University of Virginia School of Medicine in 2017. She received a Bachelor's degree in Psychology from The Johns Hopkins University in 2012, where she was elected to the Phi Beta Kappa Honor Society and chosen the captain of her cross-country team. While attending Johns Hopkins University, she interned for the forensic psychiatrist Dr. Fred Berlin and worked with sex offenders in Baltimore, Maryland. Between her university education and entering medical school, she worked as a mental health counselor at a program that specialized in patients with developmental disabilities and comorbid psychiatric diagnoses. Her academic interests include evolutionary psychology, postpartum psychosis, the insanity defense, and the broader field of forensic psychiatry. She is currently completing her Psychiatry residency at New York University, and plans to pursue a career in academic forensic psychiatry.

Rachel Boué-Widawsky, PhD, is a psychoanalyst in Advanced Training at the Institute of Psychoanalytic Training and Research, New York. She is the Associate Editor for Foreign Books Reviews in *Journal of the American Psychoanalytic Association*, in which she has written several reviews and articles on French psychoanalysis. She published a co-written article with Gail Reed in *André Green Revisited* (Routledge, 2018). She is a literary scholar in French literature and the author of books and articles on literary criticism, *La Sensation en quête de parole*, *L'éloquence du silence*, and *Etude de "Enfance" de Nathalie Sarraute*. As a Professor, she taught literature at Wesleyan University, Connecticut College, DePaul University, and at the University of Denis Diderot in Paris, where she earned her Doctorate under the direction of Julia Kristeva.

Andrea Celenza, PhD, is Assistant Clinical Professor at Harvard Medical School and Faculty at the Boston Psychoanalytic Society and Institute and Massachusetts Institute for Psychoanalysis. Dr. Celenza has consulted with, evaluated, supervised, or treated more than 100 cases of therapist–patient sexual boundary transgressions. She has authored and presented numerous papers on the evaluation and treatment of therapists who have engaged in sexual misconduct, with a focus on training and supervisory issues. She has published extensively, and has authored two books, namely, *Sexual Boundary Violations: Therapeutic, Supervisory and Academic Contexts* (Jason Aronson, 2007) and *Erotic Revelations: Clinical Applications and Perverse Scenarios* (Routledge,

2014). Dr. Celenza has been the recipient of several awards, including the Karl A. Menninger Memorial Award, the Felix and Helena Deutsch Prize, and the Symonds Prize. She is in private practice in Lexington, Massachusetts.

Lorrie Chopra, MS, is a child, adolescent and adult analyst in private practice in Livonia, Michigan. She is Associate Faculty at the Michigan Psychoanalytic Institute, where she also is serving as the MPI Secretary and is an active member of several committees. Lorrie has been involved with Walnut Lake Developmental Kindergarten and Preschool, a psychoanalytic preschool for ten years, where she volunteers as a family consultant and mentor for new family consultants. She has presented clinical material in several two-day workshops at the American Psychoanalytic Association Spring meetings. She is the Clinical Director of the Mel Bornstein Clinic for Psychoanalysis and Psychotherapy (MBC), a non-profit clinic that is allied as a sister organization to the Michigan Psychoanalytic Institute (MPI). She is passionate about the clinics mission to provide excellent mental health care to all, which led her to create a scholarship program that provides grant to individuals who would not otherwise be able to afford treatment at the MBC.

Ethan Grumbach, PhD, is Training and Supervising Analyst at the New Center for Psychoanalysis where he teaches Gender and Sexuality and Infant Observation in the Tavistock Method. He is a member of NCP's Committee on Diversities and Sociocultural Issues. Dr. Grumbach is the past chair and a current member of the American Psychoanalytic Association's Committee on Gender and Sexuality. He is a founding member and Director of the THRIVE Infant Family Program. He has a private practice in Los Angeles, where he sees adults, infants, and families in psychoanalysis and psychotherapy. Dr. Grumbach has presented nationally and internationally on Gender and Sexuality as well as Infant Psychoanalysis and Infant Observation.

Rajiv Gulati, MD, is Training and Supervising Psychoanalyst at the Institute of Psychoanalytic Education affiliated with the NYU Medical Center where he taught courses on Human Sexuality and Unconscious Phantasy. A native of New Delhi, he has a strong interest in the ways in which culture inflects the experience of selfhood, cropping up as well in the normative discourses that seek to police gender identity and sexual orientation. Dr. Gulati maintains a private analytic practice in Brooklyn, New York.

Susan McNamara, MD, is an analyst and the past co-chair of the American Psychoanalytic Association's Committee on Gender and Sexuality and of the Committee on Advocacy Relations. She serves on the editorial board of *Psychoanalytic Inquiry*, and has received the Ralph Roughton Paper Award of the American Psychoanalytic Association. Dr. McNamara is a psychiatrist at Connecticut Valley Hospital and an Assistant Clinical Professor in the Department of Psychiatry at the University of Connecticut, School of Medicine.

David Pauley, LCSW, is Training and Supervising Psychoanalyst and member of the faculty at the Psychoanalytic Psychotherapy Study Center He holds an MA in French Studies and an MSW from New York University, and completed training in psychoanalytic psychotherapy and psychoanalysis, respectively, at PPSC and Mid-Manhattan Institute for Psychoanalysis. His recent paper, "The Negative Transitional Object: Theoretical Elaboration and Clinical Illustration", is slated for publication in a 2018 issue of *Psychoanalytic Dialogues.* His clinical writing has also appeared in the *Journal of Gay and Lesbian Psychotherapy*, *Annals of Modern Psychoanalysis*, and the *Journal of College Student Psychotherapy*. He maintains a private practice in Brooklyn where he works with adults, teenagers, children, couples, and groups.

Louis Rothschild, PhD, is a clinical psychologist in Providence, Rhode Island. Dr. Rothschild moved to New England for a fellowship at Brown University, where he focused on the relationship between personality and chronic depression after completing his PhD at the New School for Social Research, where he published on the relationship between essentialist beliefs and prejudice in regard to several social categories. He maintains a private practice specializing in psychoanalytic psychotherapy in addition to providing supervision, writing articles and book reviews, and occasionally reviewing manuscripts. His publications have ranged from quantitative to qualitative, social-cognitive to psychoanalysis, and clinical to philosophical. Presently, his scholarly focus is centered on rapprochement between fathers and sons, where he has penned book chapters in three edited volumes. He is a past-President of the Rhode Island local chapter of the Division 39 (for Psychoanalysis) of the American Psychological Association. Most recently, he served as a member of the steering committee for the 38th annual spring meeting of Division 39 which took place in New Orleans, his birthplace. There he was able to feature one of his paintings entitled "Ghosts and Guardians".

Pranav Shah, MD, is a practicing psychiatrist with Southern California Permanente Group, based in Orange County, California. He completed his medical school in India, and moved to New York to undergo his psychiatric training at the Albert Einstein College of Medicine. He has been involved with teaching of medical students, residents, and psychiatrists most of his life, and has been an Associate Professor at both UCLA and Einstein. At Kaiser Permanente, he has continued to teach Behavioral Health. He has also practiced and taught mindful meditation for the past eight years. Dr. Shah is also involved with the Film and Mind series at the New Center for Psychoanalysis in Santa Monica, and runs a movie club at his home, discussing movies through a psychoanalytic perspective. He is the author of several papers on diverse topics in psychiatry and psychotherapy.

R. Dennis Shelby, MSW, PhD, is Training and Supervising Analyst at the Chicago Psychoanalytic Institute and Professor Emeritus of the Institute for

Clinical Social Work. He also maintains faculty affiliations with the Chengdu Si Chuan Institute of China and the HamAva Institute located in Tehran, Iran. Dennis has a long history of publications and interests in the areas of psychoanalysis with gay men, the psychological consequences of HIV, war-related trauma, and changing psychoanalytic views on sexuality and gender. He is currently deeply involved in international psychoanalytic education, and is currently studying how culture is negotiated in educational processes. Dennis is one of the winners of the 2019 Edith Sabshin Teaching Award.

J. Anderson Thomson Jr, MD, is a psychiatrist in Charlottesville, Virginia. He received his BA from Duke University (1970), his MD from the University of Virginia (1974), and did his adult psychiatry training at University of Virginia (1974–1977). His private practice is oriented towards individual psychoanalytic psychotherapy, forensic psychiatry, and medication consultation. He was the Assistant Director of the Center for the Study of Mind and Human Interaction at University of Virginia, which involved interdisciplinary intervention and research in large group ethnic and political conflict, primarily in the former Soviet Union. He is a staff psychiatrist at Counseling and Psychological Services at the University of Virginia Student Health Services. He serves on the clinical faculty at The Institute of Law, Psychiatry, and Public Policy at University of Virginia. He has publications on narcissistic personality disorder, evolutionary theories of depression, antidepressants, criminal behavior, the function of serotonin, post-traumatic stress disorder, religion, suicide terrorism, and the psychology of racism. In 2010, his work with Paul Andrews "Depression's Upside", on an evolutionary theory of depression was featured in *Scientific American Mind* and in *The New York Times Magazine*. He co-authored *Facing Bipolar: The Young Adult's Guide to Dealing with Bipolar Disorder* (2010) and authored *Why We Believe in God(s): A Concise Introduction to the Science of Faith* (2011), which has been translated into Spanish, German, Italian, Polish, Turkish, and Urdu. His current research interest is evolutionary psychology and its application to religious belief, well-being, resilience, suicide, the insanity defense, and psychiatric illnesses. Since 2006, he has had the privilege of serving as a trustee of the Richard Dawkins Foundation for Reason and Science.

Jason A. Wheeler Vega, PhD, is on the faculty of the Institute for Psychoanalytic Education affiliated with NYU School of Medicine. He currently teaches courses on theory and sexuality and gender. Besides his work on pornography, he has previously written about how to understand conflicting explanations of sexual violence. Most of his writing has combined psychoanalysis and modern philosophy, for example, developing systematic accounts of authority and interpretation in the analytic setting that draw upon the work of Donald Davidson. In addition, he has written psychoanalytic book, film, and theater reviews. He has also given presentations on midlife issues, hate speech, and integrating psychoanalytic therapy with dialectical behavior therapy (DBT).

Introduction

Among the various proposals made by Freud regarding the romantic and sexual life of human beings, the following four stand out:

- The process of their love object choice is biphasic. The first phase begins between the ages of two and five and is characterized by infantile sexual aims. This is brought to a halt by latency. Puberty then sets in the second phase which consists of a more explicitly sexual move towards the object (Freud, 1905a).
- There are "two currents whose union is necessary to ensure a completely normal attitude in love. . . . These two may be distinguished as the *affectionate* and the *sensual* currents" (Freud, 1912b, p. 180, italics in the original). The affectionate current is ontogenetically earlier and arises in connection with early maternal care. The sensual current represents a synthesis of infantile sexual aims during puberty; it is responsible for adult sexual passion.
- A distinction also exists between narcissistic (arising from the ego's self-affirming needs) and anaclitic (arising from the ego's desire for the object's help-giving qualities) forms of love (Freud, 1914).
- A synthesis of libidinal and aggressive aims is necessary for true love. In fact, "nature, by making use of this pair of opposites, continues to keep love ever vigilant and fresh" (Freud, 1915d, p. 299).

While these four notions are largely held valid and have been elaborated upon in the psychoanalytic literature since Freud's death in 1939, it is our sense that the second proposal (namely, that of 'affectionate' and 'sensual' currents) has remained least explored and updated. To be sure, it has been noted that the 'affectionate current' consists of concern, empathy, tenderness, optimal distance, and mutual playfulness (Akhtar, 2009) and the 'sensual current' consists of longing for physical closeness with another person, identification with the sexual excitement of the partner, overcoming of shame, desire for loss of boundaries, wish for erotic teasing and being teased, and an oscillation between privacy and exclusivity on the one hand, and a radical shifting away from sexual intimacy and return to conventionality on the other (Kernberg, 1991).

These newer proposals do transcend the confines of instinct theory to include object relations but do not go far enough. What is needed in furthering our grasp of human eroticism and love is a far more extensive approach that brings together the drastic theoretical, clinical, and cultural changes that have occurred over the last five or six decades. Here we have in mind the feminist corrective to phallocentrism of 'classical' psychoanalysis, the new insights into human subjectivity and personality development provided by the gay and lesbian movement, the contemporary de-centering of the essentialist and binary gender formulations, and the post-colonial voices of the non-Western people.

It is this agenda that our book strives to fulfill. With contributions from distinguished scholars and clinicians who view human erotic desire from the modern developmental, relational, societal, and cross-cultural vantage points, it offers a multifaceted and up-to-date glimpse into what we find sexually attractive and why. The end-point of this discourse is clinical which aims to deepen our empathy with our patients' sexual anxieties and pleasures, sharpen our understanding of their erotic dreams and transferences, and help us be in touch with (and manage) our own erotic resonance to such scenarios. By providing theoretically anchored clinical guidelines, our book becomes not only an update on the early analytic understanding of human eroticism but an advance of our clinical praxis as well.

Part I

Developmental realm

Chapter 1

Eroticism from an evolutionary perspective

Kathryn Baselice and J. Anderson Thomson

Men and women are at war. It is a silent war, often fought over dinner dates and between bedroom sheets. It is a war that is written into the fabric of our beings, right down to our DNA. It is a war that sees its participants use subtle deceit, both of self and others. Without this war, humans would cease to exist. The war is one of reproduction and relationships, the balance of which ensures the short-term survival of one's offspring and self, and the long-term survival of one's genes. And, the players of this war often do not understand the ends to which they strive. Our aim is to enlighten. But to understand this war, and the often-hidden motives of each side, we must first explore evolutionary theory and what has sculpted the differences in what men and women found to be erotic for millions of years.

Evolutionary psychology

We begin our discussion of evolutionary theory by quoting something Freud (1914) said over one hundred years ago.

> The individual does actually carry on a twofold existence: one to service his own purposes and the other as a link in a chain, which he serves against his will, or at least involuntarily. The individual himself regards sexuality as one of his own ends; whereas from another point of view he is an appendage to his germplasm, at whose disposal he puts his energies in return for a bonus of pleasure. He is the mortal vehicle of a (possibly) immortal substance – like the inheritor of an entailed property, who is only the temporary holder of an estate which survives him.
>
> (p. 78)

Evolutionary psychology is the natural progression from Darwin's (1859) evolutionary theory, originally published in his seminal work, *Origin of the Species*. Though Darwin did not have the benefit of a full understanding of DNA and genetic material, the idea behind the theory has stood the test of time. It has ensnared many of the fields of scientific pursuit and caught the eye of the father of modern mental health himself, Sigmund Freud. In 1914, Freud came close to articulating what is now known as the 'Modern Darwinian Synthesis', reflected in the quote above.

A brief overview of evolutionary theory is necessary to lay out the arguments in our main text. It is thus: traits are passed on from generation to generation. If an individual with that trait is better able to survive an environment and to reproduce, he or she is more likely to have offspring who will possess the same characteristics that allowed that individual to survive and reproduce. On and on these traits will pass, with the possessing progeny propagating the traits further. The better these traits, the more offspring will be had, and the more these traits will spread through a given species or population. These traits will be 'selected for', as those lineages that possess the least beneficial traits will ultimately die off. After millions of copies, with subtle changes throughout a species' history, these traits will be commonly found throughout that species.

Though we owe our modern evolutionary theory to Darwin, our current understanding of evolution did not occur until the genesis of the 'Modern Darwinian Synthesis' in the mid-twentieth century. By combining the basic principles of *Origin of the Species* with Mendel's theory of genetics, scientists finally understood that while traits (or phenotypes) appeared to be passed down, these traits were ultimately passed at the level of the gene. Those with genes that produced the most attractive faces, the strongest bodies, and the most socially adept individuals, were more likely to be passed on. And these genes combined to form many traits and phenotypes that trended towards the most useful in a given environment.

As we move forward, it may be easiest to think of genes and the people who possess them as having a 'goal', and that goal is to have the most copies made of themselves. Though genes, traits, and the organisms that possess them have no conscious awareness of such goals, that genes (and their resulting traits) are the driving force behind reproductive success often makes it seem as though traits/genes/organisms are in competition with one another. And the prize in these endless cycles of competition is representation throughout a given species.

The modern human is a relative latecomer to a long list, twenty-six to be exact, of hominid species who split from our common ancestor, which we shared with bonobos and chimpanzees, 5 to 7 million years ago. Imagine a twenty-four-hour day in which each hour represents 100,000 years. At midnight, our genus, *Homo*, appears in Africa. At dawn, some leave Africa for the first time. Around lunch time, some have made it into what is modern-day Europe. At dinnertime, our common ancestor with Neanderthals, *Homo heidelbergensis*, emerges in Africa. Some of them leave Africa, and by 9 p.m. have evolved into Neanderthals and the Denisovans in Europe and the northern latitudes of Asia. By 9 p.m. in Africa, 300,000 years ago, modern *Homo sapiens* appears. It is not until about 11:20 p.m., 70,000 years ago, that we fully modern *Homo sapiens* show up, and some leave Africa. Evidence suggests that around the time that our ancestors separated from the last common ancestor, the rainforests that they had once called home began to disappear (Walter, 2013). As humans made their way to the plains of Africa, they formed small coalitions that afforded survival benefits.

Imagine the world of early humans as a lifelong camping trip, with limited resources and an unending concern for safety (Cosmides and Tooby, 1992). This is our environment of evolutionary adaptedness, or EEA (Bowlby, 1969). Bowlby states that, "the only relevant criterion by which to consider the natural adaptation of any particular part of present-day man's behavioral equipment is the degree to which and the way in which it might contribute to population survival in man's primeval environment" (p. 59). As Cosmides and Tooby (2013) point out, the behaviors, cognition, and emotions that made sense in our EEA often fail to fit well with our ever-changing modern environment.

For all that time, our ancestors lived in hunter-gatherer societies. These were societies that survived by hunting game and gathering edible plants. The basic characteristics of these societies were few. The primary institution was the family, which decided how food was shared, how children were socialized, and how members were protected. The groups were small, usually only fifty or fewer people. The typical hunter-gatherer society was nomadic. They moved to follow food supplies. There was high, necessary mutual interdependence. There was a division of labor. Men hunt. Women gather and provide primary childcare.

What is clear even in the eyes of modern biology is that men and women are fundamentally different, and these differences created a divergence in the traits that would be adaptive for each gender. As such, sexuality in men and women is best understood by examining the traits that would give the most reproductive benefit to each gender. The eminent anthropologist Symons (1979) says it best:

> Men and women differ in their sexual natures because throughout the immensely long hunting and gathering phase of human evolutionary history the sexual desires and dispositions that were adaptive for either sex were for the other tickets to reproductive oblivion.
>
> (p. 2)

Erotic relationships through the lens of evolution

A core concept required to understand the fundamental difference between men and women and male and female sexuality is parental investment. This concept was first described by Trivers in 1972. He defines parental investment as "any investment by the parent in an individual offspring that increases the offspring's chance of surviving (and hence reproductive success) at the cost of the parent's ability to invest in other offspring" (p. 55). This includes both the metabolic and physical cost of producing that offspring and rearing it, as well as the cost incurred by time, protection, and resources invested in that offspring. Thus, the parent with the greater parental investment is one that invests much in a single offspring. Trivers notes that, in any species, the sex with the greater parental investment will be the limiting resource of reproduction, as their investment is time and metabolically intensive.

This was a crucial insight of Trivers. Sexual behavior is determined by parental investment, not the sex of the individual. In those few species in which the male has the greater parental investment, the difference in behavior holds true. In those species, the male is smaller than the female and choosier about with whom he mates. In these species, the females are larger and compete fiercely with one another for access to the male, the sex with the greatest parental investment.

When considering the human reproductive cycle, it should be obvious that women offer more parental investment than men. The woman must produce a nutrient-rich egg, build an expensive placenta, gestate the fetus for nine months, endure the hazards of childbirth, and burn countless calories to produce milk and breastfeed a child after birth. Even though modern women may choose not to breastfeed, the basic minimal physiologic investment is massive. Men's baseline physiologic contribution is sperm and about two and half minutes of sexual activity. This creates a massive mismatch in the number of offspring available to either a man or a woman.

Men are therefore capable of bringing more offspring into the world than women. Those women who carefully selected mates who possessed good genes and could provide valuable resources to her and her offspring would have had more children that made it to adulthood. The genes for careful selection, therefore, would have propagated. As we will see, this has led to an incredibly nuanced evaluation pattern in women, which allowed for complex levels of arousal.

Men who copulated with as many fertile women as they could find had more offspring. As we see with the male interest in pornography, the biological drive towards partner novelty and a quantitative approach is still present in the male brain. However, though this may be a strong biological drive for men, the modern family unit is reflective of other pressures in our evolutionary past, the root of which we find in our environment of evolutionary adaptedness.

Hominid communities were small, and parents and offspring often had contact with one another (Draper and Harpending, 1988). This environment was harsh and afforded little food other than mothers' milk. Babies nursed until the fourth year of life. With children in constant contact, their cries were often heard and tended to by parents. Failure to do so would mean a parent had to give up their reproductive fitness, as surrogates were not readily available (Draper and Harpending, 1988). This explanation only goes so far as to explain a mother's role in childrearing, as men are unable to produce milk to sustain an infant. So, what possible explanation can there be for a father's role?

Gathering food was a primary means of food source for the clan, and women more so than men were the primary gatherers. While women were foraging, men spent a significant amount of time watching the children (Miller and Fishkin, 1997). With the dawn of bipedalism, humans were forced to carry infants in their arms, which prevented parents from having full use of their hands. The move to the open savannah afforded hominids less protection from predators than they had enjoyed while in the forests and trees. A more proactive role by the father for both aid to the mother and protection of both the mother and the couple's offspring would have been beneficial to the father in maintaining both current and future reproductive fitness (Fisher, 1989). With women being a limiting factor in mating, longer pair bonds and male caregiving behavior were favored as fewer willing and available women meant fewer opportunities to reproduce. Fathers who invested in their offspring's protection and care were more likely to see their offspring survive to adulthood in the harsh environment that shaped these adaptations (Miller and Fishkin, 1997).

The push towards monogamy can be seen in one survey of 853 societies. While 84 percent permitted polygyny, and 44 percent of those cultures viewed it as the preferred form of marriage, only 10 percent of the men in those societies practiced polygyny (Fisher, 1989). The results of that survey speak both to the evolutionary drive towards co-parenthood as well as the strength of the female reproductive strategy to find an optimal mate and stay with her.

The importance of reproductive optimization can be seen in trends in modern US divorce rates (Fisher, 1989). Eighty-two percent of women who get divorced are under the age of forty-five, within their reproductive years. Divorce occurs more often when there are no children, less so when there is one child, and infrequently when there are more than two children. Probably the most striking trend is that the duration of a marriage that ends in divorce has a mean of four years, which, as we noted previously, is around the average time that it took to wean a child in our EEA (Fisher, 1989). This data suggest that even though modern society has childcare available outside the immediate family circle, relatively more resources, and less overt predation, the mechanism by which we remain bonded with someone depends on whether we can have future offspring and whether there are current offspring to rear, the evolutionary mechanisms that became engrained in our DNA through our EEA.

As highlighted above, there are vast differences in the basic reproductive strategies that would benefit men and women the most. And, with the balancing act of these diverging reproductive strategies, coupled with our harsh EEA, we see a consistent drive across the globe to pair bond and have a family unit. However, underneath the familiar façade of the nuclear family remains the conflict of maximizing reproductive potential. Since the mating strategies that would have maximized reproductive success for men and women are so different, this will lead them to be preferentially attracted to different attributes of their partners, as these attributes would have provided the greatest reproductive benefit in our EEA. The directions of these preferences fit with what we know about the reproductive costs garnered by each sex.

In our modern world of technology, the differences between men and women regarding mate selection and romance may best be identified in their use of dating applications. In their study of the dating application Tindr, Tyson et al. (2016) found that men indiscriminately selected women regardless of their intention to message them should a match occur. Men received more matches if they included a short biography about themselves, presumably as this would provide women with more clues as to their quality as a partner, information not as easily garnered from a photograph. The differences extended in how they used these applications – women preferred to seek out dates and relationships, men preferred one-night stands (Tyson et al., 2016).

As men require less investment in order to produce an offspring, it would stand to reason that their ideal partners would have the most to offer in terms of reproductive capacity. Women who are fertile and young would offer the most reproductive benefit as a potential mate.

Age is the strongest indicator of the reproductive potential offered by a woman. Across thirty-three countries, men were observed to prefer mates that were younger than themselves (Buss, 1989). Across cultures, men prefer neotenous features of big eyes and a relatively small nose, which are features indicative of youth and nulliparity (Cunningham, Druen, and Barbee, 1997). Women who had larger breasts and were slender with low waist-to-hip ratio were perceived as younger and more attractive, and more desirable for short- and long-term relationships; women who were heavier and had larger hips were considered less attractive and older (Singh and Young, 1995). Youthful and fertile partners, both in appearance and in age, are highly valued by men. This is reflected in literature assessing the habits of online dating: men tend to seek out women who are younger than themselves (Abramova et al., 2016).

However, there is a floor effect to this. In a study examining teenage male preferences for mate ages, teenage males were found to prefer females that were a few years older than they were. As men get older, their preference for younger women was found to increase (Buss, 2004). It turns out that it is not youthfulness itself that is attractive, but rather reproductive ability. Women, unlike men, cannot reproduce throughout most of their adult lives. Starting around age fifty, women will go through menopause, which renders them infertile and unable to bare any more children. To improve his reproductive success, a man should be inclined to mate with women who are within their optimal reproductive window. This implies not just younger than menopause, but older than menarche. This explains why teenage males prefer to date women who are slightly older, and therefore in their reproductive prime. As a man ages, and youth becomes more desirable, visual cues of youthful appearance are used to try to spot women who are still able to reproduce (Feingold, 1992).

As physical attractiveness is correlated with youth, it would stand to reason that men place a higher premium on physical attractiveness than do their female counterparts; this is borne out in the literature (Buss, 1989; Feingold, 1992). This is also reflected in online dating; men more often specify preferred partner body type and rate physical attractiveness as a key deciding factor for pursuing a date more often than women (Abramova et al., 2016). This was also seen in a 'speed dating' paradigm, where it was found that, irrespective of whether males preferred a short-term encounter or a long-term relationship, the premium on physical attractiveness did not waiver (Li et al., 2013).

The importance of physical appearance is reflected in the amount of time it takes either sex to get ready each morning. Women are more likely to alter their appearance by wearing makeup, jewelry, and stylish clothes in an effort to attract mates (Buss, 1988). One needs only ask siblings who share the bathroom with a young female of dating age to appreciate the many hours that go into preparing for an outing (and the frustrations for those who need to use the toilet).

What should be most striking in the factors perceived as most important in a man's attraction to a woman is that these cues are mostly visual. This will be important to keep in mind in our later sections as we transition to the erotica that men pursue.

Irwin Shaw's (1939) classic *New Yorker* short story, "The Girls in Their Summer Dresses", which is easily accessible online, is the most concise and evocative elucidation of the differences between men's and women's sexuality and men's focus on visual cues. We urge the reader to pause, find it, and read it.

Women's wish list for an ideal partner is understandably more complex. The most important thing to consider is that women, being the sex with the greater parental investment, must be choosier when it comes to the partners they bed. The choice centers on finding a partner who not only will stick around to protect the woman and her children, but has the capability, skills, and strength to obtain resources for his family, both social and material. Unfortunately, the cues reflecting these traits are not as objectively appreciated on the surface, as women's physique and youth are for men. In hunter-gatherer societies, if a man died at the hands of another man, in the pursuit of game, or as a result of disease or injury, his children's survival chances dropped. All women on the planet today descend from an unbroken chain of successful mothers who raised children with immeasurable help from effective fathers.

One needs only glance at the not-so-attractive appearance of many rich and powerful men compared to that of their attractive wives to appreciate that women place less of a premium on appearance than men. There is one important caveat to this: women do prefer males who are symmetrical (Thornhill and Gangestad, 1994). Symmetry is a measure of good genes and the resilience to developmental hits and illnesses the male has endured up to that time.

Women not only prefer partners who have good genes but also can access resources and are willing to share those resources with her and her offspring. This is supported by a meta-analysis of gender differences in dating preferences, as women were found to value good socioeconomic status, ambitiousness, character, and intelligence more than men (Feingold, 1992). Across a varied cultural sample, women were consistently found to have a stronger preference for ambition and 'good financial prospects' (Buss, 1989). This preference is best reflected in the signals that men use to attract their mates. Men are more likely to boast about accomplishments and future earning potential, to display athletic abilities, and to show off possessions, which are a demonstration of his resources and potential for material acquisition.

Across the animal kingdom, as in humans, there is a strong female preference for a dominant mate (Trivers, 1971; Sadalla, Kenrick, and Vershure, 1987). However, women desire a 'tender defender'. A partner who is kind and attentive to her, fiercely protective of her, and is competitive, dominant, cooperative, and if need be, violent with other men (Max and Miller, 2016).

While male dominance is related to dating desirability, prosocial behaviors and agreeableness were more important factors in attractiveness of men (Jensen-Campbell, Graziano, and West, 1995). While dominance failed to increase attractiveness of someone who was rated to be low on agreeableness, in men who were rated high on agreeableness, dominance increases their ratings on subjective physical and sexual attractiveness, dating and general social desirability, and perceived wealth later in life (Jensen-Campbell, Graziano, and West, 1995). This suggests that, rather than lose our evolutionary desire for dominance, humans evolved a desire for social cooperativeness that reflects the importance of social living. This cooperativeness would allow a man access and support from other members of the community to obtain social resources.

Male altruism and cooperation that is perceived by women to be intrinsically motivated is preferred to extrinsically motivated altruism and cooperation. Women evolved to perceive this intrinsic motivation as a potential indicator of a male's willingness to share his resources with his potential mate and offspring (Graziano et al., 1997). Thus, prosocial and cooperative behaviors, dominance, and an intrinsic willingness to share are important factors in female preference. When looking at factors that were predictive of how often women initiated sex with their male partners, correlations were found for partner determination, focus, sense of humor, motivation, and intelligence (Gallup et al., 2014).

Now that we have defined what men and women want in a partner, we turn our attention to the phenomenon of arousal, and the differences in experience of that arousal between men and women.

The nature of arousal and orgasm in men

Male heterosexual eroticism

Men, on average, report a higher sex drive than women (Lippa, 2006); this is true across cultures and does not appear to be moderated by a country's gender equality and economic development (Lippa, 2009). And though it is not as frequent as 'every seven seconds' as is often reported, men do spend more time thinking about sex than women (though it should be noted that they spent more time thinking about other physiological needs such as sleep and food as well; Fisher, Moore, Pittenger, 2012).

Further, men's sex drive appears to be more focused than women. Men have a more category-specific response to erotica, meaning that both heterosexual and homosexual men are more likely to respond to stimuli featuring their preferred gender partner than their female counterparts (Chivers et al., 2004). There is also greater concordance between genital and subjective arousal in men than in their female counterparts (Chivers et al., 2010; Chivers, Seto, and Blanchard, 2007). All things considered, men demonstrate a more focused sexual response than their female counterparts, and this response serves them well evolutionarily.

Through its depictions in popular media and culture, it is well known that men are more easily sexually aroused than their female counterparts. Ogas and Gaddam (2011) liken this response to 'Elmer Fudd', noting that men, like Elmer's Fudd and his rabbits, will act fast and sometimes foolishly when they spot a potential mate (a man, much like Mr. Fudd, always seems to be able to reload his 'gun'). Fleischman (2016) likens it to the 'Smoke Detector Principle' – it is better for a smoke detector to go off inappropriately than to miss a potential fire. Both these examples highlight the most important difference between men and women – men have a seemingly never-ending supply of sperm that are not costly to make, which provide abundant chances for reproductive success. For men, it is costlier to miss a reproductive opportunity than to 'miss-fire' on one.

In their paper on the evolution of orgasm, Gallup, Towne, and Stolz, 2018 posit that sexual pleasure evolved to ensure that species with low reproductive rates (but multiple reproductive cycles throughout a lifetime) engaged in sexual acts at a high frequency. This would have improved reproductive rates by giving a species more chances to achieve conception. As insemination must be coupled with ovulation, it would benefit a male to both have many reproductive partners and to have sex frequently to improve reproductive success (Gallup, Towne, and Stolz, 2018). Men who would have been most reinforced by orgasm would have sought out more sexual encounters, and would have gained the reproductive rewards thereafter.

Evidence suggests that female sexual pleasure arouses men (Ogas and Gaddam, 2011). This arousal and its reinforcing effects hint at a reproductive advantage for men when ensuring a female partner's orgasms. There is evidence that the female orgasm may have reproductive consequences, promoting sperm motility towards the egg and creating a more hospitable environment for sperm on their journey through the female reproductive tract (Gallup et al., 2018). Females who were sexually satisfied by male partners were more likely to not only stay with them, but to copulate repeatedly with them (Ogas and Gaddam, 2011). As noted, more copulation meant more chance of reproductive success. On the other hand, this was a sign of fidelity: "the male cue for female sexual pleasure is entirely analogous to the female cue for a man's emotional commitment" (Ogas and Gaddam, 2011, Chapter 9, "She's Gotta Have It", Paragraph 15). A male who therefore possessed traits to be psychologically rewarded, and even aroused, by female orgasm would have had much to benefit, both in terms of reproductive success and in fidelity of the partner. It is no wonder that male pornography focuses closely on dramatic displays of female orgasm and why such heated debates are raised about their veracity (Ogas and Gaddam 2011).

Male homosexual eroticism

The differences between male and female evolved reproductive strategies might best be highlighted by studying homosexual men. The innate choices highlighted previously in heterosexual men are found similarly in their homosexual counterparts. The desire for youth and physical attraction is at the forefront of casual sexual encounters among gay men (Symons, 1979). Indeed, in the domains of 'interest in uncommitted sex', 'interest in visual sexual stimuli', and 'unimportance of partner status', homosexual and heterosexual men responded quite similarly (Bailey et al., 1994). Further, in one sample, gay men tend to have more partners then their lesbian counterparts, who were found to engage in less cruising behavior or casual sex (Bell and Weinberg, 1978).

Homosexual men reported higher number of lifetime partners, were found to have greater rates of sexual concurrency, initiated sexual activity at a younger age, and formed new sexual partnerships later in life than heterosexual males or females (Glick et al., 2012). As predicted by Salmon and Symons (2003), gay men will have more sex with strangers and more sexual partners than straight men or women. This is reflected by the phone app Grindr, a platform that allows for gay men to seek out sexual encounters. If a heterosexual man proposed such an app to a woman, he would likely get slapped.

Why is casual sex more prominent among homosexual men? It may be that they are not forced to navigate innate female reproductive strategies in their partners. The reproductive strategies of woman are the proverbial 'pumping of the brakes' in a potential sexual encounter, as women tend to seek long-term and committed partners due to differences in parental investment. In essence, male homosexuals demonstrate the universal male sexual drive, unconstrained by women (Symons, 1979). This is supported by research. Although homosexual men pursued casual sexual relationships more frequently, heterosexual and homosexual men demonstrated an equally strong desire to do so (Bailey et al., 1994).

Pornography

Pornography holds a unique place in American culture. It is the contraband hidden under many teenage boys' mattresses. It is stacks of magazines found in boxes abandoned in homes of aloof elderly men. It is the content of Internet searches accessed in darkened rooms. It hides in plain sight, in subtle and culturally acceptable ways on ads and billboards, and in the butt of jokes throughout film and television. It is the worst kept secret of the media world. And it provides both a reflective cue of the evolved desires of men and gives us a hint of what happens when these desires are over-stimulated in our modern technological world.

It should not surprise the astute reader, given our discussion of the importance of objective visual cues in female mate selection, that men attune more strongly to visual cues (Bailey et al., 1994) and by and large consume more visual pornography than women (Morgan, 2011; Ogas and Gaddam, 2011; Anisimowicz and O'Sullivan, 2017). Men rely on these visual cues to seek women who are youthful, fertile, and healthy, as these are the women that will produce the most children. And the cues provided by visual pornography to its male viewers are like flames for a moth.

In their study of Internet pornography search histories (accounting for 2 million people across the globe), Ogas and Gaddam (2011) found that, by and large, what was searched for matched fairly consistently with what would be expected based on evolutionary theory. Unsurprisingly, 'youth' and 'teen' were the most often used age specifiers, as youth signifies both health and reproductive potential.[1] Men preferred overweight females to thin ones, and the authors note that this may be because overweight females have larger hips, which may give the illusion of lower waist-to-hip ratio, indicative of female health and fertility (Singh, 1993, Singh and Young, 1995; Furnham, Swami, and Shah, 2006; however see Voracek and Fisher, 2002, 2006). Ogas and Gaddam (2011) also note a strong tendency for men to view anime pornography, which was the most searched for type of erotic art across many industrialized nations. This art beautifully captures what men subconsciously seek in a mate – young, high-pitched voices, babylike eyes, sexually inexperienced, large breasts, small feet, and a low waist-to-hip ratio. It is a tinted window into the pressures of our evolutionary past, colored slightly by the imagination and possibility of the mass media market.

It is not just the content of the pornography that draws men to it but the novelty that it provides. In our evolutionary past, the man who could bed the most women would undoubtedly have the most reproductive success. Though this preference for more partners lays dormant in all men, it is quelled by other factors such as female availability and adaptive pressures by females who are seeking committed mates. There remains, however, evidence for the importance of novelty in male reproductive satisfaction. One study demonstrated that men ejaculate faster, have larger ejaculate volume, and have ejaculate that contains more motile sperm when exposed to a novel woman compared to one that the man had been habituated to (Joseph et al., 2015). As suggested by the authors, these findings are consistent with what would be expected in our evolutionary past with extra-pair copulation partners. The short time to ejaculate would have benefited a male by providing less risk of being caught. The increased number of motile sperm would have benefited the male to help him outcompete his rivals. Introduction of novel stimuli was also found to increase physiological and subjective arousal as well as absorption in the erotic material (Koukounas and Over, 1993). Men were rewarded in our evolutionary history for seeking out novelty and performing when it is present. Pornography provides this novelty in spades.

In many ways, pornography is like candy, and men are like the children who desperately seek it out. Candy hijacks our drive to seek out sweet and brightly colored fruits and briefly satisfies our needs for the carbohydrates that fuel us, firing up our reward system and making us crave it more. The cheap and over-abundant nature of candy and other junk food has led to an epidemic of obesity and diabetes, the etiology of which cannot be understood without knowledge of our evolutionary past.

In the same way, pornography is equally abundant, and equally artificial. With our increasingly digital world, pornographic material becomes easier to access.

Male desires and dispositions drive the production and consumption of pornography, not obscured by the leveling hand of women's preferences. The subjects of the pornographic media seem eager for intercourse, and do not demand the commitment and resources that a relationship would, making them ideal short-term mates. Most important, the Internet allows for an excess of novelty, a world filled with seemingly limitless available and fertile women just a click away. And as many pornographic 'sexual encounters' end in ejaculation for the viewer, the brain is tricked into the assumption that copulation and potential reproduction has been successful.

What might be the effect of such untethered access? Some research suggests that there may be consequences for relationships. One study found that the more men consume erotic material, the more likely they are to be unhappy in their long-term relationships (Morgan, 2011). Further, use of sexually explicit material was found to lead to lower scores of intimacy, commitment, and relationship satisfaction; this effect was greater for higher-frequency users (Minarcik, Wetterneck, and Short, 2016). Increased frequencies of pornography consumption were associated with decreased ratings on decision-making as a couple, sex life for couples, and marital quality; this effect was seen for male consumption of pornography but not for women (Perry, 2017). Male pornography use was associated with lower relationship stability and satisfaction and more relationship aggression; this effect was not seen for female pornography use (Willoughby et al., 2016; although this study used multiple media types for 'pornography', including written word). Distress over partner pornography use also seemed to correlate with level of commitment, with married women reporting more distress than women who were merely dating their partners (Bridges, Bergner, and Hesson-Mcinnis, 2003).[2]

The female reaction of betrayal and anger after catching their partners watching pornography may be the best proof of this. As Ogas and Gaddam (2011) point out, this reflects 'mate-guarding' that is part of a female's evolutionary software. Insult to injury may be added if the male is spending an exuberant amount of time and money on pornography, resources that would have been otherwise spent on his mate. This is supported by the fact that mutual use of pornography among couples was also associated with less distress reported by female partner (Resch and Alderson, 2014). Given the relatively recent advent of the Internet and the seemingly endless supply of pornography available, we still have a long way to go before we can understand the long-term effects it may have, if any, on romantic relationships.

The nature of arousal and orgasm in females

In synchrony with the way we approached the nature of arousal and orgasm in males, we divide our comments here into three subsections: (1) female heterosexual eroticism, (2) female homosexual eroticism, and (3) female preference for romance novels.

Female heterosexual eroticism

Arousal in women is a complicated picture, and for good reason.

> A woman's reproductive success is jeopardized by anything that interferes with her ability: to conceive no children that cannot be raised; to choose the best available father for her children; to induce males to aid her and her children; to maximize the return on sexual favors she bestows; and to minimize the risk of violence or withdrawal of support by her husband and kinsmen.
>
> (Symons, 1979, p. 92)

Through hundreds of thousands of years of our evolutionary history, women have developed in such a way to maximize their reproductive potential. The challenges that women face, in many ways, are more difficult than those of men when it comes to reproduction. Unlike in males, where an ideal partner is one that can often be assessed through objective visual cues alone, women's evaluation must go well beyond skin-deep. How a man looks cannot reliably convey whether a man will be a good provider, partner, and father. Because of this, women have developed complicated, and often unconscious, arousal mechanisms.

Before we can answer what turns women on, we must first define arousal in women. Physiologic arousal, or genital response, consists of blood rushing to the erectile tissue of the female clitoris and to the walls of the vagina. This also includes a lubricating effect, preparing women for intercourse. Psychological arousal, on the other hand, is a subjective arousal, being 'turned on' emotionally and cognitively. As the literature points out, these are not necessarily the same thing.

Women have less concordance between their genital and subjective sexual arousal than their male counterparts (Chivers et al., 2007, 2010; Carvalho et al., 2013). A study looking at a population of women with and without sexual dysfunction similarly found no correlation between physiologic sexual response and subjective sexual arousal (Palace and Gorzalka, 1990). Vilarinho et al. (2014) found that none of the measures – thoughts of sexual arousal (which were correlated with subjective sexual arousal), negative thoughts, or affect in either direction appeared to account for variance of female genital response. This data suggests that the willingness of a female, particularly her body, to engage in an erotic encounter is not connected to the subjective desire to do so. It appears that evolution has worked a safety break into the female brains. Put another way:

> It's as if carnal signals from a woman's body somehow get cut off before they enter her conscious awareness. . . . This is a profound difference in the brain software of men and women. It explains why the pharmaceutical industry's quest for female Viagra kept running into dead ends. Stimulating the

vagina or the spine does not automatically fire up desire in the conscious mind. Instead, women need to feel psychologically aroused.

(Ogas and Gaddam, 2011, "The Mind-Body Problem",
paragraphs 9–10)

There is evidence that orgasm in females may serve a broader reproductive function than initially realized. Approaching from a behaviorist model, orgasm could facilitate reproductive success by reinforcing the behavior with genetically superior mates, thus increasing the incidents of intercourse and providing a better opportunity to conceive (Fleischman, 2016). In their review of the literature, Gallup, Towne and Stolz (2018) note that female orgasm frequency was correlated to traits that could be used as proxies for good genes, fertility, and health in males, all signs of high reproductive value. In fact, the frequency with which females experienced orgasms with their sexual partner was related to partner family income, self-confidence, and humor, which are all indicators of an ability to navigate a social market and garner resources (Gallup et al., 2014).

When looking at the data for genital intercourse, which we consider here due to it being a potential reproductive event, there is a significant gender gap in the reports of orgasm between men and women in both casual sexual relationships and in committed ones, with men experiencing more orgasms than their female counterparts in both conditions. This gap narrows, however, in the case of romantic relationships (Ford and England, 2014; Armstrong, England and Fogarty, 2010). Women who were having intercourse outside of a romantic relationship were found to orgasm more if they were romantically interested in their partner. Women who were already in committed relationships were also more likely to orgasm if they felt that it was likely they would one day marry their partner (Armstrong, England and Forgarty, 2012).

Female homosexual eroticism

As we briefly touched upon male homosexuality in our previous discussion about male sexual arousal, readers may wonder if there are similar illuminating effects of evolutionary psychology when comparing sexual patterns and preferences between homosexual females and their heterosexual counterparts. In short, the nature of female homosexuality mirrors the complexity of female sexuality as a whole and affirms that our understanding of female sexuality is in its infancy.

One aspect of female sexuality that makes it so difficult to study is that it demonstrates great plasticity. Baumeister's review of the literature (2000) found that women more often change their sexual patterns (including partner preference and engagement in same-sex relationships) over the course of their lifetime, and that these patterns were more often influenced by environmental factors such as religion, education, politics, peer influence, and available resources than their male counterparts. This is echoed in a more recent study, which found that on a day-to-day basis, women were less stable in their attractions (to both men and women) than men (Diamond, Dickenson, and Blair, 2017). It is only recently that Satoshi (2017) attempted to understand female sexual fluidity from an evolutionary perspective.

Diamond (2005) argues for the exploration of alternative categories of sexual orientation, which takes into account the fluidity in sexuality that some experience over time. In her study, she notes differences in women who consistently identify as homosexual (stable lesbians), those who alternated between self-identifying as lesbian and non-lesbian (fluid lesbians), and those who never adopted the label of lesbian (non-lesbians) across domains such as physical/emotional attraction and sexual contacts (Diamond, 2005). These differences highlight the importance of recognizing the complications inherent in studying female sexuality as a whole, and female homosexuality in particular, since what it means to be a 'lesbian' may represent a different experience from one person to the next.

Even if one were to successfully categorize women based on sexual preferences, data suggests that there is great variation in response patterns to sexual stimuli. Chivers, Seto, and Blanchard (2007) found that homosexual females showed a category specific genital response to preferred genders engaging in masturbation and exercising, but their response was non-specific when it came to couples of either gender engaging in intercourse. Heterosexual women did not have a category-specific genital response to stimuli. When considering subjective sexual arousal in that study, however, heterosexual and homosexual women reported greater sexual arousal to female stimuli, and homosexual women reported some sexual response to male stimuli, further suggesting a lack of specificity in female responses (Chivers, Seto and Blanchard, 2007).

Homosexual women showed greater response in both subjective report and in ventral striatum activation for erotic pictures and video with female stimuli. The ventral striatum is an area that leads to motivation through reward incentives, including pursuit of sexual activity. Heterosexual and bisexual women appeared to be equally less preferential (Safron et al., 2018). However, in yet another study, women of either self-identified orientation, homosexual or heterosexual, were not found to have a category-specific response to their preferred stimuli either in genital response or subjective report (Peterson, Janssen, and Laan, 2010).

In testing sexual response in general, as noted earlier, women often do not have a strong correlation between their subjective sexual response and genital response to erotic stimuli. For example, in the Chivers et al. (2007) study noted above, correlations between subjective and genital responses were found to be .56 and .58 for heterosexual and homosexual women, respectively. This is lower than the concordance rates for males, which were found to be .82 (heterosexual men) and .85 (homosexual men). While Peterson, Janssen, and Laan (2010) did not find category-specific preference between heterosexual and homosexual female response to erotica, they demonstrated affective responses in a category-specific pattern. Heterosexual women reported more positive affect towards heterosexual erotica, whereas homosexual women reported more positive affect towards homosexual female erotica. And, homosexual women reported negative affect towards heterosexual erotica. This lack of concordance between genital, affective, and subjective response once again hints at the complexity of female eroticism, regardless of identified sexual orientation.

A further complication is that most of these studies used a visual medium as its erotic stimuli. As noted previously, men have a stronger preference for visual erotica than do women, and this preference needs to be considered when analyzing the results.

A careful reader will note the absence of evolutionary explanations of male and female homosexuality in the current treatment of the subject. This decision was deliberate, as the current authors feel that the subject deserves a more focused review and exploration. The brief discussions of homosexuality, though reductionist at times, were meant to affirm that homosexuality, like heterosexuality, deserves to be viewed through an evolutionary lens. As the field moves toward an understanding of sexual orientation as part of the biological fabric of an individual, one can see that the discovery of a distal evolutionary explanation can put the final punctuation on banishment of distasteful rhetoric and discrimination that has plagued the minority sexual communities. Such understanding is likely on the horizon. For a review of current evolutionary views of homosexuality see William Kremer, "The Evolutionary Puzzle of Homosexuality," *BBC Magazine*, 18 February 2014.

Female preference for romance novels

There is ample evidence (Morgan, 2011; Ogas and Gaddam, 2011; Anisimowicz, 2017) that women are not as excited about pornography as men are. In one study, women's reports of subjective arousal did not correlate with objective genital arousal when viewing sexually explicit material (Carvalho et al., 2013). Interestingly, women in that study reported more subjective sexual arousal than men. Perhaps less surprising is that the highest level of sexual arousal was reported when women viewed erotic films and were asked to fantasize about their partner, whom women had objective and longitudinal data on in terms of their partner's commitment and capacities to provide.

In light of this, it is hardly surprising that women seemed to prefer romance novels over explicit visual pornography. Indeed, between 2012 and 2015, a revolution seemed to have occurred. Women everywhere were picking up a romantic novel featuring erotic BDSM (a type of sexual practice involving bondage, dominance, submission, and masochistic practices) scenes. *Fifty Shades of Grey* (James, 2011) would ultimately boast sales of over 125 million copies and sit atop bestsellers lists everywhere. At the center of the narrative is a young, awkward female protagonist who meets a mysterious and powerful millionaire. The two begin a whirlwind romance. Despite initially proposing merely a sexual relationship, the man soon realizes that he cannot live without the protagonist, and he falls madly in love with her. Much of the story's plot focuses on his incessant need to protect the protagonist (even to the point of stalking her), providing her with a lavish lifestyle and all she could ever want, and reminding her, repeatedly, how much she means to him. Sprinkled throughout are erotic scenes of BDSM, the sexual charge of which seems all the more powerful as the man's love for the female protagonist grows. The book, and its two sequels, sparked intrigue among literary critics everywhere. People who focused on the importance of the sex itself or of the literary merits of the author seemed to miss the wealth of information the book and its response carried. The story displayed, in a somewhat dramatized way, what women want in a partner.

Romance novels give us a window into the desires of women shaped by the genes of our ancestral past (Ogas and Gaddam, 2011). Even the notorious *Fifty Shades of Grey* (James, 2011), considered an exemplar of sadomasochism, was at its core a romance novel. These windows are unhindered by the realities such as accessibility, cultural restrictions, and the female readers own mate-worth. It therefore represents an uncompromised taste of what women want (Gorry, 1999).

The popularity of romance novels in general cannot be ignored. In our recent past, romance novels were a 4- to 6-billion-dollar industry, boasting 40 percent of the paperback book market (Salmon and Symons, 2003). Often viewed as the female equivalent of male visual pornography, romance novels reflect women's dispositions and desires, unhindered by male preferences. They are simultaneously women's erotica and adventure fiction. The heroine's goal is never sex for its own sake (though the protagonist may certainly enjoy it with her male lover), and never impersonal sex with strangers. The foundation is a love story in which the heroine struggles over obstacles to find, win the heart of, and marry the man who is the right one, the hero, the soul mate.

There are two aspects of importance when considering what romance novels can tell us about evolved female psychology and eroticism: the qualities of the male hero and the signals he displays for the female protagonist that she finds irresistible. Unlike in males, where the visual cue is enough, the female brain requires weighing all potential cues of a good partner and assessing these in the context of her social situation before allowing the arousal and sexual desire to win over (Ogas and Gaddam, 2011). Both mate qualities and the signals of love he sends to the female protagonist are important because, as discussed in the previous section, females must overcome the strong and discerning cognitive brake system built in to avoid being taken advantage of by a non-committing male.

The hero embodies the characteristics known to be human universals for romantic love. A romance novel never contains a hero who is short, skinny, fat, devoid of muscles, weak, pale, penniless, effeminate, stupid, lethargic, lazy, ugly, or other opposites of the characteristics listed earlier. Instead, across 10,000 romance novels, the most frequent words describing masculine features include cheekbones, jaw, shoulders, brow, waist and hips – not the penis as the male ego would assume (Ogas and Gaddam, 2011). In a survey of forty-five romance novels, Gorry (1999) found that the most frequent descriptions of male protagonists in romance novels included words like tall, large, strong and agile. These physical descriptions serve to identify these male protagonists as capable and endowed with excellent genetics and the ability to physically protect the woman. Absent, notably, is a focus on the male sexual appendage, the female equivalent of which would not have escaped description in male-directed erotica. Further, these features indicate both good genetics (health and strength) as well as capacity to overcome physical obstacles in the environment, an important indicator of resource potential in our evolutionary past.

Moving beyond physical description, Ogas and Gaddam (2011) found that the male protagonists often had strong and dominant professions (such as surgeons, princes, or cowboys). In other words, they are 'alpha' males (Ogas and Gaddam, 2011). Even when romance heroes were described as social outcasts, they retained traits that allowed them to navigate and ultimately dominate their social environment such as intelligence and confidence (Gorry, 1999). This suggests that it is not necessarily economic status that women desire, but the capabilities of the male literary protagonist (and of males in our social environment) to obtain resources when necessary, hold onto them, and invest them in the woman and her children. In our EEA, such capacity to meet challenges and come out the victor would have been more important than short-term resources such as food (the closest comparison we have to our current monetary resource) that the male may have possessed. This desire for the capable and dominant male is seen again and again throughout women's erotic literature, such that there is very little market in this genre for the gentle hero (Salmon and Symons, 2003). Indeed, about half of the romance novels surveyed described their hero as authoritative and intimidating (Gorry, 1999).

Themes of dominance are common in romance novels, and often offer descriptions of the protagonist being physically dominated herself. In about half of the romance novels surveyed, Gorry (1999) found descriptions of the male hero being physically rough with the protagonist, and almost all described their heroes as being insistent or forceful in general with the heroine at times. Gorry goes on to note that one of the criticisms of romance novels is the aggressive way in which women are seduced. However, themes of dominance and submission are common in female fantasy and in practice. In a recent study, about half of the women survey reported having had tried BDSM activities, with another 22 percent reporting having fantasized about it (Holvoet et al., 2017). Women who viewed themselves as sexually submissive perceived themselves as more attractive than those without a reported preference (Jozifkova and Kolackova, 2017). In a more extreme example, one study found that 62 percent of women surveyed had imagined a rape fantasy, and of those fantasies reported, a little under half of these were completely erotic in nature (Bivona and Critelli, 2009). As pointed out by the authors, the highest levels of arousal were seen when the non-consent was a 'token no'. This, too, may explain why the themes of BDSM, those of control, were so tantalizing in *Fifty Shades of Grey*. Dominance in the bedroom may indicate for a heroine (and the reader) characteristics of the protagonist such as sexual prowess, dominant personality, and confidence, but may also indicate something even more important for the heroine: her own desirability in the eyes of her lover.

The male of the story sexually desires the heroine, declares his love, and wants the heroine more than he has ever wanted a woman. The irresistibility of the female protagonist is often a focus of the interaction (Ogas and Gaddam, 2011). As noted in an online chat by the same authors, although the word 'penis' is not one of the top 100 body parts mentioned in a romance novel, the authors found a focus of the blood rushing through a male penis to be an interesting pattern in female erotica (www.thedailybeast.com/what-can-the-web-teach-us-about-sex-a-live-chat-with-the-authors-of-a-billion-wicked-thoughts). This should be unsurprising when considering that this is a cue of desire for a man, and an unmistakable signal to the female protagonist of that desire. In all forty-five romance novels surveyed, the male protagonist wanted the heroine more than any woman he had sexually encountered previously and made his love, which was greater than he had ever experienced, known to the heroine (Gorry, 1999). This desire and passionate love for the female protagonist is indicative of a sustained commitment to the heroine, a commitment that would have been far more valuable than any physical resource or status (Gorry, 1999).

Was *Fifty Shades of Grey* an anomaly? Or do women seek the Christian Grey's of the world when seeking out erotic fiction? Christian Grey represented a typical hero of a romance novel: older and taller than the female protagonist, muscular, handsome, strong, large, energetic, intelligent, and socially as well as physically competent. He, like other romance heroes, has never been so much in love, has intrusive thoughts about the heroine, and is gentle with the heroine but not others. The hero feels the heroine is unique, wants to protect her, and is possessive and sexually jealous. He is the ideal partner: committed and ready to invest his time, resources, and life.

In sum, what women seek in erotic art, literature, and film likely represents an intersection, a marrying of the psychological and the genital arousal. The characters reflected and the actions portrayed will hint at the good genes, safety, and resources that can be provided by a male protagonist. No woman is erotically attracted to ineffectiveness in any man in any culture. Powerlessness, unemployment, sexual impotence, incompetence, failure to protect her or a baby, and so forth are likely to be shunned by females and by the writers of classic romance novels.

Conclusion

Eroticism emerges from our sexual biology, and nothing in biology makes sense except through the lens of evolution. Any accurate view of eroticism requires as a foundation the evolutionary history of our species and the politically incorrect acceptance of our considerable sex differences forged in our millions of years as hunter-gatherers in Africa. Women's ovulation is relatively hidden, and so natural selection favored men's capacities to assay reproductive value through visual clues. Men's reproductive success is tied to how many fertile women they can copulate with and how often. That fact is reflected in men's reproductive strategies and eroticism. Given the opportunity, men will pursue a quantity over quality reproductive behavior. Women invest substantial energy and take on terrible risks with any pregnancy. Whether they copulated with one man or a hundred men, there is a finite and small number of children any woman could have. For their survival, as well as the survival of their children, ancestral women had to choose men who had more than physical health. Their men had to have the ability to cooperate with other men, dominate allies when needed, physically protect her when required, and secure resources for survival. Ancestral women had to be choosy and pursue a quality over quantity reproductive strategy.

> A woman's reproductive success is jeopardized by anything that interferes with her ability: to conceive no children that cannot be raised; to choose the best available father for her children; to induce males to aid her and her children; to maximize the return on sexual favors she bestows; and to minimize the risk of violence or withdrawal of support by her husband and kinsmen.
>
> (Symons, 1979, p. 92)

Modern women's sexuality and eroticism contain that history and the psychology it produced.

All in all, it turns out that the aphorism 'men compete for copulations while women compete for husbands' was indeed true. A boy wants sex. A girl wants a boy. Men love sex and will use love to get sex. Women love and will use sex to get love. When marriages are founded on love, women give sex for love while men give up sex for love. No matter how you cut it, the sex differences in sexuality and eroticism are stark, and we try to conceal them with myths and misunderstandings. Men are not from Mars. Women hardly hail from Venus. We all come from Africa and carry, for good or ill, the sexual dispositions sculpted by Darwinian selection in the savannahs of our homeland.

Notes

1   A reader who may be familiar with the pornography industry may point out the many fetishes and odd searches that pornography seekers may pursue. For instance, Ogas and Gaddam (2011) found that terms like 'MILF' and 'grannies' were also consistent searches. Keep in mind that sexual attraction is a complicated and multifactorial psychological process. Inputs such as classical conditioning and environmental cues for availability, discussed earlier, may contribute to what is preferred. It is adaptive for the male brain to be somewhat malleable in its attraction as it allowed ancestors who would not have otherwise been reproductively successful (given the limited supply of perfect females) to find success. This adaptability would have been passed on as a trait to the reproductive offspring, and thus propagated through generations. Once this malleability becomes hijacked, fetishes would be born. As discussed by Ogas and Gaddam (2011), men may have the ability to pick up on various versions of female cues, and these may become further solidified by reward from ejaculation. This would allow for older women to be preferred and sought out, despite youthful women being more fertile and reproductively viable.

2   It would be important for future studies to observe how the number of children, and thus parental investment, affects the perception of partner pornography use.

Chapter 2

Maternal eroticism or the necessary risk of madness

Rachel Boué-Widawsky

The application of eroticism to maternal care is often a source of controversy because eroticism is commonly associated with sexuality. However, Eros is not sex; it is a force of desire for life. Although the focus on maternal eroticism is not new, and has been recognized by Deutsch (1944), Loewald (1971) and Laplanche (1989), it is still a taboo, perhaps as taboo as childhood sexuality once was. As Balsam (2003) often points out in her work, the female body and 'maternal embodiment' are largely ignored in contemporary psychoanalytic literature.

The condensed expression 'maternal eroticism' attributes to motherhood a bio-psychological dimension rather than a psychological function devoted to child development. The mother's subjectivity and its bodily manifestations through pregnancy, labor, childbirth, and child care imply physical and psychical trans-formations that are a source of deep disruption in the psychic organization of the mother. This chapter intends to study the roles and the risks of these disruptions which mobilize the mother's libidinal drives to the extreme.

The return to a pre-objectal and pre-symbolic stage, which motherhood implies, has been depicted in Greek mythology, ancient philosophy, biblical narratives and art as a source of fascination and mystery. Prehistoric frescoes, despite the absence of the representations of the human form or visage, depict maternal gigantic vul-vas next to bison and horses. In *Timaeus and Critias* (2008, p. 52) Plato attributes a maternal quality to the *khora*, the first receptacle (womb, matrix) of forms and things, and as such the first signifier and organizer for life. In the Bible, Sarah's and Mary's maternities are presented as divine miracles. Each of these stories and myths on the maternal origin of the human psyche can still teach us what biology and cognitive psychology cannot – namely the psychic disruption of the maternal embodiment.

From the start, psychoanalysis has been able to provide theoretical concepts and narratives underlying these ancestral and personal maternal experiences. Although Freudian psychoanalysis has focused primarily on the role of the father entering the scene at the Oedipal phase, it can help us to understand pre-Oedipal derivatives of this originary mother–child relationship.

The maternal body under siege from the physical transformations and arousal of conflicting drives experiences a form of rapture, as the body is pushed to the

limits of its mental and physical capacities. It is precisely this experience that the mother will transform, or not, in libidinal tenderness for the future infant.

Being a mother is an experience which the three mythical representations of motherhood combined – Jocasta, the seducer; Medea, the infanticide; and, Mary, the mater dolorosa – illustrate. I am not using here the myths as data evidence but as a source of inspiration to challenge and stimulate our psychoanalytic thinking about the maternal and the specific nature of its erotic dimension. Furthermore, these myths present a cathartic (it is their original function) illustration of an amoralistic or apolitical approach of the maternal. They are indeed informative of the strenuous tensions experienced by the body ego of the mother. The maternal state is not exclusively a psychic state, it is also a body experience from the very conception. This is precisely the inseparability between of the bodily and the psychic experience that provides the erotic dimension of the maternal experience where drives are aroused – life, survival, and death drives. I am here referring to Freud's late drive theory, developed in *Beyond the Pleasure Principle* (1920b), where life drives are not limited to sexual drives but include survival drives contiguous to the controversial death drive. The latter, even as a myth, as Freud himself referred to (1933, p. 95), is logically at stake in the maternal process in as much as giving birth and providing maternal care afterwards can be felt as a state of emergency to preserve body–ego cohesiveness. Thus, maternal eroticism can be understood, at its roots, as a climatic situation where Eros (life) drives wrestle with its corollary adverse ones (aggressive, destructive, and, in some instance, death drives).

Before being a function for the development of the infant, as a container of his/her not yet fully organized sensations and affects, which, since Winnicott, psychoanalytic literature has focused on, maternal eroticism can be viewed as a disruptive and chaotic state in which libidinal and aggressive drives lean on each other – thus creating a tension, close to a state of urgency. The maternal experience is at the core of a vital process – the climax of which being the labor experience – which depends on necessary destructive drives: separation, violence, and loss are parts of the delivery process. While the child has to separate from the mother's body in order to live, the mother has to lose a part of her body to give birth to another life. In this mutual operation of expulsion and separation, life and destructive drives are part of the same act.

To illustrate some points of my argument, I have inserted in the body of this article some artistic vignettes by Louise Bourgeois, whose work has been inspired over decades by the theme of motherhood.

Images of motherhood, and exploration of female functions and needs, have been pervasive in Louise Bourgeois' work and in particular in her final years where she explored at the end of her life the proximity of birth and death. Her paintings and sculptures present the inner experience of motherhood as a non-ending separation, like "My Inner Life" (2008)[1] or "Don't Abandon Me" (1999),[2] which is a horizontal sculpture of motherhood as a never-to-be-cut umbilical cord. This conception of motherhood can turn into nightmarish surrealistic versions of suffocating feelings enclosed in a glass bell jar[3] or into a birthing woman body within an egg form, "The Crossed-Eyed Woman Giving Birth" (2005).

The climactic situation of labor and delivery, where the vitality forces are bound to the destructive ones, is not only an anatomic process, it is a state of emergency where the mother has to break the bio-psychical continuum for the child to be expulsed and live. This capacity of the mother to go beyond herself and de-multiply in two, without annihilating herself or the baby, defines the primary forces at stake in motherhood. This state of erotic confusion and effervescence in the new mother might be understood as a form of identification to the infant's

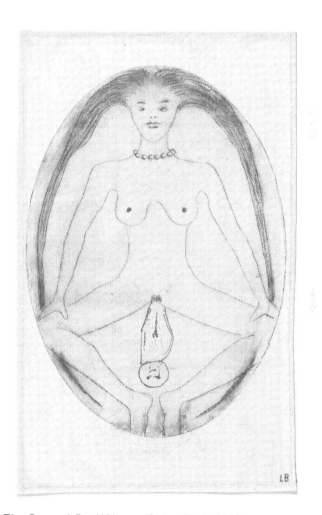

Figure 2.1 The Crossed-Eyed Woman Giving Birth, 2005

state, or even as a return to it. In his famous article "Primary Maternal Preoccupation", Winnicott (1956) described this state as a 'normal illness', like a 'dissociated state', which allows the mother to be in tune with the infant's first moment of life. The French writer Marie Darieussecq (2002) describes this state in her book *The Baby*:

> These first two months, I was half way on this earth, hearing half of what people were saying, seeing half of them, reading books understanding half of what was written. Half of my brain was his: was he warm enough, was he breathing well, did I hear him whining? . . . It was a kind of madness. I was permanently in touch with an other world, like an extra-terrestrial hearing in her skull, the echoes of her original planet. I felt ubiquitous and hypersensitive.

(My translation)

This almost schizoid (con)fusion between the mother's and the child's self states, which one of my patients called 'mad love', takes the form of an inevitable primary 'incestuous' love, where the mother, in taking care of the child's body, inevitably becomes 'the first seducer' (Freud, 1938). The references that Freud made to the biological and erotic role of the mother in the child's development are too numerous to quote, but it is pervasive in all his work, from "Three Essays on Sexuality" (1905a) to the late "Outline of Psychoanalysis" (1938), where he repeats that the mother–child relationship is "the first and strongest love object and the prototype of all later love relations – for both sexes" (p. 56). The lack of substantial theorization of these observations in Freud's work was due to his conception of primary narcissism as being in a phase of autoerotic objectless state until the emergence of the Oedipal complex and the interference of the paternal object.

Even if Freud recognized the mother as an inevitable seducer, he kept a factual view on her role (kissing, stroking, rocking), limiting it to the arousal of pre-genital sensations in the infant. Laplanche (1989) brought the concept of seduction at a psychic level, contending that the seductive role of the mother comes from her unconscious communications to the child, which can only be perceived as opaque, and therefore 'enigmatic'. This original experience received from the mother's unconscious extends the maternal role to more than a nursling function. The mother also brings her psychic, conscious and unconscious, history to the infant, whose capacity to decipher it can only be limited. According to Laplanche, this is an inevitable corporeal and mental impingement on the child that, by lack of possible translation, leads to the primary repression. Thus, according to Laplanche, the seducing mother imposes the rudiments of symbolization and communication. However, in his re-elaboration of a theory of the mind and of the object based on drives and the unconscious messages, Laplanche does not address the maternal state in its specificity, but rather as playing the role of a developmental function for the child.

After Winnicott, other psychoanalysts, like Bowlby, with the attachment theory or Mahler, with the separation/individuation process, expanded their focus on the early mother–child relationship and on child developmental needs. More recently, Green (1996) and Kristeva (2014) have centered their work on the mother's psychic upheaval. For them, in agreement with the etymological history of the word 'passion', which reflects a movement from physical suffering to a flow of affects and emotions, motherhood can be viewed, in its biological and psychical aspect, as a *passion*. For Green, passion is close to madness, ('folly'), a form of mental derailment under the sway of drives. In fact, to become a mother implies the ability to transform, or to metabolize, contradictory drives and emotions (attachment and expulsion) into an idealizing loving process. The choice of the term 'passion' by these contemporary psychoanalysts is motivated by the need to reflect the intertwined corporal and psychical specifics of the maternal experience, which the terms 'good enough mother' or 'normal illness', coined earlier by Winnicott, downplay.[4] For Green and Kristeva, the concept of passion adds, to the 'maternal preoccupation', the bodily affective derailment that characterizes the maternal experience as a body and mind transformation.

As we clinically know, some mothers recover from this passion, some get stuck in it, and some cannot allow themselves to reach it. On the spectrum between the 'dead mother' (Green, 1996), whose presence is an absence, and the overinvested and impinging mother, all mothers have to face the torments of the physical and mental upheaval of the maternal experience. We can encounter conscious or unconscious traces of the history of this maternal passion in patients' diffuse micro symptoms (psychosomatic reactions, affect regulation, difficulties to tolerate the binding relationship with the analyst, needs for a merging relationship with the analyst, fear of silence, etc.), which seem to indicate, and construe, within the transference and countertransference dynamics, an original malaise with the maternal intimacy that the psychoanalytic dyad replicates.

The maternal transformation of a woman contributes, for better or worse, to the development of the child's mental apparatus and leaves its marks in the adult's psychic organization. In *The Violence of Interpretation: From Pictogram to Statement* (1975), Aulagnier developed the concept of "pictogram" as the first psychic inscription of primary bodily experiences. This psycho-corporal experience, different from the Kleinian splitting or projective experiences, defines, in her view, the corporal origin of the mental apparatus. Aulagnier underscores the structuring role of the vicissitudes of the maternal passion in this primal process. In *Un Interpète en Quête de Sens* (1986), Aulagnier studies the early confusing (enigmatic? seducing?) process of the exchange between the child's needs/desires and the mother's desire of them (e.g. the mother desires that the child enjoys drinking the milk she gives). Aulagnier views this process, where the circulation of the two desires (the child's and the mother's) may merge (whose desire is it? is it a need (milk)? or a desire (breast)?), as seminal for the child's capacity to articulate his/her own needs and erogenous desires on his mother's conscious and unconscious ones. As a result, the primary identification to the (m)other relies on this primary biological and erotogenic exchange between mother and child. Laplanche describes this situation in his theory of 'generalized seduction', viewed as a necessary step for the primary repression, due to mother's demands or 'enigmatic messages' to the child. Furthermore, the theory of the 'generalized seduction' inscribes, at the core of the development of the child's psyche, the drive system, source–object–aim, that Freud developed in "Three Essays on the Theory of Sexuality" (1905) and in "Instincts and Their Vicissitudes" (1915a). What Laplanche, and Aulagnier add to the role of Freud's drive theory, after Lacan's unavoidable legacy in the history of French psychoanalysis, is a theory of translation of the drives' needs into a psychic process. I cannot develop, in the scope of this chapter, the importance of this theoretical point in the history of psychoanalysis, leading to the debates between Freudian and Kleinian theories around the origin and nature of the object. Briefly, Laplanche (1989, 1992) and Aulagnier (1975, with the concept of 'pictogram') introduced the theoretical necessity of a translating process to explain the 'derivation', or leaning-on process, from the self-conservative instincts (hunger), the sexual drives (erogenous pleasure), and their substitutive psychic representations, usually called hallucinations or phantasies. This unresolved debate is at the core of maternal eroticism in as much as it brings the mother back to the core of the intensity of the original vital body–psychic experience, where vital and death forces are wrestling in the body and in the psyche.

This brief review of the intricacy of the erotico-biological maternal passion is intended to outline the psychic upheaval the mother experiences in enduring pregnancy, labor, and mothering. This maternal passion brings the mother's self-cohesiveness to its extreme limits, on the threshold of dissolution of her identity markers. What was physically and psychically part of her during her pregnancy is challenged at birth by the physical struggles of life and death drives in the very act of expulsing what was inside her. It is a physical and a psychological ripping apart. This very experience is the root of maternality, as being in between a traumatic separation experience and a *relating* one, which Kristeva has named 'reliance' in her article, "Reliance or maternal eroticism" (2014), "Reliance: to link, to gather, to join, to put together; but also to adhere, to belong, to depend on; and therefore to trust, to feel safe, to share your thoughts and feelings, to assemble together, and to be yourself" (p. 79). Kristeva defines maternal reliance, like Winnicott, as a developing binding experience between mother and child but also as, primarily and continuously, an interface between libidinal and aggressive drives. This urgency of life to be lifted up to its risky limits, physically and psychically, is what Kristeva defines as the ultimate erotic maternal reliance.

According to Kristeva, the maternal reliance, nourished by opposite drives and ambivalent feelings, defines the social construction of the crazy, ordinary mother but also sets the ground for feminine *abjection* that, again, many myths, traditions,[5] religions,[6] and literature[7] have elaborated as a cultural taboo. The concept of 'abject', Kristeva develops in *The Powers of Horror* (1982) refers to a reaction (horror, disgust, repulsion) to the breakdown of meaning due to the confusion between self and other. The abject "draws me toward the place where meaning collapses" (p. 2). More directly referring to the maternal experience, she explains that "abjection preserves what existed in the archaism of the pre-objectal relationship, in the immemorial violence with which a body becomes separated from another body in order to be" (p. 10). An internal representation of this experience can be seen in Louise Bourgeois' swelling bodily fluids of "Swelling" (2008).[8]

Thus, the maternal erotic folly plays in between this abject experience and the loving one. It defines the natural ambivalence of maternal love, we all are heirs of, before we are even taken care of. However, if one can say that the maternal experience is a passion – where life and aggressive drives confront each other – it is also an extraordinary source of *desire* and *jouissance*. Although Lacan did not specifically wrote on motherhood, his concepts are useful in characterizing two aspects of maternal eroticism. Following Freud's differentiation between wish and need (*Wunsch/Befriedigung*), Lacan uses the concept of desire as being drive motivated by the impossible satisfaction which he names 'object (a)' (Lacan, 2006). This missing object is identified as the mother's womb, the prohibited object. This unconscious or conscious fantasy of rejoining the body of the mother by becoming a mother provides a frightening *jouissance* (Lacan, 1997), which embraces all at once a lack, a primal separation, and a desire for merging.

This radically regressive experience provides overexcitement, which carries the mother beyond herself to a different place, *unheimlich*: stranger to herself; separate from others, father, or other children. If this 'crazy enough mother', to mimic Winnicott's phrase, tolerates a momentary stay in that strange place, the mother won't only passively endure the situation, but will actively reach the desire to enjoy the ultimate power of defying castration through endorsing a phallic power, as the genitor. Louise Bourgeois' feminization of the martyr Saint Sebastian as a corpulent woman carrying eggs defying the arrows attacking her might be understood as an illustration of the bisexual ambivalence of motherhood: "Sainte Sébastienne" (1990).

At the same time, the mother reconnects with her own mother – with desire or reluctance – and re-experiences her own infancy. This overexcitement enmeshed with a regressive experience based on the mother's history is not an Oedipal victory but a reconnection with the most primary part of oneself in terms of drives and identification processes.

One can posit that motherhood also stimulates a return to a bisexual psychic state, in which the mother flirts with the limits of her own sexual identities, where activity and passivity, femininity and masculinity blend. In providing care to the infant, the mother may experience herself as a bisexual caregiver, mother and father at once, a "closed eternal circle",[9] which is how Louise Bourgeois qualifies her "Self-Portrait" (1990).

This complex primary form of relating, the maternal reliance, which includes incestuous desire, ambivalent *jouissance*, and bisexuality, in addition to all the torments of the maternal dissociated states, can be used too easily to associate motherhood with the experience of madness that popular culture traffics in.

Figure 2.2 Sainte Sébastienne, 1990

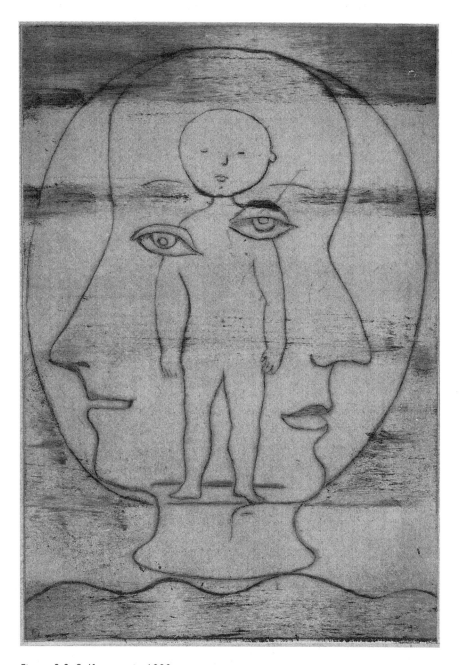

Figure 2.3 Self portrait, 1990

These transformative and regressive intrapsychic states the mother goes through can help us to understand the fear of our female patients, mothers or not, of being 'like' their mothers. In addition to the reactivation of possible traumatic wounds, phantasies around narcissistic regression, merging experience, and mental breakdown are part the maternal experience, which can be replayed in the maternal transference with the analyst. A brief clinical vignette will illustrate the trans-generational impact of the maternal madness where mothers and daughters end up in a reenactment of the difficulty of being a mother in perpetuating the abject, the hate, and somehow the infanticide wish.

Clinical vignette: I

Kate, a thirty-year-old woman, came to analysis to put an end to a life of tumultuous and abusive relationships that she felt was a threat to her capacity to be a 'good' mother. She was a single mother of a six-year-old daughter whom she had had out of wedlock.

Kate was raised in an abusive family in which women and daughters suffered sexual assault in childhood and had been in abusive relationships. Kate's eventual retraumatizing psychoanalytic understanding of her familial legacy frightened her and plunged her in a state of anger towards me for weeks during which she expressed her rage at her mother and at her insatiable longing for her love: "As much as you like me, you can't provide an unconditional love, like throwing yourself under a bus for me", she said to me.

Kate was caught in this archaic defensive splitting where love had to be absolute. It could not coexist with its opposite. In this period of her analysis, she was getting closer to her archaic maternal object with horror. She showed me pictures of her mother and was disgusted by her physical resemblance with her mother. At one session, Kate brought a letter that she wrote to her mother when she gave birth to her daughter. This letter, though sent, never received a response from her mother. Although it was Kate's intention to read the letter to me, her feelings about its content were so unsettling to her that she could not read it. She thus put me in a position of not being able to respond to her, like her mother. In other sessions, she talked about transference dreams which clearly were a second edition of her tormented relationship with her mother.

In her childhood, Kate had rescued an abandoned black kitten, to which she became much attached. One day, her mother got rid of the cat while Kate was at school. For years, Kate had a recurrent dream in which she would search for the cat endlessly in the city. After finally finding it, she would wake up, deeply disappointed by reality. At a later session, she described the following dream to me:

"Do you remember this repeated dream about the black cat in my childhood? This dream last night started with the black cat who is walking next to me along a hallway. I am coming to your office, but you don't want the black cat in the room. I leave it outside. Then I am in your room; it feels like a cage. You're here but I can't reach you. Like, nobody is there. My tongue is all tied up. I can't speak. The walls seem to move to squeeze me. No one is there in the room for me".

This dream material can be subject to multiple interpretations; the transference interpretation is the most relevant here. In this dream, I am turned into the rejecting (not accepting the black cat in the room) and unreachable one (you are here but I can't reach you). At a deeper level, the dream evokes a situation of sequestration (the room is like a cage), a horrifying but perhaps desirable wish to return to the wound (the walls seem to move to squeeze me; sexual symbol of the black cat) which no words can describe (my tongue is all tied up; I can't speak). This dream appears as an illustration of the primary ambivalent link to the mother. In Kate's mind, this primary object had to stay a bad object to be hated. She remembered throwing toys at her great-grandmother each time the latter would show affection to her. Kate and I often refer to this scene/memory as a metaphor to describe her difficulty in relating to me as a good object.

However, after months of working through these issues, Kate arrived at a compromise 'solution' by bringing her daughter to her sessions (the pretext being that she had no alternative for child care, since child support was in litigation). I arranged a playroom next to my office's waiting room for her daughter. I viewed the whole situation as an actual and inevitable inclusion of me in the midst of Kate's life. I understood that this trio revolved around the archaic maternal object through a new configuration of relationships between Kate, her daughter, and me. By coming to her sessions as an actual mother with her child, Kate was standing up against the hateful mother she had had and with whom she negatively identified.

Although Kate was a well-intentioned, caring mother, she thought she would inevitably, given her history, become a failing mother. Indeed, she came to analysis out of that fear. Being both a woman and a mother, where eroticism and motherhood collude, was thought as almost incompatible for Kate. In her fantasy, being a mother meant inevitably being a bad mother. In that context, bringing her daughter to sessions meant that she was trying to bring the two parts of herself together, the woman and the mother. Although Kate strove in her young adulthood to separate from the maternal ascendance, she was now, as a mother, joining the maternal lineage she had tried to escape from since her adolescence. At a more primary level, by bringing her daughter with her, she was also bringing herself as a child who longed for a loving mother.

In addition, to this multilayered experience which Kate was working through in her analysis, she faced her separation anxiety with her child who at six years old was starting to be more independent and less in tune with her mother's tantalizing love. Kate said that during the first years of her daughter's life she felt they were just one body and mind.

As the holder of these different layers of identification, I was identified in the transference as the surrogate mother of Kate, the grandmother of the child, and the substitute for the absent father/lover. These positions assigned by Kate placed me at the core of the complexity of the ramifications of the maternal reliance.

Motherhood is a composite of unachieved mourning from generation to generation; that is, where life comes out of loss. As mythology and literature teach us, maternality is a state of ambivalent passion that Jocasta, Medea, Mater Dolorosa, Anna Karenina, or Sophie (in *Sophie's Choice*) represent to embody the multiple facets of the primary forms of love. In our clinical work, listening to the stigma of the inherited maternal passion is opening some alternative ways to reflect on our patients relational difficulties with intimacy in the psychoanalytic dyad, to help them to understand the meanings of their sexual orientation, or to address the latent infantile depression in their adult life. Because we all come from a mother, the maternal reliance is the primary and everlasting link to humanity, whether we are men or women, mothers, or adopting parents.

Notes

1 *Louise Bourgeois, An Unfolding Portrait*, Catalog published by MOMA, New York, 2018, p 114.
2 Ibid., p 117.
3 Ibid., p 135.
4 The concept of passion, with its semantic contradictions, might have been in Winnicott's mind when he wrote "Hate in the Countertransference" (1947), in which he lists all the good reasons for a mother to hate her newborn baby whose demands are felt as annihilating for the mother.
5 Mary Douglas, *Purity and Danger: An Analysis of concepts of Pollution and Taboo* (London: Routledge and Keegan Paul, 1966).
6 As an example, see Leviticus in the Old Testament of the Bible about the feminine taboo.
7 Beckett, Kafka, Bataille, Artaud, etc.
8 MOMA catalog, p 146.
9 Ibid., p 118.

Chapter 3

Locating the father's eroticism

Susan McNamara and Ethan Grumbach

Behind its simple title, this chapter takes on multiple tasks. Much as that measure of age-appropriate behavior, 'adult', has morphed into 'adulting', more performance than stage, the meaning of 'father' has also evolved. To say the father is the male parent of a child belies the densities of fathering, gender, and parenting. "The conceptual difficulties this conversation begins to map are more complex, and more interesting than that" (Wiegman, 2015, p. 2). There are now multiple descriptive terms for father: 'baby daddy', 'birth father', 'biological father', 'posthumous father', 'putative father', 'sperm donor', 'surprise father', 'adoptive father', 'DI Dad', 'foster father', 'mother's husband', and 'stepfather'. Recent research on families shows uncertainty about parental roles and identities. Some research suggests that gendered expectations that men should prioritize their work lives and women should prioritize their marriage and home life no longer exist. Other research supports the idea that gender differences continue to exist in the division of household labor and chores, with men working more hours and women spending more time on domestic and child-care responsibilities. Research also strongly suggests that children of lesbian and gay parents engage in life with positive social relationships with peers, with parents, with grandparents, and with parents' adult friends. Fears about children of queer folk being sexually abused by adults, ostracized by peers, or isolated in single-sex lesbian or gay communities have not been validated. What, then, of mothers and fathers?

The editors have asked us to write a chapter about the father's impact on the erotic. This request immediately generated a healthy confusion in us, as we considered the complexity of the task. The subject of the father's eroticism is an occasion for thinking about psychoanalysis in general and about fathers in general and about life in general. We ourselves cherish the psychoanalytic tenets of intense curiosity while avoiding causation and category, and strive to think about fathers in this psychoanalytic context. Might the descriptive term 'father' go beyond a cisgender identification, a penetrative prick roughhousing with his child? How can we explore current and past psychoanalytic thinking about fathers while remaining open to the possibilities of deepening our understanding of material we hear in session? We consider "the different ways in which we thought about the *sexes* then, and the ways in which we think about *gender* now" (Corbett,

2011, p. 441, italics in the original). The sexed body is no longer equivalent to gender roles or identities. In a world in which there are many types of families, we challenge traditional views of fathering (and mothering) as activities based on gender and biology. Ten years ago, in " 'Fathers' and 'Daughters'", Harris (2008) questioned the categories of 'father' and 'daughter', concluding those designations are unstable and unsettled. Harris asks: "Are there still fathers . . . or just 'fathers'?" (p. 39). A decade later, we continue and elaborate upon these queries. We have constructed this chapter to parallel the experience we had in writing. Faced with many viewpoints that were steeped in tradition and did not reflect the current focus of psychoanalytic thought we were often jarred by the juxtaposition of ideas. The manner in which we constructed this chapter we hope will offer you the opportunity to share this experience with us.

Recently, some analysts have expressed concern that the father and paternal function are neglected in an overemphasis on matricentric psychoanalytic developmental theory. It is proposed that fathers be returned to their rightful place in psychoanalysis, disrupting the pre-genital mother–infant dyad. The contention is that in the psychoanalytic focus on mammocentric "conflicts having to do with symbiosis, attachment, separation, and the need for nurturance" (Diamond, 2017, p. 863), the father has disappeared in an implicit father-murder, invoking Freud's (1939) 'primal murder' and Green's (2009) 'dead father'. But is the father really neglected? Or is this part of "an intricate rationalization of sex roles as they are" (Rubin, 1975, p. 48), theory deformed by ideology? Is this yet another occasion for gender regulation? According to bell hooks (2004):

> Patriarchy is a political-social system that insists that males are inherently dominating, superior to everything and everyone deemed weak, especially females, and endowed with the right to dominate and rule over the weak and to maintain that dominance through various forms of psychological terrorism and violence.
>
> (p. 17)

As analysts, are we coerced into identifying with a mother and child dyad, ignoring the father? Are we unable to consider and explore the choices, experiences, and feelings evoked in fathers as they share the life of their newborn?

The project of psychoanalysis is distinguishing fantasy and reality, that is, facing the pain of reality. In the following sections of this chapter, we use the psychoanalytic to shed light on aspects of an erotic that is not split into the binary of masculine/feminine, or viewed through the lenses of heterosexuality or the nuclear family. "The erotic – the sensual – those physical, emotional, and psychic expressions of what is deepest and strongest and richest within each of us, being shared; the passion of love, in its deepest meanings" (Lorde, 1984b, p. 56).

Sigmund Freud and Anna Freud

In 1926, writing in "The Question of Lay Analysis," Freud said, "We know less about the sexual life of little girls than of boys. But we need not feel ashamed of this distinction; after all, the sexual life of adult women is a 'dark continent' for psychology" (p. 212). In Freud's "Analysis Terminable and Interminable" (1937), true to form and style, he leads us down one path then another about the therapeutic efficacy of psychoanalysis, given his understanding of the physiological and biological factors influencing the outcome. At the very end of the paper, Freud posits two themes from which he derives a general principle:

> The two corresponding themes are in the female, an envy for the penis – a positive striving to possess a male genital – and in the male, a struggle against his passive or feminine attitude towards another male. . . . We often have the impression that with the wish for a penis and the masculine protest we have penetrated through all the psychological strata and reached bedrock, and that thus our activities are at an end. This is probably true, since, for the psychical field, the biological field does in fact play the part of the underlying bedrock. The repudiation of femininity can be nothing else than a biological fact.
>
> (pp. 250, 252)

The bedrock of psychoanalysis is not only misogyny, but homophobia.

When one considers Freud's work, it is important to consider its intellectual, social, and personal context. Freud was well acquainted with late-nineteenth-century thought on sexuality, perversion, and pathology, as delineated in the work of Krafft-Ebing, Moll, and Havelock Ellis. In the thrall of Darwin, these men considered sexuality purely a means towards the propagation of the human species. Only procreative sexual acts were considered normal. In turn, perversion was simply defined as any sexual behavior that was non-procreative. Freud critiqued this body of thought in the first version of "Three Essays on the Theory of Sexuality" in 1905, referring to it as a fable. In later versions of the "Three Essays" and other later writings, Freud retreated from his more radical ideas about the multitude of variations in human sexual life and reintroduced a functionalist approach (Van Haute and Westerink, 2016). Freud embraced the ideas, driven by those then-current theories of categorization and evolution, that girls are defective boys and civilization requires genital heterosexual coitus leading to mutual orgasm. Other forms of sexuality are perverse aberrations, development awry. And, despite Freud's early commitment in theory to bisexuality, that is, love, hate, and rivalry with both parents, it was ultimately his stance (and still an implicit, if not explicit psychoanalytic conceit) that if all goes well, heterosexuality and the gender roles implied by heterosexuality win the day. Freud himself could not grasp the radical character of his own early thinking, and the "instability of his text seems to be the direct result of this state of affairs" (Van Haute and Westerink, 2016, p. 97).

Anna Freud's role is crucial in parsing this puzzling textual instability. We have it from Marie Bonaparte and Elisabeth Young-Bruehl that Anna Freud was her father's 'vestal', that she took refuge in asceticism rather than engaging with any of her male suitors. Their master narrative is that Anna Freud sublimated her own desires in taking on her father's mantle, especially after he was diagnosed with cancer. But a counternarrative is that Anna Freud had a fifty-year queer relationship with Dorothy Burlingham. Freud analyzed both his daughter and her life partner. Caught in a similar dilemma as when he proposed his seduction theory, Freud equivocated about what he knew about women's sexuality and retreated to culturally bound sentiments masquerading as psychoanalytic thought. Freud then imposed his improbable theories of female sexuality and neurosis on his women patients, with great harm done them in the process (Cohler, 2008).

Freud's "A Child Is Being Beaten" (1919) is thought to be based on Anna Freud's analysis with him (Lax, 1992). In the paper, Freud described three phases of a fantasy he found in women patients. Novick and Novick (1973) detail Freud's work identifying the three phases of a beating fantasy in young women, starting with my father is beating the child whom I hate, I am being beaten by my father, and finally a father representative (a teacher) is beating children (usually boys). According to Freud (1919), the third fantasy has "strong and unambiguous sexual excitement attached to it, and so provides a means for masturbatory satisfaction" (p. 186). Freud (1919) posits that when little girls "turn away from their incestuous love for their father, with its genital significance, they easily abandon their feminine role. They spur their 'masculinity complex' into activity, and from that time forward only want to be boys" (p. 191).

Jessica Benjamin (1991) describes Young-Breuhl's (1988) theory that Anna Freud wrote her own paper for admittance to the Vienna Psychoanalytic Society, "Beating Phantasies and Daydreams" (1923), at a time when she had yet to see patients, so she most likely used this material from her own analysis with her father to gain admission into his analytic world, expressing how "the wish to be son to her father, a forbidden homoerotic love, might underlie that sexual fantasy" (Benjamin, 1991, p. 290). Benjamin goes on to make a case for

> a more complex understanding of gender identification and its role in erotic life with an illustration of how identificatory love may appear in the transference and in related fantasy or dream material. This appearance may become manifest in different ways, switching between men and women, father and brother, sexual and nonsexual.
>
> (1991, p. 293)

Benjamin critiqued the simplified binary in which mother–child are fused and the father's function is to separate them in the service of adult sexuality.

Anna Freud was thirty years old when Dorothy Burlingham appeared in Vienna with her four children in 1925, hoping to get them into analysis. Previous to this, Anna Freud was clear that she was "not suitable for marriage" (Young-Bruehl, 2008, p. 121). Soon after the Burlinghams arrived, she began analyzing the children, taking on the role of parent. The usually dysphoric Anna Freud wrote to one of her friends, "Being together with Mrs. Burlingham is a great joy for me" (2008, p. 134). The Burlinghams moved to an apartment above the Freuds at Berggasse 19, and a private phone line was installed between Anna Freud's and Dorothy Burlingham's rooms. The families frequently ate dinner together. Starting in

1927, Anna and Dorothy took vacation trips together, leaving their families in Vienna; in 1930, they bought a summer cottage in the Austrian resort village of Semmering. Dorothy Burlingham was analyzed by Reik, and then by Freud himself during 1924, eventually becoming a child analyst in her own right. She had a professional as well as personal collaboration with Anna Freud, first in Vienna, then London, where Dorothy lived with the Freuds at 20 Maresfield Gardens until Burlingham's death in 1979.

There is a photograph of the two women sitting at opposite ends of a small table covered with a Persian rug. On the table between the women is a bronze statue of Buddha and an Egyptian coffin mask. Above them hangs an etching of Sigmund Freud. The two women are smiling at each other – two powerful, self-confident figures – and seem to be ignoring the camera. Grandson Michael Burlingham took the photo in 1979. Later, he reported, "They asked me where they should look, and I said they should look at each other. Anna Freud responded to Dorothy, 'I don't mind looking at you a bit'" (cited in Tylim, 2011, p. 1). Today, their ashes are next to each other in the Freud family crypt in Golders Green.

Anna Freud was an intensely private woman who detested rumors about her relationships with either her father or with Dorothy Burlingham. Both father and daughter were secretive about the analysis. Anna Freud was completely committed to her father's views on masculinity, femininity, and homosexuality. We will never truly know the complex ways in which Anna Freud or her father held these parts of their lives together; father and daughter colluded in denying the formation of the Freud–Burlingham family and in denying Anna Freud's role as parent to the Burlingham children. Freud equivocated on women's sexuality, eliding the reality – queer families are neither new to psychoanalysis nor to parenting. The erotic was denied.

According to Grossman and Kaplan's seminal paper of 1988, Freud's writings are full of reflections that "remain at some remove, indeed at some variance, from his own technical principles" (p. 341). Grossman and Kaplan use female sexuality to think about psychoanalysis in general. They note that quite a bit that Freud had to say did not succeed as technical discourse, such as the received notion of women as childlike, impressionable, and corruptible, and his eventual reliance on the conclusions of nineteenth-century sexology.

What Freud does is present a constellation of traits as though they were psychoanalytic findings rather than culturally bound opinions, and scientific conclusions rather than matters for further research. This detracts from the capacity of the analyst, difficult enough to maintain in the best of circumstances, for a neutrality consistent with the theoretical and practical matter that there is nothing technically to be done with the fact that a woman, say, is on the couch, rather than a man. Thus, gender and sex similarities and differences are given a privileged place, leading to what is a psychopathology of conformity to gender and sexual stereotypes, including about parenting; essentially psychoanalysts as regulators of gender and gender roles. Regarding development, Grossman and Kaplan point out that a crucial message of the "Three Essays" is that nothing about sexuality should be taken at face value, even though Freud subsequently backed away from the implications of that message.

Coitus interruptus

The transition from high birth rates balanced by high death rates to lower birth and death rates occurs when a country or region shifts from a pre-industrial, agrarian economic system to an industrialized urban one. Children lose their value as an overall asset as farmworkers, and instead become an economic burden. Much smaller families become the norm. This phenomenon is known by social scientists as the demographic transition, and Western Europe underwent this transition between 1880 and 1910, the years during which Freud developed psychoanalysis (Paul, 2016). The social reality changed, resulting in a cultural shift.

How does such a reduction in the reproductive rate occur? By the use of contraception. In the paper, "Is Psychoanalysis Shaped by the Cultural?" Robert Paul (2016) notes that it was "the inadequacy of these now requisite methods, as he saw it, that Freud attributed the great frequency of sexual dysfunction" (p. 825). According to Angus McLaren (1979), Freud was convinced that pathologies of sexual function, as well as anxiety and hysteria, were the result of unsatisfactory sexual experiences:

> The wave of sexual dysfunction and neurosis that he saw in his practice could be laid at the feet of the demographic transition and its requirement that sexual reproduction be curtailed; but in the absence of fully satisfactory methods of contraception, most sexual activity did not allow for full sexual release.
>
> (Paul, 2016, p. 825)

In that paradigm, sex (heterosexual coitus) was restricted to the married man and woman; the family was the institution "designed to promote legitimate reproduction" (Paul, 2016, p. 827). Women were the sum of their reproductive roles, and were to be satisfied so.

One complicating factor in heterosexual sexuality of that time was the universal, yet secret fear of syphilis. Women's bodies were seen by men as potential sources of disease, while at the same time, women avoided sex with men for fear of contracting syphilis. Doctors told husbands not to tell their wives if they were infected, so as not to threaten the stability of the marriage. Women were locked into a secret sexual double bind. In Freud's "A Case of Hysteria" (1925), we can see now the behavior of the fathers in the story as the problem, with Dora's symptoms as the effect. Her father, whom Freud previously treated for syphilis, brings Dora to Freud. Dora tells Freud of the complex relationship involving her family and the K's. The two families go on vacation together. Dora looks after the K's young children and is friendly with Frau K. Dora's father, who has encouraged the closeness between the families, is having a protracted affair with Frau K. Herr K has been sexually harassing Dora since she was fourteen, trying to kiss her and enter her bedroom. When Herr K presses his erect penis against her, Dora tells her father, who claims to not believe her. There is an unspoken (except by Dora) quid pro quo – accept my daughter, so I can have your wife. Freud accepts Dora's story, but wonders about Dora's disgust for Herr K and is of the opinion that Dora unconsciously desires him. Freud has no understanding for the possibility that Dora might not feel attracted to Herr K. He ignores Dora's concerns that her father infected her mother with syphilis and ignores her own concerns that she herself is infected. Not only did Freud retreat from his theory that incestuous sexual abuse was a hidden part of family life, he never truly grappled with the links between the fear of syphilis and women's sexuality.

Paradoxically, at the same time as the demographic transition in early and mid-twentieth-century Western Europe, the role of women as child bearers and mothers was seen as crucial after the casualties and collapse of the fertility rate of World Wars I and II and the loss of life in the 1918 flu pandemic. There was a push to repopulate Europe and Great Britain – the total number of military and civilian casualties in World War I was more than 41 million – ranking it among the deadliest conflicts in human history. It was in this context that the scientific study of the relationship between infants and their mothers was started by upper-class Englishmen who were torn from their families as young boys and sent to regimented same-sex boarding schools, the sorts of places Orwell wrote about so compellingly in "Such, Such Were the Joys" (1953). These war- and Kleinian-influenced psychoanalysts – John Bowlby, Wilfred Bion, Harry Guntrip, Ronald Fairbairn, and Donald Winnicott – emphasized the roles of mothers in children's lives, especially after observing "the effects of wartime evacuation and group nurseries that separated young children from their families" (van der Kolk, 2014, p. 110) during World War II. In particular, Bowlby's "radical claim that children's disturbed behavior was a response to actual life experiences – to neglect, brutality, and separation – rather than the product of infantile sexual fantasies" (p. 110) ostracized him from his contemporary psychoanalytic community. Although Bowlby nodded to fathers and other caregivers, his central emphasis in attachment theory was on the child's tie to the mother.

The facts of nature

Freud revered Darwin, as did the late-nineteenth-century sexologists, basing their theories on Darwin's theory of sexual selection. The Linnaean classification system, based on kingdoms, classes, orders, genera, and species, was just becoming established. Naturalists and biologists strove mightily to classify nature. In this context, Darwin is known for three claims: first, that species are related to each other by shared descent from common ancestors; second, that species change through natural selection; and third, his theory about sexual selection – that males and females obey a universal, binary template. In this template, males are passionate and females are coy, and deviations from the template are anomalies.

According to biologist Joan Roughgarden, the facts of nature contradict Darwin's sexual selection theory. In reality, there are often more than two genders, with multiple types of males and females. This real-life diversity in gender expression and sexuality challenges basic evolutionary theory as we tend to think of it. Freud prided himself on being a scientist, and many analysts today pride themselves similarly. If we do pride ourselves as scientists, we have to consider the fact that scientific knowledge has changed in many ways since Freud's time. It is just not true that the heterosexual binary is nature's way. As Roughgarden tells us, "The challenge today is to work through the implications of this diversity, which destabilizes our understanding of biological nature" (2009, p. XIV). In addition, in Western culture difference is pathologized; difference is considered a disease. Diversity as it exists is considered threatening, even though a species without variability has no evolutionary potential. When we try to limit diversity or when we pathologize diversity, we slide towards the spectrum of disappearance, eugenics, slavery, ethnic cleansing, and genocide.

Perhaps another way of looking at gender and social diversity is through 'social selection' rather than 'sexual selection'. Sexual selection emphasizes mating, focusing on who mates with whom. Social selection emphasizes participating in a social infrastructure to produce and raise offspring, with a focus on how to deliver the offspring into the next generation rather than on attracting mates. "In the social selection context, the diversity of gender and sexuality makes evolutionary sense, rather than seeming at odds with evolution, because of the valuable social (and genetic) roles the diversity represents" (Roughgarden, 2009, p. XIV). Biological diversity as it exists interferes with any attempt to force living beings into neat categories. Organisms flow across the boundaries of any categories we construct. We only have to try defining the categories of masculine/feminine to see them implode.

As humans, we do engage in categorization, the process of grouping things based on prototypes. It has even been suggested that categorization based on prototypes is the basis for human development, and that this learning relies on learning about the world via embodiment. The idea of embodiment is that many features of cognition are deeply dependent upon characteristics of the physical body, such that the beyond-the-brain body plays a significant casual role, or a physically constitutive role, in cognitive processing. However, we must also be aware that the categories we construct in this way are not objectively 'out there' in the world, but are rooted in our experiences. Conceptual categories are not identical for different cultures, or indeed, for every individual in the same culture.

"O god save all the many gendered-mothers of my heart, & all the other mothers, who do not need god or savior." (Ward, 2014)

How does anyone decide what's normal and what's deviant? In the best-seller *The Argonauts*, Maggie Nelson (2015) writes about "becoming, both mentally and physically – about what it takes to shape a self, in all its completeness and disarray" (Als, 2016, p. 30). Nelson explores the love she has for artist and performer Harry Dodge, who is fluidly gendered, as Nelson becomes pregnant and Dodge starts testosterone and has top surgery. Nelson is a queer critic, who "questions what it means to be a lover, a parent, someone's child – 'heteronormative' roles – when you don't feel heteronormative, let alone comfortable with such traditional labels as 'gay', 'straight', 'female', and 'male'" (Als, 2016, p. 31). Nelson disrupts categories, especially binary categories, and then asks, "How to explain, in a culture frantic for resolution, that sometimes shit stays messy?" (2015, p. 53). The following vignettes are examples of profound bodily experiences in relating to the complexities of parenting/fathering/mothering that are not gender or role bound.

A mental health professional in his mid-thirties, Chris, spent a year in an infant observation with Sam and his daughter, Janet. Chris was a bit older than Sam; Janet was Sam's first child. When Janet was a few weeks old, Sam and Chris were sitting in the living room with Janet resting on Sam's legs, looking up at him. Janet became fussy, crying and scrunching up her face. Sam was worried, not sure what to do, uncomfortable with Janet's distress. Sam gently rubbed Janet's tummy, wondering aloud to Chris if she had gas or a tummy ache. Janet was swaddled in a blanket, but Chris could see her struggling to move her arms. This went on for a few minutes, and Chris felt a looming and empty feeling in his stomach as he watched father and daughter. Chris struggled to sit still and was very aware of wanting to offer Sam suggestions on how to stop Janet's distress. In keeping with his role as observer, Chris chose to stay quiet and attempted to contain his feelings.

Chris's stance is consistent with the approach of Esther Bick, who was instrumental in creating the Tavistock Infant Observation Method that was incorporated into analytic training at the Institute of Psychoanalysis in London in 1960. Bick thought that, "he (the observer) must, as in the basic method of psychoanalysis, find a position from which to make his observations, a position that will introduce as little distortion as possible into what is going on in the family. He has to allow some things to happen and to resist others". Later, she continues, "He must resist being drawn into roles involving intense infantile transference and therefore countertransference" (1964, p. 559).

Sam abruptly changed his body position and tried comforting Janet by bringing her up to his shoulder. He told Chris that maybe this was a time to do kangaroo care with Janet, so they were skin-to-skin, except for Janet's diaper. Chris immediately felt his stomach and torso relax and great relief. Sam pulled his T-shirt up and over his head, keeping it around his arms and back. He then unwrapped Janet and set her on the couch next to him so he could take off her onesie. Janet continued crying and moved her arms once she was free of the blanket. Sam talked with Janet the entire time, telling her that he was going to snuggle with her and that he hoped she would feel better. As Sam was talking with Janet, Chris continued feeling anxious and restless. When Sam got Janet out of her onesie and brought her up to his chest, Chris felt a tremendous sense of relief and realized he'd been holding his breath, which he let out in a way that felt like a burst.

Janet was now skin-to-skin with Sam who hugged her against his upper chest. Janet's crying changed to a whimper, and her body relaxed into Sam's. Sam gently put the baby blanket over Janet. Sam slid down on the couch so he was at about a forty-five-degree angle, and Janet settled into his body. Her whimpering stopped and she completely relaxed. Sam talked softly to Janet, saying how nice this felt and how much he liked being skin-to-skin with her. He turned to Chris and said it was an amazing experience to feel his daughter so close, which gave him a sense of completion he'd never felt before. Sam reflected on the first time he kangaroo cared with Janet. Within a few minutes, Janet was falling asleep. Sam continued kangaroo care with her.

Margot Waddell notes that infant observation:

> Exposes the observer to ever-oscillating identifications and to perpetually changing emotions of, for example, peace and disturbance, bliss and terror, anxiety and fulfilment, discomfort and relaxation, whether in parent, baby, sibling or self. *There may be states of intense suffering, of the horror of disintegration, or of 'free-fall'* . . . Cast into the maelstrom of these emotional changes and exchanges, reliant only on internal capacities (now, perhaps, tested as never before) and on the containing structure of the weekly seminar, it is no wonder that the observer so often finds him/herself in the midst of a wholly unexpected and unanticipated learning experience.
>
> (2006, p. 1111, italics added)

Chris was able to share with the infant observation seminar leaders, but not with his classmates, that during this observation he'd been very aware of his own body and had very stirring experiences as he watched Sam and Janet. Chris does not have any children and is not sure if he will ever be a parent. He was moved and surprised to realize that his body relaxed as he observed Sam and Janet kangaroo-caring, but also that he became aware of having his own powerful bodily sensations. Chris described those feelings as extremely sensual; he had the sensation of feeling Janet's body on his own torso, and his powerful bodily response to that sensation, sensual rather than sexual. He became aware of an unarticulated longing for an intimate connection with another person. Chris linked this back to his own childhood, sharing with the seminar leaders that his own father was always busy with work or activities and never very affectionate towards him. Chris had no recollection of having ever been held by his father as he had witnessed Sam holding Janet, and was suddenly aware of a deep inner longing. He wanted to be the one kangaroo-caring for Janet, and recognized a wish that Sam would ask him to do so and leave the room. Chris told the seminar leaders that this was a profound bodily experience that was very confusing for him initially. Chris also shared that he had brought these moments in infant observation to his analytic sessions and spent a great deal of time sorting out the sensual, the erotic, and his bodily experiences, both paternal and maternal.

Winnicott proposed, "The male element *does* while the female element (in males and females) *is*" (1971, p. 109). He goes on to focus on the attributes of the good-enough mother and the breast as the symbol of being rather than doing, "The study of the pure distilled uncontaminated female element leads us to BEING, and this forms the only basis for self-discovery and a sense of existing" (p. 111). Winnicott admits that "in health, there is a variable amount of girl element in a girl, and in a boy," but cautions that "some boys and girls are doomed to grow up with a lop-sided bisexuality, loaded on the wrong side of their biological provision" (p. 112). Winnicott is problematically gender bound in his concepts of being and doing, as it is clear that a capacity for what he refers to as maternal care/holding (that turns into the basis for being and for a sense of self) can be provided by men who parent, while women who parent can provide otherness and excitement about the larger world. We have come to learn that being and doing are not sequential, as Winnicott thought, but ongoing interlinked processes throughout development, not tied to a particularly gendered parent. For Winnicott, ordinary devotion was provided by the mother, but this was a culturally bound view, anchored in a particular time and place. Parents provide ordinary devotion for their children.

In *The Argonauts*, Maggie Nelson reminds us that complex lives cannot be shoehorned into neat dichotomies and binaries. She relates the story of how a friend sees a coffee mug with a photo of Harry, Maggie (seven months pregnant), and Harry's son, Lenny, dressed up to go to the Nutcracker, which was an important family ritual for Maggie's mother. The friend comments, "I've never seen anything so heteronormative in my life" (2015, p. 13). Nelson replies that the demand that anyone live a life that's all one thing is unsustainable.

Scarfone (2012) states,

> Indeed, it would be a technical monstrosity, alien to both the spirit and the ethic of psychoanalysis, to imagine that we could maintain constant control, seamlessly guided by theory, of what will arise in the transference that knots together the two members of the analytic couple. There would be a danger of totalitarian thinking and control (pensée totalitaire et d'emprise) in place of the effort of loosening and freeing up that psychoanalysis represents.
>
> (p. 5)

Exploring the dynamics of a transference–countertransference experience is a helpful pathway in exploring the erotic feelings that arose as an analysand struggled to understand his evolving relationship with his four-year-old son. Andy presented the following clinical material in supervision. Charles was in his third year of analysis with Andy and was struggling with his sexual feelings and an intense sense of loss and loneliness that his parents never wanted him. Charles spoke of a great hole he felt inside himself in his lower belly, above his groin. He spent a great deal of time describing the desolate and lonely feelings that accompanied this sensation. Over several weeks, he noticed that his torso was extremely sensitive and that at the same time, he had a profound sense of loss. Charles reported that he was favoring his belly and protecting it, as if it was extremely vulnerable and could easily be damaged. Charles's associations in session were feelings of always being held like an object as a child, with very little body-to-body contact. At the times of these recollections, he also was aware of having the sensation of smells that reminded him of a hospital or sterile environment, as if he was being held by a nurse or doctor as an infant or newborn. There was no body-to-body contact, and everything around him was starched and scratchy. This was strongly linked to the emptiness he felt inside himself that something was missing. He was aware of having no sexual feelings and only a great hole inside. In the analysis, Charles came to realize that he longed for skin-to-skin contact, particularly with a paternal figure, and was upset that the analysis was aggravating these feelings and not gratifying them. Charles reported feeling that Andy seemed further away than ever before, only increasing the pain of the hole inside. Through the work of analysis, Charles came to realize that what he was beginning to feel were erotic feelings toward his analyst. Andy was older than Charles, and he knew Andy was a father as he had seen him with his children out in the community.

In supervision, Andy reported great countertransferential responses to the hole described by Charles. It reminded him of a time in his own analysis when he'd struggled with feelings of wanting to know what was inside himself and what it meant that he could never carry a child. He linked this to Charles's associations to feeling objectified. This took Andy back to a time when his mother was pregnant with his sister. Through his own analysis, Andy realized that at the time his mother was carrying his sister he wanted to be just like her; when his mother's belly grew, it pointed out the great difference between them as his belly stayed flat. For Andy, this reflected a deeper understanding of a confused part of him that wanted to be male and female in the same moment. He felt great connection to his mother's pregnancy and wanted to be able to have the same experience, while he also appreciated his desire to be a boy and pursue what he described as traditional boy adventures. As an adult in analysis, Andy realized that he was struggling with how limited it felt to be restricted to one gender.

The work of Katya Bloom helps us grasp how Andy was able to explore intimate feelings with Charles and find a way to utilize his own body responses to help him help Charles put into words what he was feeling. Bloom writes, "Embodiment is another way of describing the integration of parts – mind, body, feeling, internal and external worlds. Movement is a medium that gives form to, and can monitor changes in, what is occurring (often unconsciously) from moment to moment" (2006, p. xvi). Andy's awareness of his body and the sometimes intense sensations he experienced in the sessions with Charles, from pain to emptiness, increased his capacity to stay alert and curious. Andy realized he was making subtle movements in his chair while Charles was describing the empty hole in his body. Andy's attunement allowed them to create an environment where these vital feelings could become known between them.

Bloom alerts us to, "language to describe preverbal states arise naturally as a result of therapist and patient more consciously embodying their psychophysical states . . . material needs to be communicated and received on a purely non-verbal level" (p. 63). Charles and Andy struggled to grasp how associations to sensations and memories from early in his life brought Charles the capacity to begin to explore how these related to moments he was having between himself and himself, as well as his son and himself.

The analysand, Charles, realized that the feeling of a great hole inside of himself and his associations to sterile environments went beyond the experience of being an object. Charles realized that those thoughts and feelings arose as he was increasingly aware of growing sexual sensations in sessions. He reported dreams of having sex with Andy and devouring each other's bodies, accompanied by a great sense of comfort in feeling warmth and growing intimacy in the analysis. Charles also realized that these feelings were exacerbated as he interacted with his own son, who was four years old at the time. Charles reported a growing awareness that the hole reflected a gap he feared was developing between his son and himself. Charles remembered being very aware of wanting to have body-to-body contact with his son from the time he was born and that he had a sense of being a wholesome father. Yet he became aware of a struggle as his son grew and developed. Charles realized their relationship was changing and that his son would no longer want the same kind of attention from his father. Furthermore, Charles became aware of sexual stirring in himself and great worries that it would evident to his son as he struggled to see his son entering latency. We can see how Andy's capacity to allow Charles to be curious about and explore his bodily sensations created a space for growth and understanding.

Mary Target (2015) writes,

> Sexual pleasure perhaps requires waves of projective identification: realizing one's own pleasure through taking control in fantasy of thoughts and feelings of the other, possessing them momentarily, making their feelings one's own and then giving them back as one repossesses one's own desire, transformed.

(p. 51)

Might Charles's capacity to transpose himself into what he thought his son was experiencing have created a cavity within his own body and psyche to grasp earlier experiences in his own life as well as what he embodied in his analytic sessions?

The fathers' erotism

> The words *I love you* come tumbling out of my mouth in an incantation the first time you fuck me in the ass, my face smashed against the cement floor of your dank and charming bachelor pad. You had *Molloy* by your bedside and

a stack of cocks in a shadowy unused shower stall. Does it get any better? *What's your pleasure?* you asked, then stuck around for an answer.

(Nelson, 2015, p. 3)

Len was devastated when he came into my (EG) consulting room. He had just found out that the adoption he planned with great care and enthusiasm had fallen through. Len and his partner, Jim, had worked with an adoption agency for over a year. Through the agency, they made contact with Denise early in her pregnancy and supported her emotionally and financially, hopeful about adopting her baby, yet aware she could change her mind about the adoption at any time. They spoke to Denise by telephone and made repeated long-distance trips to visit, accompanying her to prenatal exams and meeting her family. Len and Jim received the call informing them that Denise's labor had begun and left immediately for the delivery. However, they missed the baby's birth and Denise refused to see them. Her mother met with them and said apologetically that her daughter had decided to keep the infant. The new mother was exhausted and distraught; she refused to meet with Len and Jim.

The hopeful dads decided to stay for a few days in a nearby hotel in case Denise changed her mind. After five days, Denise's mother informed them that they would be hearing from the adoption agency formally canceling all ties between them. Devastated, Len and Jim returned home and began a lengthy mourning process. It was not their first experience with a failed adoption, but their previous experience had not involved such a high level of participation and commitment to the infant, as they had been informed of that potential adoption only a few weeks before the scheduled delivery and were told soon after that the adoption was off.

Over the next several months, Len and Jim again explored trying to adopt a baby, as well as other options for having children. Len had strong feelings that he wanted to adopt as he felt there were too many unwanted children in the world. He felt that Jim and he could offer a wonderful home to an infant and help ease the painful challenge of an unwanted pregnancy. Len and Jim both wanted children and thoughtfully considered their options – adoption, foster to adoption, and in vitro fertilization/surrogacy (IVF). Regularly, Len brought his feelings and concerns about having children to his analysis. As Len and Jim explored their choices, it caused some friction in their relationship. Through his analytic work, Len realized that Jim and he experienced the loss in very different ways. Len was very aware that he was suffering. He was very sensitive and fragile for weeks after the loss. Jim, in contrast, endured the loss more stoically. He immediately busied himself in trying to take care of Len, and exploring what other options were available in order to have a child. From Len's perspective, Jim was unable to join him in his grief.

Len's grief about the loss of the adoption continued for several months, and he was determined to mourn the loss fully before moving forward with another adoption. Over time, Len and Jim realized that each of them had mourned the loss in their own way and were able to consider the next step together. A year later,

Len and Jim decided to try IVF. They found an egg donor and a surrogate, Jill, interested in helping in their quest to become parents and began the IVF process. After debating whose sperm would be used for the fertilization, they decided to use sperm from both men with eggs from the same donor. Several viable embryos resulted, and they let the fertility specialist pick one embryo to implant, without knowing whom the biological father was. They also decided they would try again if the procedure did not lead to a viable pregnancy.

At the start of his analysis, Len and Jim had been together for about three years. Len was interested in an analysis because previous therapies had helped him understand events and feelings in his life; he now wanted to explore his thoughts and emotions more deeply. He sought out an analyst who was openly gay and could help him integrate and explore his feelings without trying to analyze what 'made him' gay. After interviewing several analysts he decided to work with me (EG). At the time of the IVF, Len had been in analysis with me for about four years. Earlier in the analysis, we had explored Len's ideas about eroticism, sexuality, and gender, as well as how he experienced his own gender and sexuality. He described himself as sexually versatile, enjoying many different sexual practices with Jim. Len recalled some confusion about his gender in his youth and when, as an adolescent, he came out. He sometimes felt as if he was in the wrong body, that he felt much more feminine than a cisgender man, but in previous therapies and earlier work with me, Len came to understand that he had fluid feelings regarding his gender but self-identified as male. Len felt increasingly comfortable in his body, but wrestled with how he could recognize and acknowledge feminine parts of himself without resorting to artificial labeling.

With the successful implantation of the embryo came a shift in the analytic work with Len. As we explored the prospect of becoming a parent and what it was like to father a child, Len was surprised by what that was evoked in him. During the fourth month of the pregnancy, Len and Jim began telling friends and extended family that they were expecting. They had several friends with infants or who were attempting to have children, and felt a sense of community in their experience of being expectant fathers. Simultaneously, Len was surprised by his sexual cravings. Previously, Len took pride in describing himself as sexually versatile; he often shifted back and forth between receiving and inserting in his sexual activity with Jim. During a Monday session, clearly in the grip of strong emotion, Len said that he needed to tell me something that was quite difficult for him to say. He started the session with updates about the pregnancy – contacts he had with the surrogate, Jill, and reports from her that the obstetrician felt the pregnancy was going well. Len described things he and Jim had discussed in preparing their home for the new baby. Over the weekend, both he and Jim felt drawn to staying home and spending time together, something their schedules did not always allow. Len described having sex several times over the weekend and was surprised at his own demand that Jim penetrate him and what it felt like to be in that position. Len shared that over the last few weeks he had only wanted to be penetrated and was curious as to what was happening to him. In describing his feelings during sex, he said that intercourse felt unusually powerful. As he reflected on his weekend experience, he described having a sense of fullness inside his lower torso in the moment. He could not locate exactly where the fullness was. Simultaneously, as Len described these feelings, I (the analyst) became aware that my lower belly felt warm and open. I had a strong awareness of openness and silently wondered if Len felt something similar. Len continued on to say that he was deeply touched by the sensations he was having in the session, and that it was extremely hard to put those bodily perceptions into words. He continued by wondering if all of this had something to do with the pregnancy and his desire that he and Jim create something together.

Len then told me that he had several dreams over the weekend, but could not remember much about them, only that he and another man that he thought was Jim were in the dreams and that there was a sense of warmth and satisfaction in the dreams. I suggested that perhaps he was trying to grasp how he and Jim were connected to the unborn baby, imagining what Jill was experiencing, yet also coming to know the experience of their own minds making space for a new baby. Jim had shared with Len that their sexual intercourse over the weekend felt particularly powerful to him as well, and Jim felt a deep longing and love for Len. In the session with me, Len articulated how important it had felt to him to receive Jim and how much he longed to keep Jim inside him. He was aware of how sexually exciting it had been, but also how profound and sensual. Over the next weeks, we explored how Len's erotic desires and thoughts helped link him to the growing baby and had a profound impact on how he experienced his body. He reported noticing other bodily sensations, such as feeling different in workouts at the gym or when he was sitting in meetings at work or sharing dinners with Jim. The exploration of these experiences and feelings sporadically came back into the sessions over the next several weeks. Len realized that part of his desire in being penetrated was wanting some very deep part of himself seen by Jim. We explored Len's hopes that I could see those feelings and things deep inside of him, as well.

Len elaborated on the sensations of holding and containing he was having in his body. He had come to see that not only were Jim and he making room for their daughter in their house, but he was also making room in his body. Having Jim inside him made Len feel complete and whole in a profound way. Through his analytic work, Len realized that an opening was occurring in his psyche, as well as through the bodily sensations he was having. He recognized that deep within himself, it felt incredibly powerful that they had created a baby.

These sessions increased the powerful connection between us. At the same time, Len was terrified by the power of his new feelings. Through the work, we were able link this to notions he had about the birth of his baby and a sense that he was embarking on a journey where he would have many very powerful feelings, from love and joy to terror and dismay. Len was able to explore how his sexual experiences and feelings were helping him prepare for the baby in a very embodied way. He began linking the feelings of strong desire for Jim to awareness that he was excited about and simultaneously scared of the upcoming birth.

These explorations led him to consider that the bodily experiences he was having, including but not limited to erotic and overtly sexual, was a way of feeling a tremendous connection to the baby and anticipation of fatherhood.

A few months later, Len noted that his sexual experiences had completely shifted. He was now much more interested and desirous of being the penetrating partner in sexual relations with Jim. He noticed the intensity he felt with Jim when they had sex and how deeply connected he felt as the inserting partner. Jim was comfortable with the switch and appeared a willing and equal participant. In session, Len was curious what had shifted in him to make his sexual desire evolve. We explored these thoughts and he began identify the power he felt leaving something of his in someone else. He was aware of wanting something shared that could evolve and grow; while reporting these activities, Len was aware that he and Jim had continued their plans and made physical space in their home for the baby. They had created a room for the baby and shifted their belongings to make it easier for extended family to come and visit. Len and Jim were sorting through various childcare options for when the baby was born, as to what arrangements would be made between the two of them and others to take care of the baby. During this time they found out they were having a daughter. Initially, they thought they didn't want to know the sex of the baby until birth, but they had changed their minds since Jill, the surrogate, already knew. Len and Jim didn't want to create distance by having to keep secrets. Len was able to explore how being the inserting partner in their sexual relations was reflective of how he was feeling about himself.

Things had evolved for Len. Despite his discomfort in bringing it up in his analysis, Len felt the need to explore what had shifted and why he felt such a strong desire to be the inserting partner with Jim. He realized that his sexual desires and the feeling of penetrating Jim reflected a powerful link to a part of himself he had not been aware of previously. In contrast to feeling held and contained, he recognized new strengths in himself as provider, holder and caregiver. He linked the idea of being the sexually inserting partner to a part of himself that felt strong and secure. Len was amazed by how satisfying and exciting the sexual moments with Jim were because he felt able to lead and support Jim in their intimacy. At the same time, Len's confidence was growing in imagining his capacity to take care of his newborn baby. He contrasted this to earlier feeling in his life where he'd been confused and worried about how feminine or masculine he appeared to friends and family. He became more aware of deep feelings that he was now comfortable in his mind and body in awaiting the birth of his child. Jim noticed this shift and commented that Len seemed less worried or focused on the physical preparations for the baby and more comfortable in his own body. This recognition by Jim helped Len realize something even more meaningful. Len recognized that after a period of being interested in receiving Jim and then a period of wanting to penetrate Jim he was now more open and available to himself and increasingly interested in a versatile sexual intimacy. While his comfort in himself and his body would continue to fluctuate with moments of intense self-doubt and concerns to a more confident and comfortable awareness of himself it also reflected Len's growing capacity to weather these currents and not feel disrupted by them. This expanded to conversations between Len and Jim about what they each envisioned life would be like as fathers and how they could each support each other on this new voyage. They discussed practical matters, such as what they each wanted to be called and how they might coordinate daily care for their newborn baby.

Over the next months, Len and Jim decided that Len would take at least six months off from work to be with their daughter. Jim would take a couple of weeks at the birth, return to work, and then at six months they would decide if Len would extend his leave or Jim would take time and Len would go back to work. In the work of his analysis, Len discovered that part of what had become activated in him with the shift in sexual desire was connected to feelings of staying home, creating a home, and being the primary caregiver for his daughter.

Canonical psychoanalysis is ambivalent about gender and sexuality. Even the possibility that anatomy is not destiny chafes, as inevitably analysts revert to Freud's twin themes of penis envy and passivity as bedrock. It is incredibly difficult to develop our capacities to freely imagine human possibility. Into this context comes Griffin Hansbury's "The Masculine Vaginal" (2017), in which Hansbury invites us to consider men's relationship to the Vaginal, as the symbolic counterpart to the Phallic. The body is mutable (or not), but there are no limits to what can be imagined:

> the Vaginal defies boundaries, as its literal source appears to do – spreading, opening, tunneling into darkness, connecting to deeper reaches of the body, similarly conceptualized as a corresponding space in the mind, that which can expand or close, ventilate or confine, a headspace of overlapping passages and vaults.
>
> (Hansbury, 2017, p. 1010)

Hansbury brings us to a new physio-psychic reality, both queer and not. Hansbury makes space for an "empowered male vagina," and with that comes imagining, as Len does, the deeper parts of himself. It is only a slight stretch for Len not only to be an open, penetrable man, but perhaps to fantasize pregnancy and childbirth.

Conclusion

It is difficult to deviate from the "expectable ways in which body/sexuality/gender order each other" (Saketopoulou, 2017, p. 1044) and the expectable ways we see fathering/mothering/parenting. In an era in which the nuclear family is no longer the norm, how does the analyst step outside the "cultural forces of collective meaning making that organize sexual and gendered" and family life that "are carried in and through the analyst" (p. 1045). If anything, "One of the gifts of genderqueer family making . . . is the revelation of caretaking as detachable from – and attachable to – any gender, any sentient being" (Nelson, 2015, p. 72). Maggie Nelson and Harry Dodge, and their children, Lenny and Iggy, and indeed the parents/fathers/mothers described in this chapter, all participate in a long history of people (queer and not) constructing their own families:

> It reminds us that any bodily experience can be made new and strange, that nothing we do in this life need have a lid crammed on it, that no one set of practices or relations has the monopoly on the so-called radical, or the so-called normative.

(pp. 72–73)

Rather than reducing complexity, as analysts we must imagine new possibilities in time and space for locating the father.

Chapter 4

The role of innate bisexuality in adult eroticism*

Rajiv Gulati and David Pauley

This chapter investigates the discourse on psychic bisexuality as it unfolds in Freud's writings; in contemporary papers by LGBTQ psychoanalysts; and in a volume of essays, *Psychic Bisexuality*, published in 2018 by a group of prominent French and British analysts (Perelberg, 2018). The greater acceptance of non-normative sexualities and genders is reshaping the discourse on bisexuality and gender in many corners of our profession, yet – as Perelberg's volume attests – that evolution is far from universal. We aim to highlight a strain of unquestioned heteronormativity and cisgenderism in Perelberg et al.'s description of the fundamentals of psychic life, a strain that we submit has roots (via a certain one-sided reading of Lacan) in Freud's unresolved mourning over his inchoate homosexual self. We propose a more embracing vision of bisexuality that seeks to 'hold', rather than enact, the grief and anxiety associated with the development of myriad, different personal patterns.

Introduction: peering through keyholes

This chapter is about psychic bisexuality, a foundational Freudian concept of unprecedented reach, but one that is sagging under the weight of widely disparate usage in different corners of the psychoanalytic firmament at the present moment. Before turning to those different usages and their repercussions for that robust (though not unbreakable) concept, to Freud, or to our own experience as openly gay training analysts – a minority status that inevitably colors the way we frame such issues – we will introduce the concept, viscerally, via excerpts from two poems[1] from the collection *Night Sky with Exit Wounds* by the acclaimed Vietnamese-American poet, Ocean Vuong (2016). The first, "Threshold," begins:

> In the body, where everything has a price,
> 　　　　　I was a beggar. On my knees,
> I watched, through the keyhole, not
> 　　　　　the man showering, but the rain
> falling through him: guitar strings snapping
> 　　　　　over his globed shoulders.

> He was singing, which is why
>   I remember it. His voice –
> it filled me to the core
>   like a skeleton. Even my name
> knelt down within me, asking
>   to be spared.

(p. 3)

The singing man, we learn shortly, is a father; the poem's subject, the transfixed young child kneeling nearby, is his son. Vuong's poem, extending just a few more lines after the excerpt noted, traces the headwaters of the boy's desire, his birth as a sexual subject there at that exact instant at the keyhole –"for in the body, where everything has a price // I was alive. . . ." – and the ambivalence and loss that this birth engenders: "I didn't know that the cost // of entering a song – was to lose/ your way back // So I entered. So I lost, I lost it all with my eyes // wide open" (pp. 3–4).

The second poem, "Trojan," appearing a few pages later in the collection, finds the same boy (or so we imagine), older now, dancing in a red dress before a mirror in a silent apartment, the dawning light casting shadows of his movement against family photographs lining the walls. Unlike the subject of the previous poem – an awestruck, even reverential child – the boy here is in perpetual motion, twirling, "the dress/petaling off him like the skin of an apple. . . ", while a far greater combustion courses silently within. He *is* the Trojan horse (the poem's central metaphor), his "belly full of blades/& brutes. . . ", the mute awakening of the previous poem transformed within his gyrating form into an elemental force, barely contained: "How like/the wind, they will see him. They will see him/clearest/when the city burns" (p. 9).

We begin this chapter with Vuong's haunting verses in order to remind ourselves (and you) that the bisexuality in which psychoanalysis trades is its own elemental force, and that, as analysts, we are each forever peering through keyholes, struggling to come to terms with the tunes that Sigmund Freud sang long ago in the waters of his self-absorption. One of the most generative parts of those tunes for us and for many analysts (we suspect) can be found in the ambiguous word 'bisexuality' itself. As the interpersonal analyst Mark Blechner points out in an important recent paper, that term covers a wide range of territory, encompassing an identification with both polar physiological sexes and gender roles (dresses versus pants, 'passive' versus 'active', etc., a concept Blechner calls 'bigenderism'), and the more colloquial sense of the word 'bisexual' as pertaining strictly to sexual object choice (gay or straight), *and every semiotic possibility in between* (Blechner, 2015). That super-saturated term came into Freud's theoretical vocabulary, famously, during what Harold Blum recalls was the most homosexual phase of his life, his long epistolary self-analysis in the 1890s with Berlin otolaryngologist Wilhelm Fliess (Blum, 1990). The term 'bisexual' was Fliess's property (a debt which Freud continually recalls), yet the word itself spoke to something deep within Freud, a germ that he required to make sense of enigmas he was confronting simultaneously in his clinical work with patients and in his self-analysis. So important was that idea, and the lived experience of sharing a loving connection with the man who gave it to him, that Freud for a long time looked past his friend's glaring eccentricities. He longed to share his ideas and clinical experiences with Fliess, and in his letters unfolded to him, before all others in the world, the tendrils of his theory of unconscious life. At a genital level, it seems clear, their relationship remained unconsummated (though not for want of trying; Freud invited Fliess to enter his nasal cavity on multiple occasions to assuage physiological *as well as emotional* malaise, see Kris, 1954; Masson, 1985), yet with time, their vast differences, and Fliess's oddities – inevitably – brought rupture.

Freud's theory of psychic bisexuality – and with it, the whole of psychoanalysis – nonetheless came into being in this homosexual "parenthood" (Blum, 1990, p. 22), yet, from the outset, simultaneously, Freud the theorist worked to backpedal from the full implications of that procreative act. Despite his *theoretical* understanding of the wishes of *all* little boys to at times take the 'passive' position and be inseminated by their fathers (Freud, 1923, p. 250), he rarely questioned his own dominant heterosexuality or embraced his feminine side (Orgel, 1996) The tremulous possibility of homoerotic consummation (and surrender to 'passivity'. for Freud synonymous with 'femininity') was for him a leitmotif that hovered in the background, a road not taken (and perhaps one that never held much more than a fleeting interest at a conscious level). In continually *choosing* his heterosexual/'masculine' orientation in this way (a 'choice' undoubtedly made in early childhood), Freud, not unlike Vuong's kneeling subject in the "Threshold" poem cited at the outset, nonetheless foreclosed on other paths evident in his transference with Fliess, and experienced an analogous loss: "I didn't know that the cost // of entering a song – was to lose/your way back // So I entered. So I lost, I lost it all with my eyes // wide open" (Vuong, 2016, pp. 3–4).

In keeping with the searing (if unconscious) grief associated with his heterosexual object choice, Freud's theory of psychic bisexuality, for all of its many ambiguities and contradictions, keeps the memory of that other, unchosen (homosexual) possibility alive. In moments when one least expects it – the bravado of his Leonardo paper, when he all but shouts that the great artist's homosexuality is a developmental miscarriage, a narcissistic adaptation to a flawed domestic space (mother fixation; absent father), it rears up: "everyone, even the most normal person, is capable of making a homosexual object choice, and has done so at some time in his life" (Freud, 1910, p. 99 fn). Or later, in his famous "letter to an American mother," published posthumously: "[homosexuality] is nothing to be ashamed of, no vice, no degradation, it cannot be classified as an illness. . . . Many highly respectable individuals of ancient and modern times have been homosexuals, several of the greatest men among them" (Grotjahn, 1951, p. 331).

Such statements, significant not just by dint of being gay affirmative, but by acknowledging Freud's grief by not denigrating the homosexual pole of experience he valued and turned away from, exist cheek by jowl with many others that stress the pathology of same-sex object choice, a 'certain arrest in the sexual function', leaving healthful heterosexual inclinations stranded irrevocably in childhood (that pathogenic phrasing, along with another unfortunate metaphor for homosexual desire, 'blighted seeds', belongs to the same paragraph of the "Letter to an American mother" as the more affirming messages just cited). To our knowledge, there has been no published tally of the number of homophobic versus homo-normalizing utterances in Freud's written works, yet, in keeping with his dominant heteronormative framing of psychosexual development,[2] we expect that the former would predominate to a large degree. That these forceful and unexpected homo-normalizing statements exist *at all* within his writings on the dynamic unconscious, a minority message perhaps in keeping with the numerical percentage of gay or transgender people within a largely heterosexual/ cisgender society (4 to 10 percent), is the slender filament – the miracle – that has brought us and so many other LGBTQ individuals into the ranks of the psychoanalytic profession.

The thirteenth floor

Reading the recent volume *Psychic Bisexuality: A British–French Dialogue*, edited by the London-based psychoanalyst Rosine Jozef Perelberg (2018), we were reminded of a recurrent dream of a patient from many years ago. The patient hailed from another country, and lived for a short time on the thirteenth floor of a building there at a significant moment in childhood. In the dream, she recalled going back to that home, yet her childhood building merged in the dreamscape with other structures from her working life in New York City, a place where – as is well known, owing to superstition – thirteenth floors do not exist (elevators glide seamlessly from floors twelve to fourteen, precluding panic). The place she was seeking was thus unfindable.

Another association to the Perelberg volume, this one a colleague's memory from childhood in a small middle-American town, centers on the public library there, a modest cinderblock structure that at the time of this memory in the early 1980s held no more than 40,000 volumes. With flushed excitement and a degree of shame, he recalls combing the shelves of the psychology section for books that might help him understand his homosexuality. Even a textbook on abnormal psychology, however – the most promising candidate and the cause for the fleeting hopefulness – contained only a perfunctory rehashing of Freudian tropes (mother fixation; absent father; untreatable), with no sense whatsoever of how people go through their days shouldering such potent, incurable longings. Once again, a vital part of lived experience was made untraceable.

Like the thirteenth floor in the apartment building or the missing books on the library shelves, Perelberg's volume, read from the perspective of two well-traveled gay psychoanalysts, bewilders with its obdurate refusal to grapple forthrightly with gay, lesbian, bisexual, or transgender experience as part of the continuum of 'psychic bisexuality' denoted in the volume's title. Published in 2018 and including contributions from a group of clinicians that occupies the summit of a certain orthodox Lacanian[3]/Greenian sect within the British and French traditions – including the late André Green, Juliet Mitchell (one of the first writers to bring Lacan to the English-speaking psychoanalytic world), Donald Campbell (past president of the British Psychoanalytic Society), and Gregorio Kohon (a noted analyst and the most expansive and engaging writer of the bunch), as well as a number of prominent members of the Société Psychoanalytique de Paris – this is not a hack volume that one would expect to peddle conversion therapy for LGBTQ patients. The near-complete avoidance of LGBTQ experience or of contemporary gender theory in its pages (not just in its purest academic form, per Butler, 1990, but in the many articles and volumes by LGBTQ clinicians and their allies that apply such concepts fruitfully to the analytic encounter),[4] occasioned head-scratching as we browsed through its pages, and then, with a deeper reading, a mounting indignation.

Despite its bland title and encouraging promise of cross-cultural dialogue, Perelberg's volume is very much a polemic, a forceful shoring up of a crucial pillar of psychoanalytic doctrine in danger at the present moment of "a collapse into the commonplace" (Mitchell, 2018, p. xviii). The pillar in question is the bisexual unconscious, a 'psychic bisexuality' that, in a certain narrow reading, exists on an exalted plane, without errors in need of redress or concessions to shifting empirical reality, as Juliet Mitchell, who provides the volume an appreciative foreword, wrote decades ago in the text where she helped launch Lacan (and her interpretation of his ideas) to renown in the English-speaking psychoanalytic world:

> Lacan conceived of his own project differently: despite the contradictions and the impasses, there is a coherent theorist in Freud *whose ideas do not need to be diverged from*; rather they should be set within a cohesive framework that they anticipated but which, for historical reasons, Freud himself could not formulate.
>
> (Mitchell and Rose, 1982; emphasis ours)

For Lacan, as Mitchell recalls, that framework centered on Saussurian linguistics – and the irreducibility of the ur-signifer, the phallus, the axis ('law') around which all of psychic life is said to radiate: we either yearn for it, or seek to embody it, but invariably fail, a state of unceasing desire, partial satisfaction and disillusionment that is our destiny as psychic beings, the Lacanian version of original sin. The 'historical' factors Lacan meant to redress on Freud's behalf were manifold, from the de-sexed pre-Oedipal psychology of Kleinian object relations, to proto-feminist thinkers like Karen Horney or Ernst Jones, squeamish about the phallocentrism in some of Freud's later writings on female sexuality, to the 'neutered' ego psychology of Anna Freud and her British and American followers, to empiricist observers of sexual life, like Kinsey or Masters and Johnson (Mitchell and Rose, 1982; Roudinesco, 1990, 1997).

Despite his theory's Manichean overtones, Lacan's complex 'return to Freud' has many compelling parts, not least of which is his insistence on the centrality of bisexuality and its attendant grief as the major motivator of unconscious life. (Our self-representation as gendered beings invariably carries a constitutive loss; as psychic subjects, we will never be whole, a lack that no amount of 'attachment security', 'adaptation', or 'loving and working' can close.) Lacan's version of bisexuality, moreover, avoids the Darwinian reductionism evident in many places in Freud's writings; it is not biology but psychosexuality ('sexuation') that shapes our desires and our relationships to the fractured forms that we embody physically. In certain places, Lacan even chides Freud for his heterosexism, as in his interventions in the 'Dora' case, which Lacan famously (and accurately) felt overly privileged Freud's need to channel his patient's desires toward her male suitor and away from his tantalizing wife (Lacan, 1966, in Mitchell and Rose, 1982, pp. 61–63).

While Lacan, unlike numerous American analysts of the era in which he wrote and lectured (Bergler, 1944; Socarides, 1968), never sought to change the sexual orientation of his gay patients, his early writing nonetheless enshrined a potent heteronormative dualism that explicitly and repeatedly favors heterosexual and cisgender forms. His reluctance to grapple with the urgency of homosexual desire as a distinct and coequal erotic valence *in itself* (as opposed to a misguided or perverse effort to grapple with the challenges of gendering: gay men trying to become women; lesbians impersonating men) is evident in his response to the most famous clinical case that Freud devoted to lesbianism, the 1920 paper, "The Psychogenesis of a Case of Female Homosexuality". As Perelberg (2018) recalls in the present volume:

> Lacan thought that the paper was one of the most brilliant of Freud's texts. He pointed out that the young girl desired nothing from the older woman [her beloved], a relationship of *no satisfaction* that established *the relation of lack* to the feminine object. She desired in the woman she loved precisely what she did not have: what she did not have was a phallus.
>
> (p. 18, emphasis added)

How does one translate this obscure passage in terms that are not homophobic? We suppose this would start from the premise that all people, from the moment they become aware of sexual difference, enter into sexuality from a position of a 'lack'. Even small boys, who possess the flesh and blood appendage in an immature form, do not ever possess the more mystical paternal phallus; they invoke it over time through their longing to stimulate their (female) partner's reciprocal desire and its partial satisfaction, *jouissance*, but then clatter back into brokenness – yearning and striving, never reaching or attaining – not even as fathers or grandfathers in their own right.

Perelberg's summary of Lacan's response to the Freud case, however, which also alludes to the girl's 'desire' and 'love' for the older woman – a palpable tenderness that Freud emphasized in the original text, even as it bewildered him (1920a, p. 145) – suggests a different orientation: a yearning for a 'something' that exists apart from the phallus. In Perelberg's more conservative reading of Lacan, with its unbending, either-or view of the sexual binary, this 'something' is – in fact *must be* – a 'nothing' ('no *thing'*), with 'no satisfaction' possible. Thus, even if the girl in question[5] succeeds in seducing the older woman, in making love to her and reaching climax; even if (as is possible today in many places) she marries her lesbian partner and has children and lives out her days amidst the tedium and joys one associates with family life, she embodies a 'lack' that is greater than the 'lack' of her heterosexual neighbors. The lesbian partners, in their marrow, have failed to grapple with their yearning and grief at being cleaved from the essential phallus, have failed to make peace with the primordial brokenness that characterizes the human unconscious, and are thus living in a quasi-delusional denial of psychic bisexuality and thereby of their monosexual (castrated) femininity.

This type of implacable heteronormative dualism, with its brisk dismissal of homosexuality as a flawed (if sometimes unavoidable) attempt to grapple with gender differentiation, is reproduced in the present volume ceaselessly and without qualification, and is anointed – numbingly – as the unquestioned 'deepest level' of psychosexual bedrock. In replicating this discourse, its authors not only airbrush away Freud's far more complex and attenuated statements on homosexuality, but pointedly ignore four decades' worth of writing by lesbian and gay psychoanalysts (and like-minded heterosexual analysts; for an early example, see S. Mitchell, 1978) that takes up the *intense* grieving that invariably accompanies LGBTQ experience: grieving for lost heterosexual possibilities, for normative expectations and gender roles, for real-life family relationships shattered due to homo- or transphobic judgment (see Crespi,1995).

The implications of this unexamined heterosexism in the present volume are most vividly and disturbingly displayed in the book's sole extended clinical report, Donald Campbell's (2018) chapter "Alienating Identifications and Sexuality". Campbell's patient, a twenty-seven-year-old self-described gay man, presents in the consultation with complaints about ambivalence: "I can never make up my mind. I can never decide who I want to be with or what I want to do. I really can't have any meaningful relationships" (p. 227), yet does not extend this ambivalence to questions about his sexual life until a month into the analysis, when he notes that he "can't decide whether to go to a gay massage parlor or a straight one" (p. 228). Campbell does not explore whether perhaps that particular 'ambivalence' might be a *gift* to the analyst (heterosexual fantasies, we gather, were not often present in the patient's adult life until the treatment began), but latches onto that thin reed as evidence of an embryonic heterosexual identity lurking – in whole cloth – beneath the patient's outward gay presentation.

That formulation – masturbatory homosexuality as defense against generative heterosexuality[6] – guides the entirety of Campbell's participation in the case over seven years. When the patient describes heterosexual fantasies (whether from childhood or from his current life), the analyst springs to life: exploring, interpreting, parsing out a historical theory that seems to explain the patient's blighted heterosexual potentiality. That theory, when elaborated at length eighteen months into the treatment, sounds – alas – rather familiar: the patient's father, alternatively distant and explosive, was not a consistent enough presence (aka, 'phallic representation'; aka, 'law') to allow for identification and differentiation; the mother was decidedly phallic, even castrating toward the father. Eager as always to please, Mr. Jones heartily endorses these interventions and others like them – ' "*What did she do to Dad's masculinity? Why didn't Dad fight back?*"' (p. 231; emphasis added) – yet despite frequent efforts to embrace heterosexuality and validate the analyst's doctrines (masturbating to straight fantasies!), is only ever able to achieve orgasm to images of men (p. 234).

When, however, earlier in the treatment, the patient's *homosexual* desires emerge, the analyst finds himself flummoxed:

> In the second month, Mr. Jones came back after a weekend and said, "I really don't know how to say this. (Silence). I don't know. (Silence). It's really embarrassing". Then very quietly and hesitantly he said, "I love you". I acknowledged the feelings with a murmur, but said nothing. This was a moment without context, from someone who felt like a stranger, *like someone he might have met in a gay massage parlor*. It was unsettling, and I was filled with uncertainty. I did not know who he was in love with in the transference. At that moment, *I did not know who I was for him.*
>
> (Campbell, 2018, p. 228; emphasis added)

This pregnant moment, coming only weeks after the session where the patient first disclosed his heterosexual 'gift' to the analyst, is not welcomed in a similar manner. It occasions no exploration from the analyst, no interpretations or questions; only a murmur of strained acknowledgment, followed by stunned ('unsettled'; 'uncertain') silence. The analyst recovers by the next session, and comes up with a rationalization for his own 'shock and disorientation' – the patient *objectified* him by engaging him as "a masturbation phantasy" (p. 228) – yet we submit that this searing, dissociated chapter in the countertransference, a scant two months into a seven-year treatment, made the case's eventual failure foreordained. Rather than exploring the patient's avowed 'love' from an *analytic* position, as decades' worth of writing on this topic would recommend ("I wonder if telling me you love me is really a question – am I the kind of person who can be trusted to accept your desire to love other men, including, perhaps, me?"), the analyst here, for reasons he does not disclose, crumbles, leaving the patient alienated and alone.

Thus, just like the woman searching in vain for a childhood home on the thirteenth floor, like the teenager scouring bookshelves for a text that might illuminate his desires, Mr. Jones looks to his psychoanalyst for some clue about how to live his life as a sexual being, and comes away empty-handed.[7]

Staying, crossing over

If gay desire comes off poorly in Perelberg's volume – a morbid effort to deny gender difference through aping cross-gender object choice, unfortunate, yet at times unavoidable – transgender experience fares even worse. What would a theory that insists upon the acceptance of polar ('castrated') gender make of Ocean Vuong's "Trojan" boy in his red dress, dancing his heart out before the mirror in his family's apartment?[8] Or others, like the five-year-old girl the American psychoanalyst Avgi Saketopoulou (2014) describes in a riveting recent paper, whose natal male genitalia clashes completely with her invariant, subjective sense of herself as female?

Perelberg's volume takes up such questions in three moments. The first occurs early on, as the editor herself, drawing on Freud and on her background as an anthropologist, sets out data that seems to support the notion that the sexual binary is a universal feature of human cultures around the globe. Perelberg asserts that this binary – phallus/no phallus, "an inherent characteristic of all human beings" (p. 2) – may assume widely different colorings depending on context, but exists without exception from one culture to the next and within all individuals. This problematic argument,[9] anodyne on the surface, in fact aims to undercut a key claim made by European sexual minorities starting in the mid-nineteenth century as they stumbled into the light of liberal society (i.e. away from religious essentialism; see Ulrichs, 1864), and one that is resurfacing powerfully at the present moment: the possibility of a *third gender*, an 'intermediate sex' (Hirschfeld, 2000, 2017; Mancini, 2010) located somewhere between the poles of male and female. We mention Hirschfeld's theory not by way of returning to an essentialist/biological view of sexual variation, but rather to stress that sexual minorities were grasping actively for non-pathological terms in which to describe themselves well before Freud's theories came into being, creating 'folkways,' like the discourse of a third sex, that analytic models largely displaced. The roiling possibility of a 'third sex,' repeatedly dismissed by Freud in his writings (Freud, 1905b, 1910), is of course even more problematic for this orthodox Lacanian repackaging of Freud's thinking. From what organizing signifier is a *third* gender cleaved? How, without recourse to pathology, does one explain the failure of a certain subset of humans to obey the 'law' of 'bisexual' (castrated) essentialism? If perhaps that 'law' is in fact more of a *cultural code* than an immutable metapsychological reality, then what is to stop individuals from crossing over from one polar gender to another (and perhaps back again in some cases, remolding physiology in the process), or taking up residence, without apology, in the borderlands between them?

Perelberg's selective anthropological analysis in the book's introduction is one part of this volume's response. Gregorio Kohon's conclusion, "Bye-bye Sexuality", the only chapter in the volume to grapple directly (if superficially) with contemporary gender theory, is meant to be its summation, a kind of theoretical *coup de grâce* on behalf of its authors' heteronormative vision of psychic bisexuality. In between these two conceptual bookends, to which we will return, there exists one extended clinical illustration of work with a transgender individual, André Green's chapter, "The Neuter Gender", on which we will now focus.

This chapter, originally published in 2001, reappears in Perelberg's book (we imagine) both because of Green's eminence in the French psychoanalytic tradition, and because it sets out a kind of cautionary tale of the perils of denying 'psychic bisexuality'. Despite having a sustained interest in Lacan, Green, who died in 2012, was no Lacanian, and was more apt than some of his Parisian colleagues to make use of concepts drawn from the object relations tradition of Klein, Winnicott, and others across the English channel, as well as certain American thinkers, in this case, notably, Robert Stoller (1964, 1985). That somewhat more variegated pedigree is evident in his chapter here, as Green grapples with the impact of parental (and in particular, maternal) fantasies on the formation of children's gender identity and sexual object choice. This conceptual cosmopolitanism nonetheless exists in the shadow of Green's mostly unexamined bewilderment toward the patient in the case he presents, a bewilderment that, in his theoretical postmortem decades after the case unfolded, shades into repulsion.

The patient in question, described by Green at various moments as 'he' and at others as 'she', seems – as best as we can construct – to have been a natal-gendered male raised throughout childhood as female by a hostile, frequently degrading mother. A prisoner in Nazi Germany during World War II, the patient was subjected to sinister 'feminizing' experiments, including the forcible provision of estrogen to produce breasts, undoubtedly (though Green does not state this explicitly), as a preamble to rape.[10] At the time the treatment unfolded in the late 1950s, the patient sought Green's help in (perhaps) reversing this imposed gender manipulation surgically, either by having 'top surgery' to remove the breasts, and resolving into maleness (which would according to Green would deprive the patient of a major avenue for sexual stimulation, nipple play), or by having 'bottom surgery' (removing the penis/testes) and resolving into femaleness. Despite his palpable confusion faced with the patient's dilemma and history of unthinkable traumas, Green (to his credit) manages to empathically reflect the patient's subjective reality: "in fact you don't want to be a man or a woman" – a statement that aligns fully with the patient's experience: "*I think you're the first person to get to the heart of the matter: I don't want to give up any of the advantages of the two sexes*" (Green, 2018, p. 251, emphasis in original).

In his theoretical framing of the case decades later, however – a framing that constitutes the bulk of this chapter – the author gives vent to a less sympathetic reconstruction of the patient's life story. Rather than embracing Hirschfeld's long-ago vision of a third or indeterminate gender, evident from birth and manifested by cross-gender identifications that elide 'male' and 'female' (an admixture that, given the imperatives of the gender binary, almost invariably invokes virulent expressions of regulatory anxiety, per Corbett, 2009a), Green looks to his patient's infantile life to explain the pathological trap of *their*[11] transgender experience. In this reading, the patient's biological maleness was infected from birth by discordant and scalding cross-gender fantasies in the mother, who forced them to live like a female (and presumably blocked the healthful incorporation of the paternal, forestalling a psychic differentiation into 'monosexual' maleness). The patient's later traumas cascaded out from this original confusion in the realm of gender (in effect, the incorporation of a maternal delusion), leading them to unconsciously orchestrate the dramatic violation from the German soldiers in wartime:

> The search for contradictory satisfactions was evident: her attitude toward any form of authority, public authorities, for example, was one of rejection, and her need to be kept under tight rein, *to be bullied and dominated meant she longed to be in a passive position.*
>
> (Green, 2018, p. 251, emphasis added)

Not unlike Campbell in the chapter just discussed, Green sees the patient's present-day difficulties and ambivalence about how to live life as expressing a core intrapsychic pathology, a morbid type of 'neutering' (auto-castration) – inflected with derivatives of the death drive – owing to the failure to achieve a coherent psychic/bodily gender identity. Put succinctly, Green views the patient's mixed gender presentation, not as a 'something' in its own right, but as a 'nothing', an evasion of psychosexual imperatives – and an obliteration of heterosexual procreativity. In Green's heteronormative/cisgender meta-psychology, this "neutering" exists, he states explicitly, a heartbeat away from suicide (p. 256).

This dire, pathological framing, of course, depends entirely upon where one begins. If one admits the possibility of a third sex, per Hirschfeld, as a coequal variation within the core matrices of the human unconscious, then the locus of pathology within the case shifts, in this realm at least, from the patient's individual psyche and their personal history, and into the social sphere, including the unconscious life and attitudes of the cisgender, heterosexual analyst, whose alarm at the patient's 'failure to differentiate' (expressed through an incisive application of clinical theory) springs from a failure to grapple with, and grieve, the inchoate possibility of his own mixed-gender self.

The implications here are wide-ranging. Perhaps, in fact, for all of the mother's putative pathology and hatred for the child, her decision to allow them to dress in female clothing sprang, not from a delusion, but from an empathic resonance with the child's *intrinsic*[12] position outside the gender binary. This choice, not pathogenic but in fact affirming of a core expression of psychic reality (a 'bedrock' for the patient, albeit a different strata than the one from which cisgender identity is hewn) does not preclude trauma, owing to pathology in other realms or to the virulent prejudices toward transgender experience in broader society. These include the actions of the enemy troops in wartime – their 'gift' of breasts to the patient – a head-spinningly ambivalent gesture. Notwithstanding these traumatic impingements, the patient's refusal to be bound by the constraints of the gender binary, despite the lifelong pressure to do so, could be plausibly framed as a form of *resilience*, one that Green, despite the bias evident in his theoretical postmortem, nonetheless supports in his clinical interventions.

Green's nuanced if ambivalent approach to the transgender patient in his care – *analytic* in his clinical role (i.e. not allowing his strong personal distaste to dictate his responses), yet pathologizing in his subsequent theoretical reflection on the case – is far less evident in Gregorio Kohon's polemical summing up chapter, "Bye-bye Sexuality". Tying together the varied strands in this volume, and – in particular – making use of the anthropological framing on the sexual binary (phallus/no phallus) as put forward, tendentiously, by Perelberg in her introductory chapter, Kohon engages energetically, often caustically, with the voices in contemporary society that presume to critique that perspective, or to suggest that sexuality and gender might be embodied in ways that depart from its immutable laws. After listing – and parodying – the large number of gender descriptors between 'male' and 'female' that exist in various places at the present moment (including the ancient, still extant South Asian category, *hijra*), Kohon (2018) engages in a robust peroration on the primacy of biological sex and cisgenderism:

> In the end, [socially] constructed or not, alternative or straight, there are only two sexes. While it may be considered unfair, discriminatory, unjust, unreasonable, a bore or a challenge, we cannot but accept this reality. . . . In other words, we need to take responsibility for not being more than what we are, to recognize our finitude and give up omnipotence, accepting that our desires can never be fulfilled.
>
> (p. 270)

The homiletic tone of this passage, with its rhetorical appeal to a universalism ('we') built on the 'original sin' of orthodox Lacanian psychosexuality (its credo: castration into monosexuality; renunciation of 'omnipotence'), reaches a sad crescendo a few lines later:

> Things are never simple. The symbolic order and the generational difference contribute to determine the subject's destiny from the beginning of conception. The baby will arrive in an already signifying world, which was there well before delivery: parents' phantasies, wishes, anxieties and dreams; names chosen, the name finally given, and so on. If, later in life, as the result of the vicissitudes of the subject's history there is a decision to change his/her sex, to modify the original body by mutilating it or adding something to it, to choose a different gender identity, such changes take place in the present, *but they never were nor could become a past.*
>
> (p. 271; emphasis in original)

Like Green's retrospective, pathologizing reconstruction of his patient's "failure to differentiate" in the realm of gender identity, Kohon's assault on trans experience, with its scathing disparagement of gender transition surgery as *mutilation* (i.e. destructive repudiation of a primordial, cisgender essence, aka, the 'symbolic order'), proceeds from the unquestioned, privileged place of cisgender heteronormativity.

To understand how extreme this perspective is within psychoanalysis at the present moment, one need only turn briefly to a recent volume by the American Lacanian Patricia Gherovici, *Transgender Psychoanalysis* (2017). Far from enshrining the gender binary as the unquestioned bedrock of psychic life, Gherovici, making use of a vastly different reading of Lacan,[13] sees transgender experience as a coequal and creative adaptation to the process of 'gendering' that unfolds in every human life. In her reading, sympathetic in many respects to that of Blechner, Saketopoulou, and Corbett, Gherovici stresses what is all too obvious from decades' worth of empirical research: that, despite biological morphology and societal expectations, the relational narratives and physiological surfaces that enclose the transgender subject's life do not accurately reflect their profound, inner experience of themselves as gendered beings. Far from 'mutilation' or other hortatory terms applied to sexual minorities in psychoanalysis and elsewhere ('narcissism'; 'abomination'), embracing one's trans-ness and in some cases undertaking surgical intervention to change those physical attributes holds out the promise, not of 'omnipotence' (Kohon's word, a delusion), but of a profound, perhaps life-saving[14] personal liberation.

Discussion and conclusion: the 'personal pattern' in the bisexual mirror

Our work on the current chapter in recent months has evoked a degree of incredulity among those in our circle, from colleagues (clinicians, straight and gay) to children and teenagers in our midst, who, like us, live in a progressive 'bubble' largely free from the taint of trans- or homophobic utterances. That statements like Kohon's or Green's[15] could be published without qualification in the present-day literature of a profession that exists at its core to help people,[16] even for us, seems at moments to defy comprehension. As we have immersed ourselves in Perelberg's volume, however, revisiting Freud, Lacan, and a great many other writers along the way, we have come to regard such statements as an inevitable part of an honest engagement with the analytic literature on bisexuality, a literature which – we emphasize – grew out of the contradictions in one man's efforts to understand himself on the cusp of the twentieth century.

As is clear in the preceding pages, Freud is not the only patriarch whose ambiguous shadow hovers over efforts to theorize sexual and gender variation at the present moment. Even a cursory reading of history makes clear that Lacan was of equal – and very likely, greater – stature in shaping the Freudian legacy in continental Europe and particularly in France (Roudinesco, 1990; Olner, 1988). Even those thinkers who depart widely from his theoretical schema – from members of the orthodox French societies (with whom he famously broke over the issue of session length), to the writers represented in Perelberg's volume, many also heavily influenced by Green – nonetheless had to reckon with Lacan's breathtakingly complex and generative reworking of the Freudian edifice. His vocabulary – the signifier and *jouissance*, castration and lack, the name of the father and the symbolic order – though all but absent from most contemporary American theorizing, ripples through the ideas and words of those other thinkers in far-reaching ways.

In a pungent interview published in 2002, the historian and Lacanian psychoanalyst Elisabeth Roudinesco makes the case that Lacan, despite a propensity for intemperate utterances,[17] was at the core no more apt to vilify homosexuality than any other form of erotic expression. In large measure, the historical record bears out her assessment. In an era when psychoanalytic societies on every continent refused to admit lesbian, gay or bisexual candidates, making use of a cynical framing that equated homosexuality with the 'un-analyzable' condition of psychosis,[18] Lacan embraced the training and certification of gay analysts. According to retrospective testimony, he was, moreover, a sympathetic therapist to both gay and transgender patients,[19] more interested in helping tease out their subjective reality than aiding their adaptation to any pre-formed 'law'. Finally, in building up a theory of mental life whose central feature is a blistering skepticism about any claim for psychic normality – psychologies of self and other, in the Lacanian mirror (Lacan, 2006), never capture the elusive essence of the real – he leveled the semiotic playing field for alternate sexualities and gender expressions. In so doing, he provided tools for present-day thinkers, such as Gherovici, that are being used to constructively explore LGBTQ experience and situate it within the purview of human potentiality.

As Roudinesco points out, however, Lacan also wrote and said a great many things amenable to retrograde constructions, and – despite his theory's famous complexity – was willing to relinquish nuance if doing so augmented his personal prestige (Roudinesco, 2002, 2014). What Lacan would have made of the current movement for LGBTQ equality – and for inclusion within the nuclear family, an institution whose pieties he disdained – is anyone's guess. In his absence, as we have shown in these pages, a spectrum of responses has emerged: each making use of aspects of his terminology; each invoking his legacy and name.[20]

With regard to the subject of this chapter, psychic bisexuality, a concept which we would define, along with Blechner, as the *sum total of gender and erotic representations present in the human unconscious*, we believe that Lacan's ideas contain one further significant, and perhaps under-appreciated, limitation. In advancing a theory of skepticism, or indeed of protest – fulminating against the presumptions of the dominant Anglo-American theorists of his day; highlighting the 'lacks' and 'perversions' that inflect every expression of gender or erotic desire – Lacan failed to account for the starkly different impact that such words have for those whose daily lives unfold outside the privileged enclosure of the normative. Unlike Freud, whose subsidiary homosexual identifications, expressed in his relationship with Fliess and memorialized in monumental theory he bequeathed, led him to actively contest the oppression of sexual minorities,[21] Lacan never seems to have grappled with the impact of his own residual gay (or transgender) self, or with the relationship of homophobia and transphobia to the wider theory of the bisexual unconscious that he sought to advance (Roudinesco, 2002).

As Vuong's poems remind us, however, *every* expression of erotic choice and gender identity carries a penumbra of loss, as the vast reservoir of sexual and gender potentialities present in infancy gives way to what Donald Winnicott (1953), in another context, refers to as the 'personal pattern'.[22] This type of differentiation, an essential and often mysterious chapter in development, comes as individuals linger at certain keyholes and thresholds, while leaving others unexplored: other avenues of erotic and affective affiliation; other potential gender expressions, residing both within and outside of the polar binary. In adult life, the residue of those primeval, unadulterated vistas – and the grief surrounding their relinquishment – persists. It animates not only the flickering forms that populate our nightly dreamscapes, but the beliefs we adopt to justify the naturalness of our 'choices', whether in matters of private eroticism (Dimen, 2000, 2005) or in the sweeping claims of clinical theories.

As our critique of Perelberg's volume makes clear, those clinical theories within psychoanalysis have always been of two minds on this issue: attempting to make space for gender and erotic expressions at odds with normative expectations, while also registering – and often enacting – the regulatory anxieties that an encounter with the deep bisexual unconscious, and with the dizzying fact of difference, invariably provokes. In removing LGBTQ experience from its pages, Perelberg's volume offers a sanitized 'psychic bisexuality' in keeping with one pole in the history of analytic thinking; our critique of that volume, and the work of a great many other thinkers active at the present moment, strives to embody its opposite. If Lacan's writings on 'lack' and 'loss' teach us anything, however, it would be to recall (with Hegel) that such roiling dialectics in conscious life seldom yield a satisfying resolution. Rather than attempting to expunge heterosexism or transphobia, to uphold the sanctity of the normative or usher in a transgressive, queer utopia, the best psychoanalysis may afford us at the present moment is the authenticity of the individual gaze: the grace to admit our anxiety faced with the fathomless depths of our bisexual inheritance, and the willingness to grieve, and perhaps strive to understand, the myriad patterns expressed in other lives.[23]

Notes

* This chapter was originally published as: Rajiv Gulati and David Pauley (2019). The half embrace of psychic bisexuality. *Journal of American Psychoanalytic Association* 67(1): 97–121.
1 Credit: Ocean Vuong, "Threshold" and "Trojan" from Night Sky with Exit Wounds. Copyright © 2016 by Ocean Vuong. Reprinted with the permission of The Permissions Company, LLC on behalf of Copper Canyon Press, www.coppercanyonpress.org.
2 Especially the Oedipal drama and the adaptation (via identification) to the objective physiology of the genitals and their putative (if debatable) meanings and expectations (i.e. heterosexual genitality).
3 We use the term 'orthodox Lacanian' to denote a subset of thinkers who rely on Lacan's early work in the service of explicit heteronormative/binary constructions of psychic life. We contrast them with other thinkers, and our own reading of Lacan, in the pages that follow (see Gherovici, 2017; Roudinesco, 2002).

4 An extremely pared-down, far from comprehensive, list: Fonagy & Allison, 2015; Lemma & Lynch, 2015; Drescher, 2008; Brady, 2011; Chodorow, 1992; Corbett, 2009a,b; Dimen and Goldner, 2004; Ehrensaft, 2007, 2009; Goldsmith, 1995; Harris, 2000; Kiersky, 1996; Layton, 2000; Saketopoulou, 2014; Isay, 1989; Blechner, 2015.

5 Freud insists that the patient, "a beautiful and clever" eighteen-year-old, is healthy and suffers of no neurotic symptoms. (Freud, 1920a, p. 145). The sad later life of Margarethe Csonka (the patient in question), her failure to find a suitable female partner, and her resigned acceptance of a loveless marriage, is described in Roudinesco's essential recent biography of Freud (Roudinesco, 2016, 244–247).

6 *"The anxiety [Mr. Jones felt about] intercourse with a woman led him to escape into homosexual fantasies"* (Campbell, 2018, p. 239; emphasis ours). Campbell variously describes heterosexual coupling as "generative" and "creative", and contrasts it with the patient's "passive, homosexual" submission to the analyst resulting in a "sterile" analysis (p. 235). The possibility of homosexual relationships as having generativity or creativity does not figure in Campbell's metapsychology or in his paper. Neither does Campbell explore the impact of the 'lack of recognition' from the analyst (a key Lacanian concept, akin to Winnicottian 'holding') as an iatrogenic factor in the case's 'sterility'.

7 This patient's intense need to anticipate and fulfill the wishes of the analyst and presumably both parents before him would seem to be the 'unthought known' (per Bollas, 1987) that lies at the center of his quasi-existential ambivalence. It undoubtedly extends far beyond the issue of sexual object choice, scrambling his psychic life to a near psychotic degree. Rather than investigating the destructive enactment of this theme in the transference, however, Campbell takes an active position (be straight!), colluding in an anti-analytic repetition rather than promoting understanding and clinical progress.

8 Contemporary psychoanalytic theory on gender variation, most especially Ken Corbett's generative writing on 'girlyboys' (Corbett, 1996, 2009a, 2009b; Erhensaft, 2007) understands that kind of gesture as a creative effort to encode an intrinsic non-normative experience of gender and (inchoate) sexual object choice, set against the backdrop of a society that is still deeply uncomfortable and not infrequently hostile toward children who transgress the gender binary. A reservoir of empirical research on gender variant children makes clear that the vast majority (i.e. two-thirds of boys like Vuong's poetic subject) end up in adulthood coming out as gay men (Ehrensaft, 2007).

9 Perelberg's use of anthropology inexplicably omits significant examples from non-Western cultures, such as India, where a 'third sex', in the form of the *hijras* (natal males who occupy a 'feminized' place between the two genders), has been part of the fabric of culture and religious rites for millennia (Reddy, 2005). For other examples of gender expressions that fall between or blend the poles of 'male' and 'female' in cultures around the globe, see the volume of essays edited by anthropologist Gilbert Herdt (1994).

10 Gherovici (2017, pp. 87–89) describes a similar case treated, with evident humanity, by Lacan in the 1950s.

11 In keeping with the current preference of some transgender individuals, we employ the non-specific pronoun 'they' for this patient, while acknowledging that this option was unavailable to them or to Green at the time treatment unfolded in the 1950s. Perelberg, discussing the same pronoun in her introduction, acknowledges the current usage in such instances of "hybridization" (p. 57) and the (seemingly onerous) requirement to apply it.

12 Not necessarily inborn, but patterned deeply as an authentic facet of experience (akin to the Winnicottian 'true self') from earliest infancy.

13 Stressing in particular his late concept of the 'sinthome' – a Gallic play on words with 'symptom', but lacking the latter term's pathologizing bite; we view it as somewhat

analogous to the ego psychological concept of 'compromise formation' or the Kohutian 'structure of accommodation' (Gherovici, 2017, 8–9).

14 Gherovici (p. 20) reminds us that the rate of suicide attempts among the transgender population is *ten times* that of their cisgender peers, and that 'coming out' as trans and taking steps to alter one's gender presentation (whether through pronoun changes or physiological interventions like hormones or surgery) can be correlated with decreased depression and better overall functioning.

15 From Green's chapter in Perelberg's volume: "The vicissitudes of biological and psychical development present us with a range of structures (real hermaphroditism, pseudo-hermaphroditism, transvestism, homosexuality, fetishism), *each of which lays claim to a distinct pathogeny and different therapeutic responses*" (p. 248, emphasis added).

16 Perelberg disputes this, noting that the purpose of psychoanalysis is 'understanding psychosexuality,' a doctrinal, rather than therapeutic framing.

17 Having, notoriously, referred in one of his public lectures to the speakers in Plato's *Symposium* as "a gathering of old fairies" (Roudinesco, 2002).

18 The legacy of Ernst Jones (Fonagy & Allison, 2015, p. 128).

19 See Roudinesco's description of Lacan's analysis of Francois Wahl, editor of *Ecrits* and an openly gay man (Roudinesco, 1997, pp. 320–323) as well as Gherovici's description of his consultations with trans patient Henri/Anne-Henriette (Gherovici, 2017, pp. 87–89).

20 Maggie Nelson cites floridly homophobic/transphobic statements from Julia Kristeva and Slavoj Zizek, eminent thinkers both heavily influenced by Lacan (see Nelson, 2015, pp. 76–77). Other members of the Lacanian circles espousing such ideas include Catherine Millot (Gherovici, 2017, p. 95), Charles Melman, and Jean-Pierre Winter. These last two thinkers, according to Roudinesco (2002), "launched a real media crusade against homosexuals in the name of Lacanism and psychoanalysis . . . in order to reestablish the lost figure of the authoritarian father which, in their view, is threatened by the new homosexual order".

21 "It is a great injustice to persecute homosexuality as a crime and cruelty too", Freud, "Letter to an American Mother" (Grotjahn, 1951, p. 331).

22 The idea of the 'personal pattern' features in Winnicott's classic paper on transitional phenomena, as he describes the constellation of circumstances that inspire the infant's anointing of a seemingly random inanimate object – a piece of fluff, corner of a blanket, etc. – for that important developmental role. He emphasizes that the transitional object always arises from the child's *spontaneous gesture*, though assigns the parents a crucial role in helping to foster the patterning of that symbolic node through family rituals and play into the infant's inchoate 'true self' (Winnicott, 1953; Pauley, 2018a, 2018b). Gherovici and other writers make generative use of Winnicott's concept of the 'true self' to shed light on trans identities, despite the fact that Winnicott himself seems to have held rather conventional attitudes toward gender and gender nonconformity.

23 The importance of such personal perspectives is far from just theoretical. A growing body of research suggests that the public witness of LGBTQ individuals and allies through groups such as 'Gay-Straight Alliances' in schools is having far-reaching, positive impact on the emotional lives of LGBTQ youth, a population typically at heightened risk for depression and suicide. Anecdotal evidence also suggests that such groups contribute to disrupting the projective processes that fuel homophobic/transphobic violence (Sadowski, 2013).

Part II

Cultural realm

Chapter 5

Cross-cultural variations of eroticism

Pranav Shah

Eroticism is a concept much easier to detect and describe than to define and delineate. Attempts to distinguish eroticism from sexuality, romance, love, and other related terms and concepts always fall short of their aim. One of the more elegant categorizations is by Octavio Paz (1996), who writes in his book, *The Double Flame*, that human sexuality has three domains. The first domain is the sex drive itself, which is primordial and animalistic. This is the part that we share with our genetic ancestors and works to ensure the survival of our species. Eroticism, the second domain, is 'sexuality socialized', the sex drive turned into human desire through imagination. The third domain is love, which is sexuality turned into human relationships. But, as human sexuality is pervasive and present in all relationships, and is always moderated by fantasy, the erotic element permeates all domains of human sexuality and relationships.

Eroticism then is a derivative of the sex drive that transforms the animal instinct through imagination and fantasy to fit within the constraints of our society, often turning it into something unrecognizable as sexual. Eroticism also subverts the reproductive aim of sexuality and puts it (back) in the service of the id, insofar as it has pleasure as its immediate, and often sole, aim. As essential as sexuality is to our existence, it also threatens it with its seemingly insatiable thirst. Hence, all societies and cultures have regulations, in the form of laws, taboos, prohibitions, and moral codes, which curtail and control sexuality and most of its derivatives. We have created entire institutions and ritual practices to manage our sex drive and tame it to work within our culture. Sexuality and its derivatives, and the forces working against them, shape our society into what it is. Thus, eroticism as a concept includes both license and repression, sublimation and perversion, life and death (Paz, 1996).

Since the dawn of civilization, there has been a tension between 'traditionalists' (or 'puritans') and 'romantics'. The religious traditionalists, especially in the Western world, have sought to restrict the expression of the sexual desire and confine it to a narrow sphere, namely to the institution of marriage between a man and a woman, and even then, only in the interest of reproduction. The romantics, on the other hand, see erotic activity as adding to the gloss of life, and coupling, in all its permutations, as a central life-affirming force (Narayan, 2017).

This struggle is paralleled in our individual selves. The mystery, prohibitions, and taboos surrounding sexuality, the society's reluctance to talk about it openly, and the constant need to repress and regulate it is something we all struggle with individually. The contradictions within our society are readily apparent – we are bombarded with overt and covert sexual signals on a daily basis, and yet there seems to be a conspiratorial silence regarding talking about it. Most parents are surprisingly indifferent about exposing their children to violent content in the media but become prudish when it comes to sexual content. We struggle with even the idea of educating our children on sexuality, and they end up learning about it from their friends, or worse, as it is becoming increasingly common, from porn. Even married couples shy away from talking about their sexual lives. There is something about our sexual desires that is hard for us to reconcile; that we often hide from ourselves or fail to acknowledge fully; that can delight us and/or horrify us; that gives us pleasure but also makes us feel guilty or ashamed.

Even though sexuality has always been central to our existence, science has also avoided looking too closely at it. Until recently, there has been surprisingly little systematic research done on the nature of eroticism. When anthropologists and other academics have ventured into studying the sexual practices of any society, even their own, the tone and conclusions are jarring, as they are too prejudiced and devoid of any attempts at neutrality. More recent, and objective, interest in the sexual practices in cultures around the world, as well as emerging knowledge of the biological, social, and psychological nature of sexuality has brought into question some of the basic assumptions about the very nature of sexuality. It has turned upside down our notions of what is normal and abnormal, acceptable and taboo, perverse and pathological. No wonder Internet porn has become so popular – in the anonymity afforded by the Internet, people are able to express their wildest fantasies, and find that they are not alone.

A brief historical perspective

In ancient India and China, sexuality and eroticism were not only celebrated but were regarded as a part of, or a path to, the divine. A passage from the *Rigveda* (circa 1500 BCE), one of the oldest Hindu religious texts, is illustrative: 'Gods: "Why does sex exist?" Brahma (the Hindu God of creation): "We need the erotic because without it the world is dusty – it lacks gloss"' (cited in Narayan, 2017, xvii). The *Bhakti marg*, in Hindu tradition, is a path to eternal salvation through emotional and often rapturous devotion to God that is frequently eroticized and occasionally outright sexual. The Khajuraho temples in North India, built in the tenth through twelfth centuries, are justly famous for the intricate, erotic, even pornographic, sculptures adorning the inner and outer walls that depict various poses for heterosexual intercourse, homosexuality, ménage a trois, group sex, and even bestiality. The placement of these sculptures amongst hundreds of others which depict the quotidian activities of life suggest that, at least back then, for Hinduism *kama* (pleasure and love) was truly one of the four aims of life; the others being *artha* (materialism), *dharma* (ethics), and *moksha* (eternal salvation). While Khajuraho is by far the most famous temple with erotic carvings, there are dozens more scattered throughout India, and it is estimated that, at one point circa the twelfth century, there were hundreds, if not thousands of them throughout the region. India also had multiple and elaborate sex manuals that were meant to educate people in the ways of sexual ecstasy and lead to a path of cosmic enlightenment. Most of these writings have not survived in their original forms with the exception of the Kamasutra (which is believed to be a condensation of the original works written circa 1000 BCE). These books elaborately describe the rituals of seduction, foreplay, sexual techniques, and positions. One could argue that in ancient India sex was treated as either profound and/or mundane, but never profane.

Similarly, in ancient China, in the Taoist philosophy, the sexual union was the union between yin and yang, the female and male essences, to create a harmony and allow the flow of chi energy. Men were to prolong the intercourse as long as possible and abstain from ejaculation, so as to absorb the yin essence from the woman's orgasm.

In the Western world, Judeo-Christian sensibility has long defined monogamous heterosexuality in the service of procreation as the 'normal' or 'ideal'. Starting around 400 CE, the Christian church established itself as the dominant doctrine replacing the Roman Empire. In doing so, it also infused the otherwise unstable and uneducated European society with its brand of morality, equating chastity with godliness and sex with sin. Sex was for the weak, and was to be practiced without any passion, only for reproduction, and only within the confines of marriage. Women were created by God to benefit and serve men, but they were also creatures to be feared and suppressed for their aberrant sexuality and ability to seduce and corrupt men. All other sexual practices, including teen sex, homosexuality, bisexuality, sexual relations with relatives, polygamy, polyandry, etc. were regarded as 'taboos', 'perversions', or 'pathological' forms of sexuality. These transgressions against God were a ticket to hellfire and eternal damnation (Tannahill, 1980).

The Church slowly lost its grip on society through the Renaissance and Enlightenment periods, but the puritanical notions had infiltrated the Western world's thinking about sexuality, defined their norms, informed their legal system, and even influenced their sciences, for well over a millennium (the Middle Ages), and continue to influence our views to this day.

We have credible evidence that the attitude towards sexuality, even in the West, was not always so. The ancient Greeks were known to be tolerant of a wide variety of sexual practices which were later condemned as perversions or made taboo, such as homosexuality, pederasty, masturbation, sodomy, etc. More important, perhaps, eroticism was elemental and pervasive through their entire mythology, and there is tantalizing evidence that the Minoan women were able to celebrate their sexuality (Chyrstal, 2016). In the mid-1970s, Italy revealed to the rest of the world the wonders of the city of Pompeii that was buried under ashes from the eruption of Vesuvius in 79 CE. These included phallic symbols which appeared to be omens for fertility and good luck and erotic sculptures and murals. More interestingly, it also unearthed erotic carvings and paintings on everyday household items such as vases, lamps, dishware, mirrors, etc., suggesting that eroticism was a vital part of their daily life (Grant and Mulas, 1997).

More recent developments

The more modern era of the study of the essential nature of sexuality started approximately 150 years ago, possibly with the publication of Charles Darwin's (1871) *The Descent of Man, and Selection In Relation to Sex*. Darwin was puzzled by the existence of characteristics in certain species that were not necessarily in the best interest of their survival, like the peacock's decorous but awkward tail. He therefore formulated the 'sexual selection theory' that explained that these traits had developed to facilitate sexual selection and the propagation of species.

The sexual selection theory postulated that men have a natural inclination to feel aroused by potential mates who display visible cues proving their health and reproductive fitness. These cues are therefore interpreted by the male brain as 'beauty' – in other words, what men find naturally beautiful in women are the very attributes that are signs of their physical and reproductive abilities. These include youth; physical fitness; an hourglass-shaped body with wide hips, narrow waist, and big breasts; smooth skin; shiny long hair; and symmetrical features. Women, on the other hand, are not so visually oriented, and what they look for in potential mates are social status, ability to provide and protect, dependability, and compatibility – qualities that will ensure the long-term survival of their young. Athleticism and height, attributes that allude to physical strength and protection, have become more important in the last century or so, especially when women are looking for a short-term erotic encounter rather than a long-term commitment – a trend that illustrates that the sexual selection theory can no longer be separated from societal influence and our perception of love.

The sociobiologists (or the Essentialists) of today continue and extend this explanation of our mating behaviors and espouse that all of our erotic and sexual behaviors derive from the drive for survival of the 'selfish gene'. The Social Constructivists, on the other hand, acknowledge the basic sexual drive, but believe that eroticism, or how that drive manifests itself in our complex society, is shaped mainly by culture and the process of socialization, and is mediated by language. So what is desired, and the degree or strength of that desire, and even more important, the expression of that desire, are all functions of the particular culture and time (Baumeister, 2000).

Social construction therefore means that our ideas about what is beautiful and sexy are derived from extensive collective experiences of the society. These notions then become standards by which we evaluate each other and become part of our belief systems. For example, during my lifetime, what is considered sexy in the Bollywood world (Indian movie industry) has gone from curvy voluptu-ous figures to thinner, athletic, and more Westernized women. Whereas a woman showing her ankle, or the sight of her belly button, was considered sexy forty years ago, scantily clad women have become much more of a frequent sight now. Our concept of 'beauty' and expression of eroticism becomes reactionary to each generation's rules and taboos – and is further constricted to the *visual* appear-ance of women by the power of the patriarchy. There is no doubt that the focus on woman's beauty has been exacerbated by oppressive patriarchal sources that maintain a woman's place in beauty connected to her role as wife and mother, rather than in the workplace.

Psychoanalysis is a relatively young science and has struggled with the con-cepts of eroticism and love. Freud (1905a, 1915a, 1924a) talked about psychosex-ual development, wherein sexuality organizes our intrapsychic experiences even as we go through early attachment relations. Our sexuality unfolds in the context of these relations, and is in turn shaped by these interactions. Freud (1905a) also captured the normative abnormality of sexuality. 'Perverse' aspects get incorpo-rated into various expressions of 'normal' sexuality, whether it's in the process to find pleasure, in fore-pleasure, or in the sexual fantasies that are played out during the act of having sex. Stoller (1979) further helped us to see that we are all 'perverts' to an extent. Freud also talks about the notion of an inherent bisexual-ity; hence, diversity and complexity are at the core of human sexual experience (Lemma and Lynch, 2015).

Contemporary social influences

In the last century, there have been many developments around the world that have influenced our ideas of beauty, mating practices, and sexual norms.

Marketing/beauty and fashion industry

The twentieth century saw a big boost in marketing efforts through direct adver-tising. Now, we are constantly bombarded with marketing efforts through TV ads, radio, billboards, e-mails, social media, and mailings. These are designed to cre-ate a desire for consumer products, and the way this is often done is by eroticizing the products – showing us images of young, beautiful, and sexy people enjoying their lives and getting love, presumably because they are using these products. A significant portion of these products are aimed at women, mainly to enhance their attractiveness and make them as desirable as the women in the advertise-ments. These messages are internalized by women (and men), who then build unrealistic illusions of idealized beauty and feel inadequate in comparison, con-tributing perhaps to rates of depression, low self-esteem, eating disorders, etc. Concurrently, men internalize these same messages, eliciting toxic expectations of a consumer-driven beauty that propagate disappointment, dissatisfaction, and disrespect to both partners in a sexual relationship.

Cosmetic surgery

Cosmetic surgery has made it possible for women (men also, but 84% of these surgeries worldwide are performed on women) to alter their appearance in an attempt to conform to the societal (global/Western) norms of beauty and be more attractive to men. Although cosmetic procedures have been recorded as far back as 3000 BCE, there has been an explosion of these procedures over the last few decades.

Breast augmentation is the world's most popular cosmetic procedure, followed by liposuction (tummy tuck, for that slender appearance) and eyelid surgery (to conform to Western standards of large, round, and symmetrical eyes). The most popular non-surgical procedures continue to be injectables with Botulinum toxin (to create a more youthful looking face san wrinkles). The top five countries – the US, Brazil, Japan, Mexico, and Italy – account for 38.4 percent of the world's cosmetic procedures, followed by Germany, Colombia, and Thailand. Labiaplasty and lip enhancement surgeries are also becoming increasingly common (ISAPS, 2017; International Study Cosmetic Procedures, 2018). Alongside this trend, there is growing concern that the West is exporting its beauty standards to the rest of the world, an addition to the supremacist standards the Western world holds. This creates a sense of inequality and inadequacy amongst people from these countries (especially the erstwhile 'colonies' of Western imperialism) who are trying to emulate them.

Internet and pornography

The Internet has been adopted by the porn industry perhaps more than any other industry. The relative anonymity of the Internet has allowed the expression and indulgence of the most secret and most bizarre sexual fantasies. The ubiquity of pornography and pornographic images of genitalia have created a "pornographication" of Western culture (Jeffreys, cited in Kenny and Nichols, 2017, p. 187). In 1991, when the Internet was introduced, there were some ninety adult magazines. Before the turn of the century, there were around 1,000 porn websites, and this number has ballooned up to around 2.5 million porn websites as of a few years ago. As the puppets in the Broadway musical *Avenue Q* sing, "The Internet is for porn".

Pornhub, the world's biggest porn site, releases data on their most searched for terms every year. The most-searched-for term from 2014–2017 was 'lesbian', but included in the top 10 are: *hentai*, mom, MILF, GILF, stepmom, and stepsister. GILF, or Grandmothers I'd Like to F*ck, appears to be most common in England and Kenya. MILF, or Mothers I'd Like to F*ck, another frequently searched term worldwide, refers to 'Cougar' women, often married, between the ages of 35 and 50. The search terms for 2018 remain about the same (Pornhub Insights 2018).

The popular Indian cartoon porn site *Savita Bhabhi* (Bhabhi means one's elder brother's wife but is also often used for a friend's wife) stars a married woman in her thirties with an hourglass figure, voluptuous and curvy. Japanese *hentai* cartoon porn appears to be popular all over the world, with its exaggerated sex organs on teenage bodies. Although skinny athletic bodies dominate the advertising world, online what men look for much more often are voluptuous or curvy women.

As expected, the majority of the viewers of this very visual form of erotica are male. However, about 26 percent of the porn viewers are women (Pornhub Insights 2018, 2018). It is interesting to note that outside of lesbian sex, the porn that sells the most tends to be incestuous in nature. It cannot be a coincidence that our most secret fantasies are related to what our society considers the most taboo.

The pill

For thousands of years, various potions were used all over the world to try and prevent unwanted pregnancies, although not very successfully. In the 1800s, coitus interruptus and the condom remained the two main ways of preventing pregnancies – unfortunately for women, both depended on the man. It was not until the 1800s that the society as a whole became concerned with birth control, mostly in response to dire predictions of impending overpopulation and food shortages. By the end of the nineteenth century, latex condoms and the diaphragm had been added to birth control measures. Then, in 1956, George Pincus developed the first oral contraceptive, 'the pill'. This revolutionized birth control – for the first time, the means of preventing pregnancy was separated from the act of intercourse, thus avoiding some of the moral condemnation associated with using birth control. It also put women in control of the decision to get pregnant and finally separated the reproductive function of sex from its more pleasurable aim. The pill essentially freed women from the biological, financial, and population burden of unplanned pregnancies, allowing them to indulge in sex for pleasure. It was in this climate that the sexual revolution (also called the feminist revolution) took place (Gregersen, 1994).

The sexual revolution

Patriarchal societies around the world have long suppressed women, not considering them as equal to man. Women have been treated as physically and intellectually inferior to men by most societies. They have been accused of being evil, burnt as witches, treated as slaves, and repeatedly violated by men. Until 1929, they were not given a voice in the political process in the US.

The Kinsey Reports (1948 and 1953) exploded the romantic ideal of marriage and family and demonstrated that 70 percent of men had visited prostitutes, and 40 percent of husbands had been unfaithful to their wives. Soon after, with the introduction of the pill and the IUD, women finally took control of their reproductive capacity and sexuality, no longer at the mercy of their husbands. The 1960s and 1970s then gave way to a robust feminist movement that saw women standing up against the patriarchy, refusing to fit into the stereotypes created by men. What the sexual revolution meant was that marriage was no longer tied to the production of children. Women entered the workforce and started demanding equal rights. They also felt much freer to express their sexuality, indulge in pre-marital sex, and learned to love themselves more.

Beauty is in the eye of the beholder

Our societal trajectory of beauty continues to undulate as it is influenced by the Internet, social media, increasing global connections, and changing taboos surrounding sexual behaviors. When does a universal beauty standard cease to compel and preference begin?

As the oft-repeated saying goes, 'beauty is in the eye of the beholder'. Without a doubt there are some universals (or near-universals) when it comes to who or what is considered beautiful. However, even with that consensus, there is still so much room for societal and individual preferences around the concept of beauty that this saying holds true.

The vast majority of the following examples relate to women. This is not a coincidence. As noted earlier, when it comes to eroticism, men tend to be 'simple-minded' and single-minded in being led by the visual and physical beauty of the female. As Paulo Coehlo (REF) has said, "beauty is the greatest seducer of man". This may be the reason why in most societies, women adorn themselves with fashionable clothing and jewelry, use makeup, get cosmetic surgery, and wear high heels. Women, on the other hand, are much more deliberate in their choice of mate, and evaluate potential mates for social status, ability to provide, generosity, emotional maturity, and so on. And this is why a lot of men tend to lie about these attributes when dating.

Symmetry

Symmetrical, well-proportioned faces and bodies are preferred almost every-where globally, even though the actual body shape and size may differ according to culture. Studies show that people, when asked to rank images of other people according to relative attractiveness, rank composite images of faces and bodies that demonstrate symmetry higher than any single image. Euclid, the Greek phi-losopher and mathematician, has described this idea of symmetry as represented by 'the golden ratio'. This ratio can be seen in the ancient sculptures of the Par-thenon, the dimensions of da Vinci's Vitruvian Man, and the face of the Mona Lisa. Research has demonstrated that when infants are shown images of people, they stare longer at images of people with symmetrical faces than asymmetrical ones. Adults prefer symmetrical bodies as well, associating them positively with beauty, physical health, and strength. (Savacool, 2009). Paradoxically, studies show that people respond negatively to computer-generated perfectly symmetri-cal human faces. This phenomenon is known as the 'uncanny valley hypothesis'.

It appears that while humans equate symmetry with beauty, they also prefer some measure of imperfection to recognize it as human (Kenny, 2017). That mole on Cindy Crawford's face, most people agree, has made her even more beautiful.

The hourglass figure

Historically, various cultures have devised ways to shape a woman's body. Some examples include corsets, chest-flattening bandages, butt enhancements, implants, etc. A study conducted by Singh et al. (2010) compared female attractiveness with sample groups composed of both men and women participants from Cameroon (Africa), Komodo Island (Indonesia), Samoa, and New Zealand. The researchers showed line-drawing outlines of twelve silhouettes with a range of waist-to-hip ratios (WHRs) and asked participants to pick the most attractive woman. Their findings suggested that people in these countries found women of normal weight with a WHR of 0.7 to be the most attractive. These findings mirror the findings of similar studies conducted in Germany, the United Kingdom, and the US, where ideal WHR was judged to be 0.67 to 0.80 (Kenny, 2017). However, similar studies conducted in Indonesia, the Azore Islands, Guinea Bissau, China, Uganda, Peru, and the Shiwiar tribe of Ecuador suggest that men in these groups prefer women with a higher WHR (Kenny, 2017).

Light skin

A number of cultures and societies around the world, including China, Japan, Indonesia, Korea, Africa, India, and Brazil, show a preference for lighter skin. Women in these societies spend billions of dollars on cosmetics that make their skin appear lighter in color. Light skin is viewed in these countries as signaling high-class status, beauty, success, and empowerment. For both men and women, lighter skin is more desirable not only in their quest to find a desirable partner, but also to achieve personal and professional success.

Light skin has been highly valued historically in many of these cultures. However, it also appears this desire certainly became more prominent as a result of colonialism and the increasing Western influence from globalization. The 'Black Is Beautiful' movement started in the 1960s along with the civil rights movement is an attempt to reclaim pride in dark skin and to forge an alternative to the prevailing white beauty standards.

What about 'remote' cultures?

Let's now turn our attention to some individual societies around the world, looking at their beauty standards and what they consider attractive. Here, I am listing cultures that are relatively insulated from Western influence and the effects of globalization, as it is in these examples we find that diversity of sexual practices has been somewhat preserved.

In many cultures within the 'ethnographic' Africa, beauty is defined as unison (or harmony) of physical attractiveness and good conduct. True African beauty is also about taking pride in your own body. Women are more desirable when they are voluptuous, proving their sensuality and fertility. Ethnic traditions of ornamentation, painting, and bodily modifications are used to make both men and women more attractive, and also to convey group membership. Among the Annang of Nigeria it is normal for a girl to be 'fattened up' before she is married. The young woman is sent to the 'fattening room' where she is isolated from her village and fed calorie-rich food to maximize her weight. She also gets schooled in the art of being a good wife. She becomes more desirable and attractive as a mate as she gains a round lustrous body. Body fattening is also practiced in several other cultures in Africa and around the world, including Nauru (an island in the South Pacific), Tuareg and Moorish peoples of West Africa, Azagwah Arabs, and the Siriono people of eastern Bolivia (Kenny, 2017). Within Africa itself, this trend is now on the decline except amongst the wealthy (Kenny, 2017).

Hair

Hair has been an important measure of beauty and attractiveness in most societies across the world throughout history. Hair frames our face, and is enormously versatile – we can dye it, oil it, grow it to our liking, style it, and decorate it with a variety of hairpieces. In African societies, hair styling often becomes a social symbol, with braids and adornments conveying not just beauty, but also lineage, romantic availability, age, social status, and personality (Kenny, 2017).

The men from Tchambuli of Papua New Guinea compete for the women by trying out new hairdos and decorating themselves with flowers and ornaments. At their festivals they even dress up as women and join in raunchy homosexual dancing and sex play. Women, in this matriarchal society, hunt, while men dance, paint, and play the flute. There are several such matriarchal enclaves where what we consider as traditional gender roles are reversed (Brodman, 2017).

Body adornment, modification, and mutilation

Many cultures paint, tattoo, even scar their bodies to enhance their appearance. Then there are cultures where people have invented ways to modify their body parts, such as the lips, skull, labia, teeth, etc. Often there are historical reasons for these traditions, but they have become an integral part of these cultures, signifying belonging, tradition, and beauty. The world has not always looked kindly at these practices, sometimes denouncing them, at other times treating them as 'curiosities from the savage lands'. Some of these traditions are fading as visitors flock to them and in the process bring in influences from their own cultures.

Body painting is one of the oldest art forms in Africa, used by both sexes to adorn their bodies. Various patterns and designs are used to both beautify and convey marital and social status (Kenny, 2017). Members of the Maasai tribe in

Africa are known for their black gums and elongated earlobes. Women stretch their earlobes by wearing heavy stone jewelry. As time goes by, a woman's status in the Maasai tribe, as well as other tribes in Africa, is heightened by how large and elongated her earlobes have become (What Men Think is Attractive in Different Parts of the World, 2019).

Elongated lower lips or lip plates are considered very attractive on Mursi women in Ethiopia – they also denote female reproductive maturity and availability. The process includes the removal of the two lower front teeth before a piercing is made to allow a heavy clay or wooden disk to adorn and stretch the lower lip. Like ear stretching, larger and larger disks are inserted over time to further elongate the lip. The larger the disk becomes, the greater the beauty of the woman (Kenny, 2017).

Scarification is similar to tattooing, both resulting in permanent marks on the skin. A sharp tool is used to cut the skin in the desired pattern, which then leaves a raised scar as it heals. A number of ethnic groups across West Africa strategically cut into the skin of the forehead, thighs, calves, cheeks, between the breasts, in the small of the back, and on the shoulders to produce scars (*iwu*) and enhance attractiveness. "As part of the cultural geography of the body, *iwu* mapped out ethnic terrain and transformed the self, inscribed male and female personhood, denoted stratification by pedigree, and delineated selected occupational roles" (Nevandomsky and Aisien, 1995, p. 68, as cited in Kenny, 2017).

Elongated labia, sometimes referred to as the 'hottentot apron', is a tradition in Burundi, Rwanda, Malawi, Mozambique, Zimbabwe, Zambia, Jamaica, and Uganda. Labia are stretched gradually from a young age. It is believed to improve the aesthetics and symmetry of female genitals. The stretched labia can reach up to four inches in length, and is reportedly associated with enhanced sexual pleasure, increased intensity of female orgasm, and female ejaculation. Ethnographic data suggests that 65 percent of women in the southeastern area of Africa actively worked to lengthen their vaginal labia to prepare for sexual intercourse and to satisfy their sexual partner by stimulating erection (Bagnol and Mariano, 2012, as cited in Kenny, 2017).

The Maori women of New Zealand tattoo and paint their lips, often blue, to be considered beautiful and desirable. Tattooing is an art form in some parts of Japan. Women in India use henna, a plant-based dye, to paint temporary tattoos on their bodies, especially at festive occasions (Kenny, 2017).

Dancehalls in Jamaica hold 'skin-out' competitions to identify the most *mampy* (overweight), *trang* (tight), and beautifully sexual woman at the club. The competing women are also judged on their *phatness*, a term that refers to the erotic appeal of their hips, backsides, breasts, and labia (the acronym PHAT sometimes stands for P*ssy, Hips, A**, and Tits). Women also sport elongated labia to make themselves more appealing (Hope, cited in Kenny, 2017).

Foot-binding was practiced by wealthy Chinese women for most of the second millennium. It's not clear how the practice started, but it soon became a very erotic practice, and the bound foot was affectionately referred to as the 'golden lotus' foot. People were so enamored with this practice that at one point it had become a national fetish.

The word 'sexy' is used to describe a desirable quality that is sexually appealing. No doubt physical attractiveness is often a part of this, especially for men. However, what makes a person sexy can also be associated with a number of different characteristics, including how they walk, talk, dress, their level of confidence, intelligence, accomplishments, social status, and even how much others desire them. A sense of humor is often seen as being sexy. In the end, what each of us finds 'sexy' appears to be governed by a combination of individual experiences and societal norms that often defy purely evolutionary or biological explanations.

Concluding remarks

The enormous degree of diversity in beauty standards, with those just discussed being a small representation of it, naturally brings to question any theories proposing the existence of evolution-based normative standards of beauty and the expression of human sexuality. History has also shown us that sexual and erotic practices within any society are fluid and often change as they come into contact with other cultures. Tension clearly exists between views that uphold 'hard-wired' and those that subscribe to 'internalized' origins of eroticism. Often in making these arguments, the example that's used is that of our taste in food. We have an innate ability to differentiate five kinds of tastes. However, we eat an amazing variety of food with complex and layered tastes. And our likes and dislikes in our food selection are largely based on how and where we are brought up, what foods we are exposed to, and the associations we have with these foods. Similarly, we are born with a basic sex drive, but the vicissitudes of desire, or the erotic expressions of this, are based on our upbringing, nurturance, prevalent cultural norms, and ongoing life experiences.

Our brain continues to mature for years after birth, and during this time is shaped by our individual experiences and by prevailing societal norms and attitudes. Recent evidence points to a lifelong neuroplasticity where our brain continues to adapt and grow from our life experiences. In that sense, it's more like a fluid, taking up the shape of the vessel it is occupying. The nature versus nurture debate is almost always nature *and* nurture, both influencing us in fluid ways through a constant feedback loop. Nature has no 'edges' but rather blurred lines with no clear demarcations.

The complexity of the civilization we have created has shaped our sexuality and its myriad expressions. While animal sex is always the same, human eroticism involves innovation, variation, and diverse forms of pleasure. The manifestations of such eroticism are infinite. And eroticism has subverted the aim of sex, replacing it with pleasure which, to wit, at times, includes pain. It can never be contained fully, and it rebels against any attempts to contain it. Because it works through our imagination, it cannot be stopped by merely putting limitations on our behaviors. When a particular society tries to curtail it, eroticism takes on the form of 'perversions'. In this context, Kohut's (1977) proposal that the 'pleasure principle' is actually a degradation product of the environment's failure to uphold the child's 'reality principle' is highly pertinent.

Even as we have become an eroticized society, with easy access to actualizating our sexual fantasies, we are having less sex. This is true for adults, but especially true for the younger generation in their teens and twenties. Kate Julian's (2018) recent article in *The Atlantic*, "Why Are Young People Having So Little Sex?" addresses this conundrum. She attributes this global decline in sex primarily to the proliferation of the Internet. This is the generation that has grown up being glued to their computers or phones and has mostly experienced only a virtual social life. They are often uncomfortable interacting with strangers in real-life situations. Correlates with an increase in anxiety and depression as a result of social media use can also explain this phenomenon – and while sex boosts your happiness, unhappiness inhibits your sex drive. Hook-ups have replaced dating, taking romance out of these relationship – a 'zipless fuck' à la Erica Jong (1973). Add to this the easy availability of porn, and suddenly the idea of making the effort to go out and meet someone seems too burdensome. Masturbating with porn is way easier and serves more or less the same purpose. Not having much of a sex education and not having real friends to learn about sex from, their ideas about sex are based on what they see on porn videos. This creates two problems: they feel inadequate and self-conscious in real-life sexual encounters, and they have completely unrealistic notions of how such an encounter is supposed to play out. It is much easier to watch porn, masturbate, and go to sleep. Perhaps this trend is not paradoxical at all, and sex is simply not as desirable when it loses its taboo. The drive to pursue the unattainable dissolves when the object becomes freely available. Or perhaps the concerted efforts of millennia of civilizations have finally succeeded in the sublimated forms of sexuality meeting most of its demands. Ironically, then, the biggest 'discontent' (Freud, 1930) civilization might have cost is for human beings to become 'content' without sex. Extending this line of thinking, one wonders if the 'uncivilized' of the world are less alienated from their erotic desires.

Chapter 6

Fantasy, sadism, and the fetish in pornography

Jason A. Wheeler Vega

In a condensed summary of the contribution of psychoanalysis to modern thought and culture, Laplanche (1970) writes: *"what is accepted is repression but what is repressed is . . . the repressed; and the repressed is sexuality"* (p. 27, italics in original). If sexuality is the repressed of culture, then pornography is the repressed of sexuality – the cream on the milk, or the scum on the stock, depending on your taste. For what seems on the face of it to be an enormously popular genre of enter-tainment that promises unrestricted pleasure, pornography presents a wide range and profound depth of problems. Pornography raises questions and reveals para-doxes that are as difficult as any in the field of sexuality. It is especially because pornography seems to hide nothing that its complexity can be underappreciated.

I will refer to *current pornography* or *contemporary pornography* in this chap-ter with the assumption that the Internet is the predominant method of distribution and consumption of pornography today. Though other forms still exist, they have acquired something of the status of vinyl records for the consumer of popular music – a quirky item for collectors and aficionados.

The question of erotism in relation to current pornography can be seen as open-ing up into many related questions: to what extent does pornography reflect the sexual desires of its users; to what extent does it in turn shape them? These ques-tions may be asked both at the level of contents and at the level of process: how much does porn reflect existing aims and objects of a user's sexual desire, and how much does it introduce new aims and objects, or alter the degree of invest-ment in ones such that they appear new? To what degree does the use of porn reveal the operation of ordinary ego processes and defenses, and to what degree does it alter defensive mechanisms or even fundamental ego functions such as perception, memory, and reality testing? There are both empirical and theoretical aspects to these questions, as well as elements relating uniquely to pornography on the Internet in contrast with earlier forms.

This is a lot, too much to tackle in one place, so I will focus in this chapter on a few topics that I believe are fundamental to pornography as well as being heavily overdetermined, and by which I hope to illuminate a few of these questions. Also, I will be using mostly Freudian concepts and methods of analysis, though many other routes to these questions are possible and have been taken, which I think are suitable for this task though not without their tensions.

I will begin by examining the structure of masturbation, given that pornography is typically, though not always, used as an adjunct in masturbation. While psychoanalysts have had relatively little to say about porn so far, there is an older and larger literature on masturbation which can be used to inform an investigation of the former. This initial investigation will point towards the crucial and differing roles of fantasy in the use of porn.

Against this background, I will examine two long-standing questions in the field of sexuality that are made especially vivid by contemporary porn, which I will term *the problem of sadism* and *the question of fetishism*. Both areas will require attention to the vicissitudes of the drives as well as defensive processes, and a reconsideration of some persistent ideas about sexuality. The problem of sadism, though it may appear unitary, will be seen to include two related subproblems, which I will pose as the problems of *the combination of sex and aggression* and *the separation of love and sex*.

The question of fetishism has many possible aspects. I will have to set aside the many baroque, fascinating, and disturbing contents that often go under this too-broad heading in pornography, and focus instead on a couple of key themes. First will be the role of fetishism in its broadest psychoanalytic sense in relation to the process of using porn. Second, an example of one striking contemporary 'fetish' will be argued to have several implications for our understanding of human sexuality as represented in current pornography and beyond.

Masturbation and fantasy

Pornography is generally used as an aid to masturbation. Analysts since Freud have been interested in the topic of masturbation from several perspectives, and have clarified its distinct structure in a way that is both unique and clinically indispensable. Where pornography is not used for masturbation, we will be interested in the reasons why it is not.

In a fairly early paper, Freud (1908a) was interested not in masturbation per se, or in masturbation as a problem, but in the role masturbation played in the development of hysterical symptoms. Freud clarified as part of his study that the structure of masturbation is a compound of two essential parts: an autoerotic *motor behavior* and some *conscious fantasy material* to which it had become contingently associated, "merely soldered together" (p. 161) in a favorite phrase. This material is usually later connected with a fantasy about a love object, hence the turn of most masturbatory fantasies outwards towards other people. Masturbatory abstinence may lead to conscious fantasies becoming repressed and then seeking indirect, symptomatic, satisfaction. Thus, Freud argued, many neurotic symptoms are formed on the basis of unconscious fantasies that were once conscious masturbatory fantasies.

In his later discussion of a group of papers on the topic of masturbation in 1911 and 1912, Freud (1912a) noted that members of the distributed symposium could not agree on whether masturbation was injurious. By masturbation they meant in adulthood, and by injury they meant causing neurosis, in particular the *actual neuroses* (Freud, 1896), which have since become of mostly historical interest. Freud asserted there that masturbation is an infantile activity and clearly inferior to sexual intercourse. This apparently left no room for masturbation as a healthy adult activity. One particular pitfall with a developed habit of masturbation after infancy is what Freud described there as "the laying down of a psychical pattern according to which there is no necessity for trying to alter the external world in order to satisfy a great need" (1912a, pp. 251–252).

Let us consider this dangerous role for masturbation that Freud is referring to here. Freud saw conscious fantasying as work done by the mind in consequence of its encounters with an unwilling world, which reveals both the universality of frustration and the conservatism of the mind in trying to hold on to our original sources of pleasure (Freud, 1911, p. 222). In general, Freud saw *conscious daydreaming* as a compensatory mechanism: "We may lay it down that a happy person never phantasies, only an unsatisfied one" (1908b, p. 146). And in a later work, Freud (1917) introduces one of his memorable analogies for this activity:

> The creation of the mental realm of phantasy finds a perfect parallel in the establishment of 'reservations' or 'nature reserves' in places where the requirements of agriculture, communications and industry threaten to bring about changes in the original face of the earth which will quickly make it unrecognizable. A nature reserve preserves its original state which everywhere else has to our regret been sacrificed to necessity. Everything, including what is useless and even what is noxious, can grow and proliferate as it pleases.
>
> (p. 372)

What Freud refers to here as fantasy's role as a "nature reserve" has the harmful potential of leading to what he elsewhere calls a kind of *introversion*, a turning to fantasy away from engaging with reality due to frustration (1912b, p. 182; 1912c, p. 232; 1917, p. 374). His reference to "even what is noxious" refers to the fact that repression operates most assiduously upon the most unacceptable and taboo ideas, so that sexual fantasies often relate to what Freud called "perverse" acts: "only recall the world-famous performances of the Roman Emperors, the wild excesses of which were, of course, determined [made possible] only by the enormous and unrestrained power possessed by the authors of the phantasies" (1908a, p. 162).

Early contributors tended to echo Freud, both in his major theoretical assertions and in his generally pathological view of masturbation, though adding some important observations. For instance, Tausk (1912) draws our attention to what would now be called excessive part–object relating: "masturbation directs the individual's exclusive attention to the genitals . . . the whole striving of these individuals was directed to the conquest of female genitals and not to that of a woman in her total personality" (p. 76); and similarly, "Many a man will confess that he masturbates with his penis in the vagina of the woman" (pp. 61–62). This appallingly apt phrase fits the reports of several male patients of mine almost verbatim. Writing much later, Stoller (1976) provides a matching example from his treatment of a female patient, for whom sex was "masturbating on her partner's penis to the bidding of her fantasy, ignoring him as he pushed grimly on" (p. 905). These two examples also show the way in which introversive fantasy may be used not just in masturbation but also in sex with others.

Somewhat later, Anna Freud (1936) also saw conscious fantasy and daydreaming as a normal developmental phase in children with possible defensive uses, but in adults as either a dangerous regression bordering on psychosis, or else as rather trivial. She describes adult daydreaming, for instance, as a "game, a kind of by-product with but a slight libidinal cathexis; at most it serves to master quite trifling quantities of discomfort or to give the subject an illusory relief from some minor unpleasure" (p. 81).

Reviewing the topic of masturbation at mid-century, Reich (1951) highlights the dangers of introversion in relation to masturbation fantasy and, like Freud and Tausk, especially the problems of non-object relatedness in compulsive masturbation:

> Idealized fantasy images are preserved, to which no object in reality can live up, and which are but the lightly disguised incestuous objects. The step from fantasy objects to reality objects is not made, and reality in general need not be fully accepted.
>
> (p. 87)

The dangers of introversion and part–object relating in the use of current pornography are quite apparent. If porn depicts the most repressed aspects of human sexuality, the ones that can never or rarely find expression in actual sexual lives, we could expect enormously powerful attractions to it. Borrowing from Freud: ordinary users of the Internet today are made as powerful as Roman emperors, at least in relation to their fantasy lives, able to find almost any fantasy made flesh.

Even in the most basic model of sexual desire, such usually repressed material would then be rerepressed and take up a role in the formation of new derivative unconscious fantasies. These then in turn prompt a search for their revised conscious counterparts. This is part of an explanation for why novelty is one of the key desiderata in contemporary porn. Like the rivers into which we may never step twice, fresh waters are ever rushing in upon us and through us.

Other psychoanalytic writers have made further contributions to this early work on masturbation, including some suggested theoretical revisions and the addition of further clinical insights which expand our perspective on masturbation and fantasy beyond the strictly pathological.

In his work of tying together the biological and social aspects of development, Hartmann (1939) attempted some correction of a strictly defensive or trivializing view of conscious fantasying with his notion of a "detour" through fantasy in the service of the individual's adaptation to the environment: "though fantasy always implies an initial turning away from a real situation, it can also be a preparation for reality and may lead to a better mastery of it" (p. 18). Here Hartmann introduces a function for fantasy as a kind of trial action, along with other kinds of thinking. Even more interestingly, he goes on: "It is well known that there are fantasies which, while they remove man from external reality, *open up for him his internal reality*" (pp. 18–19, my italics). Here Hartmann extends the possibility that fantasying could be more than just a wild "nature reserve" in Freud's sense, but something more like a good zoo, where valuable learning might be accomplished.

In disagreement with some of the earliest writers on masturbation (influenced by their preoccupation with the problems of the actual neuroses), Laufer argued that masturbation may have an important positive developmental role, specifically organizing the individual around genitality. He describes several cases of disturbances of masturbation in adolescent patients, who failed to use masturbation fantasies as a kind of "trial action" (1968, p. 115), borrowing Freud's term, and following Hartmann's lead.

Laufer is better known for his later contribution to this area, which is the concept of the *central masturbation fantasy*. For Laufer, the crystallization of the adult genital organization before latency also crystalizes "the [central masturbation] fantasy whose content contains the various regressive [pre-genital] satisfactions and the main sexual identifications [and object choices]" (1976, p. 300). This fantasy, he asserts, remains largely unchanged throughout latency, and may manifest itself in that phase and afterwards in derivative forms in daydreams, play, and conscious masturbatory fantasies.

In adolescence, masturbation can help to consolidate the forms of sexual desire, at a time when incestuous unconscious fantasies are given new energy by coming into possession of a body capable of really carrying out both sexual and aggressive Oedipal wishes towards their primary objects. It is worth being reminded here that in addition to parents, siblings also often form a part of early sexual fantasies (Tausk, 1912).

Taking up the concept of the central masturbation fantasy and its developmental role in adolescence, Shapiro (2008) argues for and offers case examples of a particular mechanism by which central masturbation fantasies may become normalized and available, not just for trial action but for the real thing. He draws on Sullivan's concept of the *chumship*, a group of two, often referred to as a best friend relationship. These late latency and early adolescent relationships (implicitly for boys in Shapiro) are social spaces within which fantasies can be tried out and normalized in a small trusted setting, allowing them to move out of the realm of daydreaming and into reality. Failures in developing such relationships can leave adolescents isolated with fantasies they dare not bring out into the social world, and hence leading to restricted lives of solitary masturbation.

In a similar paper with a wider focus, Hull and Lane (1996) clarify usefully that Laufer's concept is broader than initially put. In their account, the central masturbation fantasy is better understood as a "central or core fantasy that expresses the person's earliest paradigm for interpersonal relationships" (p. 675). It is important to remain aware, as Hull and Lane suggest, that sexual fantasies are not just about sex, but also about manners of relating or not relating to another person, and likely a particular person in someone's history – just as one finds of transference fantasies in psychoanalytic work. There may be a danger in the definiteness of the definite article and overly narrowing one's focus in settling upon *the* central masturbation fantasy, rather than attending to the range of wishes and their derivatives usually present, as one would think today of *transferences* rather than *the transference* in an analysis.

Masturbation and fantasy may well be more valuable both in development and in adulthood than the earliest analytic writers allowed. In fact, they might be essential for development. The dangers of introversive turns away from reality accepted, for many people there may be a problem with too little fantasying also. As well as encouraging a turn away from reality to fantasy in its depiction of impossible, tabooed opportunities and ways of relating to others who are not even others, pornography may also diminish the user's ability to employ their own fantasying functions as a component of masturbation and sex. As Zeavin (2011) puts it, "The image on the screen saves the viewer from doing the often psychically demanding work of making his own dream" (p. 285). Though as we will see in the section on fetishism, the analogy of porn with dreaming is not a complete one, and this is an important caveat. Many people who use porn compulsively find that they cannot masturbate without it; that is, they cannot mobilize the necessary component of fantasy for the full masturbatory or sexual act to come about.

Some early contributions of Eidelberg (1945) to the study of problems in masturbation are still helpful here. Eidelberg distinguishes *neurotic* masturbation fantasy from *normal* masturbation fantasy: he describes the former as adding an element of aggressive energy to genital excitement, decreasing interest in real objects, being rigid and fixed, and experienced in the present ('I am having sex'); whereas, in contrast, normal masturbation fantasy remains predominantly sexual without strong aggressive components, increases interest in real sexual objects, changes with experience, and is future oriented ('I shall have sex').

Clinical vignette: I

A patient wanted help, among other things, with his compulsive use of Internet pornography. His girlfriend had discovered his extensive use and was frustrated by his turning away from her over time and "seeming to prefer the computer". In exploring his online preferences, we found a relatively circumscribed interest in women with large breasts. His girlfriend had notably small breasts.

In a brief therapy, we did not try to discover everything about the particular meaning to him of large or small breasts, eschewing symbolic content interpretation on this occasion. Instead, we focused on the ways that he was responding to internal feelings of arousal. When he had an aroused feeling, he would not approach his girlfriend for sex, or masturbate to a fantasy, but would instead go and look at porn. Searching for just the right kind of large breasts would lead to long periods of partial masturbation without climax, and the eventual 'edged' orgasm was then particularly intense, reinforcing this way of doing things. He had replaced sex with masturbation, and replaced private fantasy with porn.

We worked on reinterpreting his aroused feelings not as an urge to go and look at porn, but as an urge to have sex, or, failing that, an urge to masturbate. If it were possible, he would try instead to approach his girlfriend, and if it were not, to masturbate with some private fantasy.

In bed with his girlfriend, we also considered his being able to enjoy her breasts instead of, in a kind of negative hallucination (discussed further in the section on fetishism) not seeing that they were there; small breasts are still breasts. He particularly enjoyed porn in which women were having their nipples sucked, and we considered that this was something that he and his girlfriend might try to do together. Or, if the timing were not right, that he might try to masturbate without porn but with a fantasy of sucking her breasts.

The evident oral phase and part–object relating seem to have been components of his introversive preference, which as a compromise allowed some but not too much excitement. With time, and the interpretation of defensive obstacles he produced to making these changes, he began to use porn less and fantasy more, and fantasy more as a practice for action in Laufer's (1976) terms, and in Eidelberg's (1945) terms as something future oriented and object related.

As in this clinical example, people generally approach Internet pornography with some conscious intent to find arousing material for masturbation. But that is not always the case.

Clinical vignette: 2

For instance, another patient of mine established a large collection of images of nude men that he would catalogue and curate on his computer. He would search various websites for these images, which always stayed just on the erotica or art side of the art-or-porn divide. In other words, you could have put them on the wall in an uptown gallery or in a coffee table book without much kerfuffle.

What is most notable about his activity is that although it was conducted with a compulsive energy, often for hours at a time, he did so without any conscious awareness of sexual arousal and never masturbated to the images. On the other hand, he would think about his collection as soon as he woke up in the morning. He felt like something was wrong when he would be searching for pictures, describing it as "a waste of time and energy", but didn't recognize the images as porn. On a couple of occasions, he deleted his entire collection, only to collect them again over another long period of time.

The treatment revealed that his sexual life was mostly inhibited, with very rare masturbation and no sexual activity with his partner. Searching for these images seemed to serve a more narcissistic than object-related function for him, of looking for an ideal figure whom he had wanted to be when younger and still in unconscious fantasy wished to be. His relative lack of object relatedness, in contrast to the previously mentioned case, complicates treatment further.

Work in this case had to proceed first by understanding the patient's relationship to his own ego and body, his narcissistic difficulties, before developing fantasies about other people – about doing things 'with' and 'to' and 'being done to'. Pornography, though facilitating narcissistic defenses, may be used as a tool in this regard: there is much at least partly object related and at least a little well-related pornography, interestingly especially in gay porn, where it has been suggested that actors often seem more genuine and engaged than women in straight porn (Salmon, 2004). Initial work with this patient took advantage of this opportunity furnished by contemporary porn. This additional first step may then be followed along the trajectory described earlier: from porn to fantasy, from isolative fantasy to practicing for action, and from trial action (masturbation) to real action with other people.

The problem of sadism

Eidelberg (1945) introduces a complex notion as simple when he asserts, "As Freud (1924[b]) has said, sadism does not present so great a problem as masochism does" (p. 133). It is routinely observed that contemporary pornography is objectifying, indifferent, and callous towards its participants, which attitudes shade into the coercive, humiliating, degrading, and directly violent elements that are now quite the mainstream, and no longer a rare kink or 'fetish'. The problem of sadism in pornography trenches upon unresolved debates about evident gender differences in the use of pornography and the treatment of its actors – men consume porn and women are mistreated in it.

Disagreements about how to understand these stark differences have tended to become polemical and entrenched, and writers have diverged as widely as possible on such questions as the essence of pornography: "Pornography is the graphic, sexually explicit subordination of women and girls" (Elman, 1997, p. 257); "Pornography is about sex, and not about violence or the degradation of women" (Salmon, 2004, p. 211). One way of understanding such stalemates is that they may be related to difficulties with the naturalistic fallacy: mistaking an explanation of a phenomenon for a justification of it (Wheeler Vega, 2001).

On closer examination, and from a Freudian perspective, the apparent unity of the problem of sadism in pornography is actually the resultant of two processes, both of which invite investigation: the *combination of sex and aggression* and the *separation of sex and love*. Understanding each requires some exploration of the vicissitudes of the drives, within and between them, and of some common defensive operations.

The combination of sex and aggression

In a series of influential articles, Stoller (1970, 1976, 1979b, 1987) restates and extends some of Freud's observations about sexuality to the domain of pornography and adds some of his own formulations. In an early paper bursting with ideas, Stoller (1970) argued that within each porn user's fantasy is represented a victim and the overcoming of a fear, such that in all porn viewers observe a "disaster [that] became a triumph" (p. 493). All sexual objects are frustrating, and particularly the earliest ones. It is this frustration that, in a traditional model, generates the aggression which is manifested in porn, which then serves as an external scaffolding for it. Pornography is essentially a revenge play, in which the frustrated child has bided his time and now gets to turn the tables on those who frustrated him.

Stoller further argues that in all pornography there is a distinct element of *hostility* (not mere activity). Even in relatively 'normal' pornography, for Stoller, there is always a victim or victims: any couple becomes the parents in a primal scene being voyeuristically observed without their knowledge (c.f. Arlow, 1980); any woman in a porn scene is conquered by any man.

In subsequent papers, Stoller (1976, 1979b) fills out his model of the function of pornography further, though it remains essentially a generalization of the defense of *sexualization*, the transformation of historical pain or frustration into present pleasure or triumph, combined with the defense of *identification with the aggressor*. In a later piece, Stoller (1987) shifts his focus from representations of past trauma to managing the effects of humiliation.

Peterson (1991) offers a kind of case example of Stoller's theory, whom he cites. In a formulation that emphasizes the centrality of the repetition compulsion, Peterson describes the case of a man addicted to pornographic films viewed in porn film theaters. As a boy and young man, who lost his father in infancy, he was exposed to repeated examples of what Peterson calls 'primal scenes' between his mother and various boyfriends in their home. (The length and scale of exposure described probably warrants another term, like 'abuse', rather than the more normative term 'primal scene'.) His addiction to pornography replaced any development towards sexual relations with others (he became *introverted*), and of particular interest to Peterson, was confined mostly to big-screen films in porn theaters. These were, on Peterson's interpretation, attempts to repeat and master the experience of a small boy watching full-sized bodies having sex.

Sadism in pornography would be for writers like Stoller, Peterson (and Arlow), a *secondary* defensive reaction to previous trauma, with either a large 'T' or a small 't', which the user is attempting to master through repetition and the defenses of sexualization and identification with the aggressor. This has been probably the most influential general approach in psychoanalysis to these themes. Another way in which aggression and sexuality might become combined is further upstream, in the id, at the origins of both forces.

Sadism is a ubiquitous component of contemporary pornography. When Freud (1905a) first seriously tackled the problem of sadism, he called it the "most common and the most significant of all the perversions" (p. 157), along with masochism, as a pair more accurately termed *sadomasochism*. He grouped them with the sexual aberrations, whose main feature was a replacement of the final adult sexual aim of reproduction with some developmentally earlier sexual aim. In this case, causing or receiving pain would become the chief sexual aim rather than reproductive sex.

Sadism for Freud (1905a), in his *first* attempt at systematic understanding, was not just an easier phenomenon to explain than masochism but practically self-evident:

> . . . the roots [of sadism] are easy to detect in the normal. The sexuality of most male human beings contains an element of *aggressiveness* – a desire to subjugate; the biological significance of it seems to lie in the need for overcoming the resistance of the sexual object by means other than the process of wooing.
>
> (pp. 157–158, italics in the original)

Reinforcing this view, he also signals that one should distinguish between what might be called ordinary or incidental sadism, on the one hand, and what on the other would then have been termed a sadistic perversion, or now a paraphilia:

> In ordinary speech, the connotation of sadism oscillates between, on the one hand, cases merely characterized by an active or violent attitude to the sexual object, and, on the other hand, cases in which satisfaction is entirely conditional on the humiliation and maltreatment of the object. Strictly speaking, it is only this last extreme instance which deserves to be described as a perversion.
>
> (1905a, p. 158)

Within this first account an explanation for the difference between ordinary and perverse sadism is gestured at, but without detail:

> Thus [perverse] sadism would correspond to an aggressive component of the sexual instinct which has become independent and exaggerated and, by displacement, has usurped the leading position.
>
> (op. cit.)

Freud does not make clear what this aggressive component of the sexual instinct is, whether it was joined with it from the start or at some later time, nor what has happened to it such that it has split from and overtaken the main sexual line and become a disorder. This is also quite clearly a theory of sadism in men, of incidental sadism occurring as a part of man's phylogenetic legacy, and of cases of exclusive disordered sadism emerging from that base.

Freud's first attempt at explaining sadism leaves us with some significant questions. He admits in this first pass that little has been done to explain the connection of sexuality with cruelty, "apart from laying emphasis on the aggressive factor in the libido" (1905a, p. 159). Freud made two further attempts at explaining sadism, through both phases of his theory of the drives, which, as Laplanche (1970) notes, may be traced through two pairs of papers: (Freud, 1915a, 1919) and then (Freud, 1920b, 1924b). In both pairs, his focus is not on sadism per se, but on its reverse, masochism.

The title of his later work states the nagging difficulty for Freud: "The Economic Problem of Masochism" (1924b). Masochism is an economic problem, one of quantities of psychic energy in the terms of Freud's metapsychology, because the pleasure principle implies that all behavior should increase pleasure and decrease unpleasure. How is it then that masochistic behavior, receiving pain from another, which should cause unpleasure, can come about and persist?

In his *second* attempt at explaining sadomasochism, Freud leans on a concept introduced lightly in the "Three Essays" (1905a). He notes briefly there a suggestion that the aggression in (male) sexuality is a holdover from a developmentally earlier desire, to literally eat the object, an oral phase component, which he called "the apparatus for obtaining mastery [*Bemächtigungsapparates*]" (p. 159). He then casually asserts later in that text: "It may be assumed that the impulse of cruelty arises from the *instinct for mastery* [*Bemächtigungstrieb*]" (p. 193), and that is early on, when the infant is quite ruthless and has yet to develop the capacity for pity. The infant doesn't set out to hurt the object; pain is just an incidental effect of being eaten.

At the beginning of "Instincts and Their Vicissitudes", Freud (1915a) writes that the most general task of the nervous system is "mastering stimuli" (p. 121), locating mastery in its many forms at the base of his theorizing. On this first revision, an instinct for mastery, or non-sexual *hetero-aggression* in Laplanche's (1970) terms, is primary. There are two groups of instincts in Freud's metapsychology at this point, the *ego or self-preservative* group, on the one hand, and the *sexual* on the other: mastery belongs to the former

Freud then traces the phenomena of sadism and masochism as they come into being through the vicissitudes of *reversal* and *turning against the self*. First (1) a primary hetero-aggression or mastery instinct is frustrated by an object and so (2) turns around, exchanging the object of the aggression for one's own self. Then (3) a new object is put in the place of the subject. Thus (1) 'I master you' becomes (2) 'I hurt myself' becomes (3) 'You hurt me'.

Freud adds in his discussion a fourth transformation, in which, following the arrival at a masochistic position, sadism can arise then, as he puts it, "retrogressively": "for while these pains are being inflicted on people, they are enjoyed masochistically by the subject through his identification of himself with the suffering object" (1915a, p. 129). Sadism is explained as a consequence of masochism: (3) 'You hurt me' becomes (4) 'I hurt you (and me)'.

Laplanche (1970) highlights some details of this sequence of transformations. First, the reflexive turn at (2), from mastering the other to hurting the self, is like the turn from feeding at the breast to sucking the thumb (Freud, 1905a, p. 182). In that seminal example, the sexual emerges where the self-preservative is left behind, at the auto-erotic turn – where pleasure for its own sake, taken in sensual thumb sucking, diverges from the vital need for nourishment. Mastery, the old self-preservative aim, is left behind for a brand new sexual aim: inflicting pain. Second, the exchange of the subject for a new object at (3) replaces the external object from (1) with an internal fantasy of the object, the object "*reflected* within the subject" (1970, p. 88). So fantasy arises at the very same moment as human sexuality, in its specifically psychoanalytic sense.

Though an account of the puzzling origin of masochism, and offering one explanation for the origin of sexual sadism, the economic problem remains unresolved. Though masochism can now be seen as a function of the sexual instincts, how to derive pleasure from pain still seems unclear. Never satisfied, Freud solves the problem in two ways in his *third* attempt at explaining sadomasochism. In "The Economic Problem of Masochism", Freud (1924b) puts his new dual theory of the *life* and *death* drives to work, formulated in "Beyond the Pleasure Principle" (1920b) and refined in "The Ego and the Id" (1923). In a rich passage, Freud states:

> The libido [energy of the life drive] has the task of making the destroying instinct innocuous, and it fulfills the task by diverting that instinct to a great extent outwards – soon with the help of a special organic system, the muscular apparatus – towards objects in the external world. The instinct is then called the destructive instinct, the instinct for mastery, or the will to power. A portion of the [death] instinct is placed directly in the service of the sexual function, where it has an important part to play. This is sadism proper. Another portion does not share in this transposition outwards; it remains inside the organism.
>
> (1924b, p. 163)

No longer part of the group of self-preservative instincts, the instinct for mastery is now grouped within the separate death drive. Two portions of the destroying instinct are directed outwards to work on the world: one operates with some independence as mastery and destruction, and the second fuses with the life drives to further man's phylogenetic destiny of sexual conquest. Also, however, some energy of the death instinct remains oriented inward and becomes "libidinally bound there. . . [as] the original, erotogenic masochism" (1924b, p. 164). In addition, some *secondary* masochism may also be formed, on this new theory, as a result of the introjection of previously projected death instinct energy, producing, now as with sadism, the necessity of differentiating two species (primary and secondary) of the genus.

Just as the life drives constantly press for satisfaction, Freud now theorizes a destructive drive continuously acting along with and interacting with them. Hartmann, Kris, and Loewenstein (1949) comment about this idea of a primary destructive force in the mind: "The vicissitudes of aggression resemble those of sexuality to such a degree that the assumption of a constant driving power comparable to that of libido seems appropriate" (p. 28). Along with this introduction of a separate destructive drive whose energy may by directed inwards from the start, another part of the solution of the economic difficulty is prompted by an idea that Freud initially passed over (1905a, pp. 204–205), that all stimuli that reach above some threshold, including pain, energize the sexual drive to some degree. He refers to this later as "libidinal sympathetic excitation" (1924b, p. 163), and this sexual energy caused by pain combines with the energy of the destructive instinct inside the person to create the ground for primary masochism.

On this third theory, the life drives and death drives become fused at the roots and *in both directions*, with some libido joining with the death drive to moderate it, and some death drive energy joining with the life drive to power its hetero-erotic sexual functions. Though Freud's emphasis tends to linger on the "taming of the death-instinct by the libido" (1924b, p. 164), the girding of the life instincts with aggression is an equal part of the model. Freud does also highlight the close relation between the two new classes of drives:

> So far as the psycho-analytic field of ideas is concerned, we can only assume that a very extensive fusion and amalgamation, in varying proportions, of the two classes of instincts takes place, so that we never have to deal with pure life instincts or pure death instincts but only with mixtures of them in different amounts. Corresponding to a fusion of instincts of this kind, there may, as a result of certain influences, be a *de*fusion of them. How large the portions of the death instincts are which refuse to be tamed in this way by being bound to admixtures of libido we cannot at present guess.
>
> (Freud, 1924b, p. 164)

Distinct features of fusion (*Triebsmischung*) and defusion (*Triebsentmischung*) in relation to the two classes of drives have further implications. Given that the life instincts' inherent tendency are to binding or fusion, and the death instincts' to dissolution or defusion, the greater the contribution of Eros then the greater the degree of fusion, and vice versa (Laplanche and Pontalis, 1967). Hence:

> . . . the essence of a regression of libido (e.g. from the genital to the sadistic-anal phase) lies in a defusion of instincts, just as, conversely, the advance from the earlier phase to the definitive genital one would be conditioned by an accession [entering in] of erotic components.
>
> (Freud, 1923, p. 42)

Movements up and down the developmental phases of the sexual drive in reaction to trauma or frustration may be expected to affect the quality of relating to the erotic objects, with earlier oral and anal phases characterized by more aggressivization of sexuality and the later genital phase with more libidinization of object relating.

This sequence of three accounts of sadomasochism may connect with Laplanche's (1970) suggestion that there are movements in Freud's thinking about the drives whose eventual forms are *chiastic* (crossing), borrowing the classical term for the rhetorical form and rhyme scheme ABBA ('Ask not what your country can do for you, ask what you can do for your country'). This may be seen in his second attempt at understanding sadomasochism, where we can trace the shifting orientation of the organism: (1) outwards, (2) inwards, (3) inwards, (4) outwards (and also perhaps, but less clearly, in the roles of activity and passivity). A similar form, though more a tercet (ABA), can be seen in the movement through Freud's three accounts of sadomasochism, and of the sadistic pole in particular. In the theoretical sequence from "the need for overcoming the resistance of the sexual object" (1905a, p. 158) to sadism arising "retrogressively" (1915a, p. 129) from masochism, to "sadism proper" (1924b, p. 163) we can trace the passage: (1) *primary* sadism becomes (2) *secondary* to masochism, and then (3) again (along with masochism) becomes *primary* again.

Alongside these theoretical distinctions, at least part of the riddle of masochism for Freud may have been the disturbing unnaturalness of men taking a feminine (passive) position in masochism, whereas the sadistic (active, masculine) role seemed self-evident. While examples of male masochism and domination of men by women are common 'fetishes' in contemporary pornography, they are far less common than male sadism and the forced masochism of women, which are now mainstream. The return within the third account of sadism to the first, to sadism understood as a primary male sexual form, may be a reassertion of the natural order of things for Freud, whereas the second account made it a subsidiary of a passive, feminine, form.

Clinical vignette: 3

One does not have to venture into the extremes of sadomasochistic pornography in order to appreciate the appeal of degrees of sadism, such as coercion, in much that is frankly or even nearly pornographic. For example, one patient had several favorite types of porn, including often the genre of 'straight-to-gay', where an ostensibly straight actor is apparently seduced, somewhat against his will, by a gay man into having sex with him. Escoffier (2011) also notes that this trope is central to 'she/male' porn, where it is referred to as the 'surprise', wherein a 'straight' male actor 'discovers' that his partner is she/male and is somewhat unwillingly 'seduced' anyway.

The subtle shade of willingness sought would vary for this patient, sometimes unwillingly willing, other times willingly unwilling, with a shift from seduction to coercion happening somewhere in between. It was the presence of at least some degree of unwillingness that indicated the seduced man's 'straightness', and hence his greater desirability than a just plain willing gay actor. Multiple identifications are likely in this use of porn as masturbatory fantasy material.

This patient often consciously identified with the gay man seducing the straight man (me in the transference, his father in the past, perhaps a brother still in the shadows). Guilt about this seducing role and fear of terrible, murderous punishment by the outraged straight man would sometimes deflate the fantasy and masturbation prematurely. The other obvious identification is with the straight actor as the boy longing to be seduced by the father/brother, who loves him not just tenderly but erotically, too. Notably, some degree of tenderness was also arousing to this patient in such scenes, alternating (oscillating) with someone being placed forcefully in the passive (erotically loved) rather than active (loving) role.

There was also some conflict for this patient with the idea that he enjoyed watching straight-to-gay or sometimes mainstream straight porn, and felt that this was something he should 'give up' in order to be 'really gay'. We were able to find through our work, particularly in the erotic transference, that his idea of giving up wanting 'the straight man' would actually amount to giving up men, or the man as such, in the form of the original man (father/brother) and that this was a wish to conform to what his family had wanted. Therapy did not help him to change or give up his use of porn, but to become more accepting of his underlying object choice, as well as to keep porn from being used as an introversive barrier between him and his partner.

Clinical vignette: 4

As another example, a patient described a habit of masturbating in the shower in the mornings, and that this had taken precedence over having sex with her boyfriend of several years. A compelling masturbation fantasy had been 'borrowed' from a scene in a TV show. While not strictly pornography, this material serves the same functions for this patient. In that scene, a sexually confident young woman asked her boyfriend to play a sex game with her in which she would tell him to 'stop' and 'don't come inside me' while they were having intercourse, but in which he should continue and disregard her protestations. They did so, with intense climaxes for both. My patient's first association to this scene and fantasy was that she might want her boyfriend or me in the transference to force her to have sex 'against her will', to hide what she in fact wanted. Other associations included recently thinking about stopping her birth control, with possible risk/achievement of pregnancy as a result. She noted that in sex with her boyfriend she usually preferred a female superior position, which she thought made her more like the man in the scene. Another association was to her position in the shower, usually bending over at the waist, which she connected with wanting to be able to enjoy that more passive position in intercourse.

The fantasy also has obvious resonances with a primal scene, especially of an imagined time before or at her own conception, and, too, with her projection of herself into the roles of both of her parents in that scene in beginning to contemplate having children of her own. This near-pornographic material has clearly made its way into this patient's conscious fantasy life and is now being used self-consciously for masturbation. Rather than being something entirely new this material seems to have brought about the reinvestment of already established unconscious fantasy material, primarily of the primal scene, and done so at a time when, developmentally, the possibilities of becoming a parent are coming especially alive.

For my patient, the point of orgasm in the fantasy masturbation compound was usually when the man would continue in the face of the woman's objections, apparently forcing himself on her and impregnating her against her protests. This fantasy encapsulates the full both/and of sadomasochism, including identifications with both the doer (father/boyfriend/analyst) and the done-to (mother/patient), the man forcing and impregnating and the woman being impregnated and forced, with pleasure taken from both the sadistic and masochistic roles in the scene, culminating in a powerful masturbatory orgasm in which the patient is, in a sense, coming twice. In terms of treatment, this patient did not want to use this fantasy for trial action, to introduce this as a role-play or sex game with her boyfriend – indeed this exemplifies how not all sexual fantasy must – but did want to try to interpret her urges to masturbate more often as urges to have sex, to risk approaching her boyfriend more often, and to explore more of a mixture of active and passive roles with him.

The separation of love and sex

Previously mentioned features of current pornography – its typical objectification of and indifference towards its participants, and its divestiture of almost all traces of affection, tenderness, romance, or love – may coincide with a problem touched on in Freud's "Three Essays" (1905a, p. 200, p. 207) and later tackled at length in his paper "On the Universal Tendency to Debasement in the Sphere of Love" (Freud, 1912b). There, within Freud's first drive theory, rather than the blending of sexuality and aggression we find struggles with some kind of separation of two aspects of Eros: of sensuality (*Sinnlichkeit*) on the one hand and affection or tenderness (*Zärtlichkeit*) on the other.

There, Freud explores the symptom of psychological impotence in men caused by a disjunction between the affectionate and sensual currents of the life drive. In his account, an affectionate bond is made in infancy to an incestuous object, usually the mother, but also perhaps an older sister. With puberty, a great increase in the sensual current intensifies these cathexes. New love objects become overvalued. The incest taboo creates a conflict causing frustration in reality. Impotence is a sign of real love in a way, in the sense that real love is transference love, which is love of a primary object. Men thus affected may become impotent or, in order to develop a real sexual life, find a devalued object for sex, so keeping affectionate and sensual currents apart. Delivering a famous epigram (in chiastic form), Freud (1912b) remarks: "The whole sphere of love in such people remains divided in the two directions personified in art as sacred and profane (or animal) love. *Where they love they do not desire and where they desire they cannot love*" (p. 183, my italics).

Freud also comments that it is common to find perverse (non-reproductive) sexual aims in such men "whose non-fulfillment is felt as a serious loss of pleasure, and whose fulfillment on the other hand seems possible only with a debased and despised sexual object" (op. cit.).

Filling out the account of the vicissitudes of the drives in our discussion of sadomasochism, we find that in Freud's account of the emergence of sexuality the first relation of the subject to the primary object is anaclitic, in which love and nourishment coincide. The original self-preservative component of the life instinct that ties the child to the mother's milk, and then to the breast that provides it, precedes the auto-erotic turn in which the child's own body can become a source of sensual satisfaction as a representative of the now fantasied mother's milk and breast, reflected within the self. The relation of tenderness belongs to the self-preservative instinct and the relation of sensuality to the sexual, which originates within and then diverges from it (Freud, 1905a).

The turn towards independent autoerotic sexual (sensual) satisfaction begins to separate this initial unity, in which the primary object is the focus of both currents. Too much divergence can leave these two components of the life drive poorly integrated. This begins as early as the Oedipal phase for Freud, in which: "from the point of view of the drives, what is in the foreground is not the erotic relation, but the relation of 'tenderness'" (Laplanche, 1970, p. 101). During the latency period, the affectionate trends and bonds to the primary objects are strengthened as the sensual trends are relatively repressed (Laplanche and Pontalis, 1967). Later, with puberty and the energizing of the sensual currents, the new sexual objects and desired sexual aims develop relatively independently of the affectionate trends, and must slowly draw together again, infusing the new objects with affection.

Schematically, we might say that in early infancy the sensual (sexual) emerges from the tender (self-preservative), and both coexist in the orientation towards the primary object, though in fantasy within the subject. In the Oedipal period, they begin to diverge, with the affectionate trend beginning to predominate as the erotic trends are repressed as the complex is relatively resolved. During latency, the sensual is further repressed, and the tender solidly foregrounded. In puberty, the sensual current is reinvested with energy and oriented towards new objects and genital aims, and ideally reintegrated with the tender, though slowly and with some effort. Hence, it can be seen that the reintegration of sensual and affectionate trends, specifically bringing tenderness into the realm of other-directed sensuality, is a developmental task of puberty and adolescence.

As noted previously by Laufer, Shapiro, and others, masturbation during adolescence may be an important factor in the development of a stable integrated adult sexuality, including, as observed here, the unified admixture of tenderness and sensuality. An introversive turn to tabooed fantasy found in pornography in adolescence, particularly to incestuous objects and pre-genital aims, may represent a failure, and cause a failure even to find a real debased sexual object who is invested with erotic energy if not tenderness. Such adolescents may accept some satisfaction instead in masturbation with non-object-related sexual aims or incestuous objects, and with a compulsive quality due to the never-ending pressure of powerful unconscious fantasies.

Some work on masturbation conflicts in girls has expanded our understanding of differences in development. For example, it has been argued that identification of the girl's own hand with that of the mother can make masturbation dangerous and lead to its inhibition, or to the development of a dominant homosexual object choice (M. E. Laufer, 1982). Similarly, it has been suggested that girls may be especially sensitive to early anal and urethral sensations which merge with genital ones and form a compound that can be manifested in conflicts for the young girl which extend into adulthood, in particular fantasies of 'holding back' from the anal/urethral phase, and fears of genital injury, distinct from castration anxiety, may extend to experiences of genital excitement in adolescence and adulthood and inhibit the 'letting go' required for orgasm (Pelaccio, 1996).

Anna Freud (1923) offers an example of how the tender and sensual currents may become defensively separated in a paper on daydreams in a young female patient. Disguised beating fantasies accompanied by masturbation in early childhood later came to take the place of the masturbation itself due to feelings of guilt. A following set of fantasies later in childhood with a reversal of features – from 'nasty' fantasies to 'nice' ones – eventually came to replace the first set, which were becoming too transparent to the patient's ego. She explains:

> While the phantasies of beating thus represent a return of the repressed, i.e., of the incestuous [Oedipal] wish-fantasy, the nice stories on the other hand represent a sublimation of it. The beating-phantasies constitute a [sadomasochistic] gratification for the directly sexual tendencies, the nice stories for those which Freud describes as "inhibited in their aim". Just as in the development of a child's love for its parents, the originally complete sexual current is divided into sensual tendencies which undergo repression (here represented by the beating phantasies) and into a sublimated and purely tender emotional tie (represented by the nice stories).
>
> (p. 99)

In this example, each of the currents found successive satisfaction after an initial period of joint inhibition, first with evidence of a kind of defensive mixture of sex and aggression in a sadomasochistic beating fantasy, and then second in a form very close to that of popular romance novels. It is not clear if the patient was ever able to unify both aspects into a more integrated sexual life.

The achievement of an integration of the affectionate and sensual currents, both directed towards the same object and aim, is far from trivial. Freud (1905a) gives an appropriately daunting analogy: "It is like the completion of a tunnel which has been driven through a hill from both directions" (p. 207). There is room for mismeeting on every bearing.

Clinical vignette: 5

One patient of mine who struggled with compulsive porn viewing tended to use it in binges, as she did with food; both for her had a feeling of excess and being bad, a giving in to urges that she wished she didn't have. Over a long time and with considerable shame, she eventually confessed to me that her preferred form of porn was 'threesomes' involving a man and two women. She herself had had sexual and ongoing relationships with both men and women (though never in a threesome), all of them intensely conflictual and none of them stable or enduring.

With women, she described an erotic intensity that she felt was lacking in sex with men, but also an excessive, agitated excitement that she could not contain. She was drawn to breasts but repulsed by vaginas and by cunnilingus in particular, especially in the active role. Intense ambivalence infused every part of her life. She did not identify as gay or bisexual but could never be sure: "Am I gay? I'm not gay!" With men, she described more calm and romantically toned relationships but never truly satisfying sex.

Her sexual desire illustrated something like the splits we are discussing here in the currents of the life drive, but for her the division was gendered rather than idealizing/devaluing: men for love and women for sex. Her history was marked by intense and difficult relations throughout life with her competitive, critical mother ("Have you gained weight again?", "You'd look nicer with more makeup") and later with female friends, bosses, and colleagues. The transference was often similarly intense and angry. Her father had been less critical than her mother, but never really interested in her. With considerable shame, late in the treatment, she reported a primal scene (screen) memory from early puberty of hearing loud noises from her parent's bedroom and going to investigate, finding them engaged in raucous sex. She had begun masturbating about this time and did so afterwards to fantasies of this scene.

More specifics about her preferred porn use clarified things further. Watching threesome porn, she preferred harder-to-find imbalanced tableaux (current pornography tending towards an obsessional inclusivity: everything with everyone at all times) in which one woman was left out. Finding such a scene while masturbating would immediately bring her to orgasm. Her own primal scene experience, encountered at a time when Oedipal conflicts were being re-energized in the light of her developing body and desires, had a profound effect on this patient, intensifying earlier investments of both parents as sexual objects and a role for herself as overexcited, excluded voyeur.

Her adult romantic/sexual life reflected this left-out position, fitting in with no one and no group, left with her intense sensual desires and forlorn affectionate desires, neither of which she could fulfill or give up. Work with her on this aspect of her difficulties focused with moderate success on turning more towards the use of fantasy for masturbation rather than porn, and away from fantasies of threesomes and exclusion toward fantasies of intimate sexuality with another person.

The question of fetishism

'Fetish' is one of the most popular categories in contemporary pornography, but covers material so diverse as to be of little use, often meaning not much more than an interest in some one thing in particular. Researchers have looked at some of the very many kinds of 'fetishes' present online, including: schoolgirls and soccer moms (Vannier, Currie, and O'Sullivan, 2014), bestiality (Grebowicz, 2015), Asian women (Zhou and Paul, 2016), revenge porn (Kamal and Newman, 2016), disabled women (Elman, 1997), and she/males (Escoffier, 2011), to name but a few. Classic fetishes – rubber, leather, shoes, feet, bondage, underwear, etc., are also all solidly represented in Internet porn, as are more baroque and dreadful preoccupations such as kidnap, rape, murder, cannibalism, and child abuse.

It has been observed that pornography categorizes women in a few ways, often by *acts*, or *attributes*, or both: "*Anal nymphos . . . Older women . . . Afro She-male Gang Bang*" (Strager, 2003, p. 53). This kind of categorization is standard on

Internet porn sites. Strager adds that the breaking of some obvious *taboo* is usually also included: "Search as much as you wish, but you will never find *Women Who Fuck Only Their Husbands* or *Missionary Position Sluts*" (p. 54). Similarly, Gagnon and Simon (1973, p. 199) interpret as a pornographic norm that either the *act* or the *context* must be unconventional, so that, for example, both *Women Who Fuck Only Their Husbands – with Strapons* or *Women Who Fuck Only Their Husbands – in Elevators* would be vastly more likely to appear as a pornographic theme than just the first clause alone. In this light, all pornography is fetishistic, being focused on some act or attribute of a person rather than a whole person, and requiring some element of taboo or odd context for it to draw interest.

Fetishism in psychoanalysis, however, is something different from either this myriad of contents or even some convincing set of delimiting features, and is very specific. Continuing the work from his "Three Essays" (1905a), Freud comments that one does not see a lot of fetishism in treatment because it is a *perversion* not a *symptom* – a perversion is the opposite of a symptom, a relatively stable way of attaining pleasure that does not distress the fetishist as a symptom might. In Freud's (1927) classic formulation, "the fetish is a substitute for the woman's (the mother's) penis that the little boy once believed in and – for reasons familiar to us [castration anxiety] – does not want to give up" (pp. 152–153). The fetish is not an act or attribute of or context for a person, but an object in the everyday sense of the word, a thing chosen through a contingent connection (association) with the female genital, for example underwear, which might "crystallize the moment of undressing, the last moment in which the woman could still be regarded as phallic" (p. 155).

A broader idea implied by Freud's account is that pornography is fetishistic not just in its *contents*, as exemplified here, but in the *process* of using pornography and in particular in its relationship to reality testing. For instance, Freud (1927) suggests that the general structure of a fetish allows the fetishist to maintain a dual relationship to the woman and to reality: "The attitude which fitted in with the wish and the attitude which fitted in with reality existed side by side" (p. 156).

A trenchant commentator on this topic, Bass (1997, 2000) explores a generalization of Freud's concept of the fetish and perversion (see also Adair, 1993, for an interesting account that relates fetishism to psychosis). Particularly in relation to the analyst's interpretive work, some patients can be *concrete* in Bass's terms. Making use of the mechanism of *disavowal* (*Verleugnung*), a relatively late concept in Freud's thinking, concrete patients eradicate the analyst's interpretations and separate existence, imposing instead their own certainty about the analyst and his or her mind. Disavowal may be paired with repression as a primary defense against external reality, in complement to repression's primary role as defense against the demands of the id (Laplanche and Pontalis, 1967, p. 119).

Bass (1997) carefully traces the relationship between fetishism and perception in Freud's thinking. In the early metapsychology of the "Project for a Scientific Psychology" (Freud, 1895a), reality testing is accomplished when the secondary process of the ego inhibits the hallucinatory satisfaction of wishes by the primary process of the id, allowing external reality to be cathected (invested with drive energy) instead of psychic reality. In hallucinatory wish fulfillment the perception-consciousness system (*Pcpt.-Cs.*) is cathected from within as if by a perception from without. I will return to this idea presently.

Bass works also with the somewhat obscure concept of *negative hallucination*: as positive hallucination is seeing something that is not there, negative hallucination is not seeing something there that is. The originary example of negative hallucination in Freud's discussion of fetishism is the boy not seeing the vulva due to castration anxiety. The fetish object (a shoe, for example), in turn, is a kind of positive hallucination of the maternal phallus in symbolic form. A fetish is somewhat like a dream, associated with a wish or wishes. However, "The fetishist, unlike the dreamer, of course, creates a perceptual identity between an actual object and a fantasy in waking life" (Bass, 1997, p. 655). For instance, the boy is excited by the shoe that has come to represent the imagined female phallic body. (This is how the analogy of the dream for pornography, used by Zeavin, 2011, is incomplete: the dreamer is working with fantasy objects during sleep, the fetishist with part fantasy and part reality while awake.)

Bass (1997) also clarifies Freud's observation that wish and reality exist 'side by side' using Freud's concept of disavowal. Both negative and positive hallucination are involved in this process: the negative to eradicate the unwanted perception, and the positive to replace it with a fantasy object. This is not a stable arrangement in neurosis, however, as "the ego both acknowledges a piece of reality and rejects it, and then oscillates between the two states" (p. 656). A psychotic patient might actually remain in a more stable state, in this regard.

Extending Freud's concept, Bass (1997) suggests that it is not merely the phallus but more generally the difference between the sexes that is disavowed. In particular, for both the child and the adult fetishist, "sexual difference is replaced with the fantasy of phallic monism" (p. 658): everyone has a phallus. Thus, the difference between fantasy and perception is eradicated through this two-stage process of disavowal and replacement, negative and positive hallucination, and by the way that they are held in an oscillating tension by the fetishist. Further encroachments upon reality may occur, leading to borderline states within those whom Bass terms concrete patients, who may need at times to erase the most fundamental difference: that between subject and object.

Other work on the fundamental ego mechanisms of perception, memory, and reality testing, may also be useful here. We have already discussed the importance of fantasy for Freud and some later writers in its relationship to masturbation, and by extension to sexual situations with others also.

To take up first the topic of perception, in his late "New Introductory Lectures", Freud (1933) outlines a model of the mind in which the *Pcpt.-Cs.* system is the outermost structure of the ego. It receives perceptions from the external world and also receives stimuli from within the mind. The ego represents the outside world to the id and produces memories of perceptions of the world. The ego must accomplish reality testing, which, in attempting to represent the world, must "put aside whatever in this picture of the external world is an addition derived from internal sources of excitation" (p. 75).

Arlow (1969a) clarifies this central idea: "fantasy activity, conscious or unconscious, is a constant feature of mental life. In one part of our minds we are daydreaming all the time" (p. 5). He introduces a vivid and influential metaphor. Arlow describes being at a party and seeing a home-movie projector from a distance:

> It occurred to me that an interesting effect could be obtained if another movie projector were used to flash another set of images from the opposite side of the screen. If the second set of images were of equal intensity to the first and had a totally unrelated content, the effect of fusing the two images would, of course, be chaotic. On the other hand, however, if the material and the essential characters which were being projected from the outside and the inside were appropriately synchronized according to time and content, all sorts of final effects could be achieved, depending upon the relative intensity of the contribution from the two sources.
>
> (1969a, p. 24)

Here Arlow creates a memorable picture of inner and outer experience, fantasy and perception, fusing on the screen of the *Pcpt.-Cs.* system. This idea allows us to refine our earlier discussion of *introversive* uses of fantasy. The language of *turning to* fantasy and *turning away* from reality might be better replaced with something more relative and expressing compromise: someone in an introversive state has *turned down* the incoming stream of external perceptions, and *turned up* that of the internal perceptual channel.

Second, on the subject of memory, we can observe that although Arlow draws from many places in Freud and later psychoanalytic writing, one of his most important sources is Freud's (1899) extraordinary early paper on "Screen Memories". Arlow (1969b) describes screen memories as an "exquisite example of the mingling of fantasy with perception and memory . . . disguised and rearranged in keeping with the defensive needs of the ego" (p. 38). He also quotes approvingly from the most surprising formulation of Freud in the "Screen Memories" paper:

> The recognition of this fact [that some vivid childhood memories are falsified by adult observers] must diminish the distinction we have drawn between screen memories and other memories derived from our childhood. It may indeed be questioned whether we have any memories at all *from* our childhood: memories *relating* to our childhood may be all that we possess.
>
> (cited in Arlow, 1969b, pp. 37–38)

In essence, Arlow expands and extends Freud's account of the function and construction of screen memories into an account of all conscious experience. In doing so, he leverages the most radical elements of Freud's account, implying that we have no pure perceptions from which memories may be formed, only ones relating to the world. For Arlow, the world is continuously created as a compromise – between fantasy, memory, and perception, between discovery and construction. Arlow's integrative work helps us see that it is misleading to state these functions as opposing processes or generating entirely different kinds of psychical products.

Third, to take up again the topic of reality testing, as noted earlier the idea was introduced by Freud (1895a) in the baroque vocabulary of the "Project" as a way for the psyche to differentiate between external perceptions, on the one hand, and wishful ideas or memories (taken as the same at this point), on the other. Later, in his pivotal chapter on "The Psychology of the Dream-Processes", Freud (1900) observes that "the bitter experience of life" (p. 566), reality, interrupts the first efforts at thinking, which aim to reproduce a perception as a means of satisfying a wish. But a memory or fantasy leaves us hungry:

> An internal cathexis [of a wish for nourishment] could only have the same value as an external one [a perception of nourishment] if it were maintained unceasingly, as in fact occurs in hallucinatory psychoses and hunger phantasies, which exhaust their whole psychical activity in clinging to the object of their wish. In order to arrive at a more efficient expenditure of psychical force, it is necessary to bring the [topographical] regression [from feeling of hunger to hallucination of nourishment] to a halt before it becomes complete, so that it does not proceed beyond the mnemic image [and become a hallucination], and so is able to seek out other paths which lead eventually to [actions that cause] the desired perceptual identity [actual repetition of the remembered state of feeding] being established from the direction of the external world.
>
> (p. 566)

Reality testing is the mechanism whereby remembering an event is interrupted so that one can orient oneself to the world to seek a real satisfaction, preventing a deadly introversion. With a continuous stimulus, one may never turn outward to the world, remaining in an introverted state. As noted earlier, people usually come to pornography with some conscious intention to find arousing material for masturbation. But soon, unconscious fantasy themes steer them through a kind of associative process that is facilitated by the most common method of presenting Internet pornography, the thumbnail gallery – an Internet page containing small clickable links that preview larger pictures or video clips. Porn surfers may click from link to link to link in a roughly free associative manner (though constrained by advertising and other hidden algorithms), sometimes arriving at places they had not consciously set out to find.

In watching pornography, intense images may stay with us in the form of memories that are as clear as if they were of actual experiences – clearer even, being expertly lit, filmed, and acted – exciting and vicariously satisfying experiences that we have lived through, in a fashion, and that may be retained as a form of screen memory, representing something wished for. Memories of wishes can be indistinguishable in form and power from (what we may need to keep calling) veridical memories. Wishing then operates, in its usual way, to try to bring about again the remembered scene, as if of a 'real' past experience. Searching to refind the remembered experiences, one goes back to the origin of the memory, to the pornographic sources, with new memories and new derivative wishes melded with unconscious fantasies, with all the power of the drives behind them.

Despite these clarifications of the general structure of fetishism and its relationship to central ego functions like reality testing, still somewhat obscure is Freud's (1927) following remark on a primary function of the fetish: "It also saves the fetishist from becoming a homosexual, by endowing women with the characteristic [a penis] which makes them tolerable as sexual objects" (p. 154).

Clinical vignette: 6

A consultee came to me for a single appointment for help with marital problems. He and his wife of some years were no longer sexually active. He, however, was actively masturbating to online pornography. I explored with him what kinds of pornography he would look at, and he said all sorts, but especially images of 'muscular women'. When I asked if there was any particular kind of imagery that would be most exciting and maybe bring him to orgasm while porn surfing he responded, "muscular women with penises", Sometimes the images were drawings, not photographs or videos, as the latter could be hard to find. I will take a break from the case at this point to discuss some additional helpful ideas.

Escoffier (2011) and a paired commentary by Zeavin (2011) explore some paradoxes about the burgeoning genre of 'she/male' pornography. This term used within pornographic content (more usually 'shemale' or 'she-male', and usually derogatory) generally refers to material featuring partly transitioned male-to-female transgender actors with both breasts and a penis. Escoffier observes that this type of porn, somewhat counterintuitively, is almost universally treated as a genre of 'straight' pornography, but notes that trying to think within typical binaries like 'straight or gay' produces confusion when engaging with this kind of sexuality. This is perhaps one of the more vivid recent examples of long familiar struggles with binary categories for non-binary phenomena (Schafer, 2002).

Escoffier notes that, in contrast, 'bisexual' porn – group sex with men and women who all have sex with one another – is usually considered a genre of gay porn, in that it contains men having sex with men. One variation that Escoffier does not discuss is the genre of female-to-male or trans man porn, which is also generally considered a variety of gay porn.

Take for an almost unique example the genre-defining trans man, porn actor, and activist, Buck Angel (Wikipedia, "Buck Angel"). Born Susan, he began transitioning to Jake in his late twenties, but did not pursue having a constructed penis. Buck is handsome, muscular, tattooed, goateed, cigar-chewing, and bald. He has performed extensively with gay men. Trans man performers like Buck are very rare, and almost never found on straight porn websites. Conversely, trans women are very rarely found on gay porn sites, and are now ubiquitous in mainstream porn.

Escoffier (2011) quotes a pornographer on why he thinks most she/male porn is consumed by straight men: "The reason is simple: Even though she/males have a penis, they look and act like women" (p. 276). What seems to make the most difference in assignment to binary 'straight or gay' porn categories is generally secondary sexual characteristics (breasts, muscles, beards, etc.), rather than primary genitalia. Buck looks, as he marketed himself early on, just like "The Man With a Pussy" (Wikipedia, "Buck Angel"): viewers do not notice the pussy so much as they notice the man. But they must notice the pussy, at least a bit; just as viewers of she/male porn must notice the cock, at least a bit.

Let us return at this point to Freud's (1908a) essay on the formation of hysterical symptoms in which he commented on the role of fantasy in their formation. Particularly, he noted there that many symptoms combine both a masculine and a feminine sexual fantasy, hence, Freud asserted, we find bisexuality in unconscious fantasies underlying hysterical symptoms. Freud observed such bisexuality also in conscious masturbatory fantasies, expressed in contrary masculine and feminine identifications and action, for example:

> . . . when a person who is masturbating tries in his conscious phantasies to have the feelings of both the man and the woman in the situation which he is picturing. . . [as in] one case which I observed . . . the patient pressed her dress up against her body with one hand (as the woman), while she tried to tear it off with the other (as the man).
>
> (p. 166)

This account is continuous with earlier and later writing by Freud on the centrality of psychical bisexuality to both normal and neurotic psychology. Freud's original account of bisexuality in the "Three Essays" lacks nuance which he refines in a 1915 footnote, when he elaborates: "By studying sexual excitations other than those that are manifestly displayed, it [psychoanalysis] has found that all human beings are capable of making a homosexual object-choice and have in fact made one in their unconscious" (1905a, fn. p. 145).

Following this, Freud observes: "Thus, from the point of view of psycho-analysis *the exclusive sexual interest felt by men for women is also a problem that needs elucidating* and is not a self-evident fact based upon an attraction that is ultimately of a chemical nature" (fn. 1905a, p. 146, my italics). As a biological fact, heterosexual behavior as such does not need explaining in a sexually repro-ducing species. But in the psychological domain of human sexuality, the pleasure-maximizing potential of bisexuality, of *inclusive* forms of sexuality, would seem a more optimal outcome (see Young-Bruehl, 2001). It is the pleasure-restricting *exclusivity* of the apparent predominance of human heterosexuality that is puz-zling in this light.

The object choice already made in the unconscious to which Freud (1923) is referring is spelled out later in "The Ego and the Id", in his account of the ori-gins of the superego in the dissolution of the Oedipus complex. With rhetorical skill, Freud begins with an account of the "simple positive Oedipus complex in a boy" (p. 32), and then complicates the account paragraph by paragraph. First, Freud notes that the typical outcome of the resolution of the Oedipus complex (identifying with the same-sex parent, not the lost love object) is a surprise, given the model of object loss and introjection observed in melancholia. However, he adds that one does in fact, on close analysis, find that the abandoned love object (opposite-sex parent) is brought into the ego by way of some degree of identifi-cation. As for example when a girl in the positive Oedipal resolution will "bring her masculinity into prominence" (op. cit.). How much this happens depends, for Freud, on her innate dispositions towards masculine and feminine characters.

That each child has a psychically bisexual disposition, of a unique blend, means that each will make identifications with both parents and retain them both as love objects to some degree. (Freud assumes a male-female two-parent family, as one might expect he would. But the precise membership of a family is unimportant. Children identify with minds as well as bodies, and minds are bisexual. Humans are like this all the way down, like Russian dolls, as far back as you like.) Hence Freud asserts, "In my opinion it is advisable in general . . . to assume the existence of *the complete Oedipus complex*" (1923, p. 33, my italics). Further, and prefigur-ing the ideas of Kinsey (1948, 1953), Freud describes the working through of the Oedipal phase as producing individuals who collectively form

> . . . a series with the normal positive Oedipal complex at one end and the inverted negative one at the other, while its intermediate members exhibit the complete form with one or other of its two components preponderating. . . . The relative intensity of the two identifications in any individual will reflect the preponderance . . . of one or the other of the two sexual dispositions.
>
> (1923, p. 34)

Though stopping short of recent theorizing on gender fluidity (e.g. Butler, 1990) in that it assumes the desirable achievement of some stable structure of gender identifications and object choices, Freud's argument makes binary assumptions about gender identity – male or female – and sexual object choice – straight or gay – incoherent, except as a not-very-informative shorthand (see also Young-Bruehl, 2001). As Kinsey's work showed, heterosexuality is a modal point in a multimodal distribution of other- and same-sex behaviors. In both psychological and behavioral terms, exclusive heterosexuality is a myth. It makes less sense to ask, 'Straight or gay?', the standard bipolar assumption, and more sense to ask instead, 'How *inclusive* or *exclusive* is someone's sexuality?'.

For an example, note one of Peterson's (1991) observations about his patient with a fascination for big-screen porn, especially his interest in images of men on the screen: "Awesome gigantic phalluses and coarse, dense chest hair loomed larger than life" (p. 415). Peterson interprets this as an attempt at identification with a wished for father. In an interesting reversal of standard interpretations of straight porn, rather than take the woman or even the woman's body parts as the focal elements of pornographic visual materials, Strager (2003) centers upon the penis, and in particular the penis in orgasm. For example, common to much mainstream porn is the man's ejaculation, usually onto the woman's body: "The audience must see the money shot, must see the penis in action, which transforms a shared, internal, concealed, heterosexual act into a solitary, external, visible, homoerotic one . . . presenting and watching the full sexual satisfaction of other men" (2003, p. 56).

Strager's provocative conclusion follows: "All of this flows unceasingly towards a single, simple, syllogism: Pornography highlights the penis; men watch pornography; therefore, men must be watching the penis" (2003, p. 58). There may (should) be some irony in the simplicity of Strager's thesis for such complex phenomena. We can see his emphasis, though, on the object-choice component of the complete Oedipus in the man, as complementary to Peterson's emphasis on identification. As with many attempts at correction, overcorrection is always a risk.

Though the great popularity of the genre of she/male porn clearly says something about erotism, it doesn't show that most men are bisexual or gay (as Strager might infer): for these concepts are too discrete. Escoffier prefers the somewhat more nuanced (and playful) term "straight with a twist" (2011, p. 278) to describe the men who seek out she/male pornography. Some of these viewers might also be fans of Buck Angel. Some fans of either could be what one might call 'gay with a twist'.

To return after this discussion to my consultee (see Clinical vignette 6): recall that he was apparently interested in viewing and masturbating to images of (1) women, with (2) mostly feminine secondary sexual characteristics, but (3) some masculine secondary characters (their muscularity), and especially those (4) with male genitals. Zeavin (2011), responding to Escoffier's article, outlines a number of possible configurations of unconscious fantasy that may be involved in the use of she/male pornography:

> . . . [1] is the body in question a concretization of a very early fantasy, a body that is simultaneously mother and father. . . . [2] a female body with a penis,

the 'uncastrated' woman of archaic fantasy. . . . [3] a male marker [penis] joined to female secondary characteristics – breasts and femininity. . . . [4] the body that has everything. . . . A body that precedes lack, precedes sexual differentiation, precedes separateness.

(p. 282)

It is not possible to say with any confidence which of these unconscious fantasy configurations may have been involved in driving my consultee's pornography use and diverting him from sex with his wife. He considered himself straight, but perhaps he would fit among the group of ostensibly straight fans of she/male porn who are 'straight with a twist'; however, the masculine secondary characters (muscles) that he also preferred blur things further; perhaps he would be better described as 'gay with a twist'? He, though, at least in this one consultation, identified himself as straight, was married to a woman, and his conscious sexual object choice was 'women', albeit now quite singular ones.

Returning to the puzzle set by Freud's remark about homosexuality and the fetish at the beginning of this section, we can revise the obvious pathologizing interpretation (being 'saved' from homosexuality) by thinking here about saving psychical bisexuality, inclusivity, from the restrictions of exclusivity, rather than as saving (healthy) heterosexuality from (unhealthy) homosexuality. The blurring achieved in the pornographic images my consultee used for masturbation allowed him to both remain 'straight' by his own lights and functionally 'potent' (not restricted by fear of being 'homosexual', which Freud may also have had in mind), albeit with 'a twist', and in masturbation not with another person. His arousal by the bisexual object (Young-Bruehl, 2001) – perhaps the mother who could remain unimpaired and valued (phallic), or maybe by a 'body that has everything', or perhaps a body with just enough secondary femininity to count as female – allowed him to retain his apparently stable gender identity and 'heterosexual' object choice, though in isolation from other people in life as sexual objects. His 'fetish' became a problem for him only in relation to his wife's dissatisfaction with his withdrawal from her, and then maybe only briefly.

We might call this person's pornographic preoccupation a fetish in terms of psychical *processes* – being aroused by something that he sees and does not see as real and possible at the same time. In contrast, and perhaps surprisingly, we cannot say that she/male pornography, as *content*, is fetishistic, despite its usual categorization and seeming, if anything would, to exemplify the genre. On the face of it she/male porn presents the canonical image of fetishism – the phallic woman, a positive hallucination encountered as perceptually identical to an unconscious fantasy. But, it is also not a fetish in that it *pictures* rather than *symbolically* representing (as with feet, underwear, etc.) something like the fantasy of the phallic mother or some theory like phallic monism. We could say that it is the direct presentation of some repressed fantasy and some theory of sexual non-differentiation, part of a set of fantasies and theories that is apparently large and influential.

This very popular, practically mainstream category of 'straight' porn, reveals not so much the obvious manifest 'twistiness' of its apparent focus, the trans woman performer, nor even that of its regular and enthusiastic consumers, but more the latent twistiness of our seemingly straightforward ideas of 'male', 'female', 'straight', 'gay', and 'bisexual'. All of these concepts are Euclidean forms in a larger space that is elliptical, in which many lines intersect.

Summary and conclusions

1   Pornography represents the repressed, sexuality, in its most dangerous and exciting forms. Porn is most often used for masturbation, and masturbation is best understood as an act compounded of two essential elements: physical self-stimulation and an arousing conscious fantasy. Masturbation fantasies are, like dreams, variously disguised wish-fulfillments, and may operate as a kind of nature reserve, containing all kinds of normally unacceptable and tabooed contents. Immersion in such fantasies can lead to introversion and a turning away from all real human objects or to only part-objects – genitals – or both. They may also, on the other hand, provide a useful opportunity for engaging in trial action and for exploration of one's internal world. A clear danger is that porn consumption may inhibit active fantasying by saving us from psychic exercise, leaving our minds out of shape and unfit for dealing with the world.

Masturbation fantasies often tend to orbit around one or a few central themes, though care should be taken to avoid too reductive or simplistic an interpretation of these, as with other conflicts in someone's life. It should also be kept in mind that sexual fantasies, like transference fantasies, are at the same time and always fantasies of ways of relating or not relating to specific other people. Masturbation may serve an important role in adolescence in helping to form one's relationship to the newly-sexual body, and may be helped or hindered in that role by how socially engaged versus socially isolated one is at that time. The facilitation of introversion by pornography is a present danger in leading adolescents away from the compromises and limitations of real-world sex with others and towards the imperial orgy promised by Internet porn.

Much ordinary work with people who struggle with excessive porn use may consist of helping them to reorient themselves to real possibilities of satisfaction, with people actually available to them. This includes increasing the use of one's own powers of imagination in creating sexual fantasies for oneself, rather than looking for ready-made pornographic material, and in particular fantasies that are future oriented and object related, either for use in masturbation or as trial action for sex with another person.

2   Some of the most striking aspects of contemporary pornography are the predominance of sadomasochistic content, in what is now the mainstream of Internet pornography, and the almost complete separation of sex and love, or sensuality and affection.

The problem of sadomasochism in pornography has been approached mostly as a secondary defensive reaction to trauma, where the mechanisms of sexualization, reversal, and identification with the aggressor predominate.

Looking further upstream for some understanding of the ubiquity of sadism in current porn, we can trace a sequence of three accounts of sadomasochism in Freud's writing. On the first account, sadism is primary, as a part of man's phylogenetic legacy. Special cases of exclusive sadism emerge from this base.

On the second model, aimed particularly at understanding masochism, a sequence of transformations, involving both the self-preservative and erotic drives, occur. These lead from attempts to control the real object of self-preservation to a frustrated turn against the self, leading to a masochistic position in which a now fantasied other replaces the subject, and then around again into a fully sadomasochistic sexual relation to the object. Both sexuality and fantasy arise at the first moment of reflection, as the subject turns his aggression around against his own self.

Following out the implications of Freud's second theory of the drives has further implications. On this account, sex and aggression are fused at the root, and bidirectionally. Some energy of the death drive is infused into the life drives to power their striving for sexual conquest, and some energy of the life drives is bound to the death drives to bridle their destructive and disintegrating tendency. As no 'pure forms' of the life or death drives are preserved or quarantined from each other, consequently sadomasochism is to be understood as an ordinary and inevitable part of sexual-object relating and of human erotism.

As in all psychoanalytic work, we strive for individualized understanding rather than formulaic ciphers, and so expect to find various admixtures of primary and secondary, driven and defensive, aspects of sadomasochism in the sex lives, including the pornography use, of our patients. Ordinary examples of sadomasochism, particularly elements of coercion and degrees of unwillingness, are very common in sexual fantasy catalyzed by porn or near-porn, which reinvest established but perhaps quiescent unconscious fantasies.

3   In a related aspect, contemporary porn quintessentially represents the one whom 'where he desires cannot love'. It seems that an initial unity of tender – self-preservative – and sensual – distinctly erotic – trends is disrupted throughout development, beginning to come apart in early childhood and diverging quite far by adolescence. At that point, where the two currents might reconverge, is when most adolescents find their way to Internet pornography, if they have not done so already.

Porn, presenting sex without love, reflects and reinforces an adolescent phase of the life drives, such that the two, sensuality and tenderness, may seem to traverse quite parallel courses. Individuals may face differing challenges in this period, with some struggling more to bring tenderness to their sexual objects, and others facing more the task of foregrounding the sensual apart from affectionate ties. The ideal resolution of this phase would allow one to love whom one desires and desire whom one loves.

4   The term 'fetish' is so widely used in pornography as to be useless. Some have argued that all pornography must contain some deviant or perverse elements, and so is fetishistic in that sense. Freud's much more specific concept of fetishism points not just towards particular perverse interests, but towards wide-reaching changes in fundamental ego functions, including reality testing. Bass clarifies and extends Freud's initial observations and later concept of disavowal to show that that the fetishist accomplishes, albeit in an unstable, oscillating manner, the impossible feat of locating a wish and an inconsistent reality at the same space and time. This initially limited process may encroach upon all reality testing and lead to the eradication of such fundamental differences as those between subject and object, with concrete patients attempting to assimilate the object.

Some earlier work by Arlow is also relevant here. His famous home movie projector analogy for the operation of the mind pictures consciousness as a screen that is constantly receiving images from the outside and inside worlds, from perception and fantasy. The constant operation of these processes has radical implications – that there is no pure perception of the world, and consequently no purely veridical memories: all are infused with fantasy and wishes at their inception. The intense and vivid qualities of film, a major medium for Internet pornography, apply great stress to processes of reality testing. This makes it especially likely that pornographic material will modify conscious and unconscious fantasies and shape the forms of derivative wishes. These may then seem capable of being satisfied only through their original fictive sources, and propel a compulsive return to pornography to refind their objects.

A remark by Freud on one function of the fetish, and the great popularity of the genre of she/male pornography, both prompt a specific investigation of one currently striking form of 'fetishism'.

She/male pornography is currently located within straight porn. Its complement, trans man pornography, is much less popular, and located within gay porn. Though both are examples of bisexuality, traditionally speaking, they are clearly not equally so, which, in turn, flags the normally singular concept of 'bisexual' as problematic.

Freud had noted examples of bisexuality in sexual fantasy, such as identifications with both the man and the woman in a typical sexual scene. His underemphasized concept of the *complete Oedipus complex*, including varying degrees of identification and object love towards both parents, influenced strongly by constitutional factors, also implies a puzzle about the preponderance of *exclusive* heterosexuality. Given that sex is so pleasurable and so desired, why do humans not maximize their pleasure with as *inclusive* a range of objects as possible?

Some have suggested that all mainstream straight porn is, in fact, because of its implicit or explicit focus on the penis, actually concealing tabooed homosexual desire in plain sight. While interesting, a simple pendulum swing away from the standard view of mainstream pornography, as revealing heterosexuality in its purest form, can also only be partially correct.

A clinical case of an apparent 'fetishist' reveals a host of blurred psychological boundaries and defies routine categorization. Even more interestingly, the substantial popularity of the genre of she/male pornography reveals blurred conceptual boundaries. While it is tempting to locate any manifest 'twistiness' in the contents of some part of current pornography or some patient's fantasies, it more likely resides latently in many of our own seemingly straightforward concepts about sexuality.

Chapter 7

Swipe, woof, flirt, and the erotics of the handheld device

R. Dennis Shelby

It has been some eighteen years since I first explored the phenomenon of cruising among gay men (Shelby, 2002). The underlying assumption at that time was that it involved traveling to a geographically defined place, as well as a state of mind of partner seeking – 'of feeling lost and needing to be found'. A primary motivation to address the phenomenon at that time was the presence of rather alarmist, if not hysterical literature on male (read 'homosexual') cruising in the psychoanalytic literature (see Socarides, 1978; Calef and Weinshel, 1984; Willick, 1988; Bollas, 1992). The literature did not view 'cruising' as one of the myriad human endeavors – sexual or otherwise – that potentially emerges during a psychoanalysis. Rather, it was treated as something alien, something fantastic that clearly had evoked something in the – we can assume – heterosexual male authors. What was missed was seeing an analysand's accounts and associations to their cruising activities as an opportunity for deeper engagement. Let alone a comparison to heterosexual partner seeking as if heterosexual couples were merely holding hands on the porch swing, prostitution was not the world's oldest profession, and unwanted pregnancies are an age-old challenge.

Technology that assists in partner seeking has advanced considerably since that time. The advent of the Internet brought with it chat rooms, dating sites, what are commonly known as 'hookup sites' – some highly specialized in terms of types of men and women who used them. One no longer had to go to a 'place' other than their computer. But, one had to take what happened on the computer into the 'real' world of people with motivations and capacities that may or may not line up with what was portrayed online or evoked in one or both users. For the remainder of this chapter I will used the term global social networks (GSNs) used by Beymer et al. (2014). This term better captures the scope and usage of dating and hookup apps. Technology has evolved to the point where dating, or for some people 'hookup', GSNs are available on smartphones. Now men and women can simply engage a GSN on a highly mobile handheld device (smartphone) at any time, day or night, during boring meetings, or while passing time, acutely lonely or 'horny'. Many profiles and pictures of potential sexual and/or romantic partners are there for perusing and engaging at any time, in any city or country. The handheld device is a mode of entrance into a vast network of potential mates; the reach is global, and they end up providing an array of social functions – not just sexual gratification or the less charged term, 'dating'.

GSNs employ various means to draw the attention of another user: on some, one swipes left, others the user can send a 'woof' or a 'flirt' to get the attention of a potential mate. Something in their photo or wording of their profile has captured attention, and the user reaches out in hope of a response. These initial engagements can lead to long-term chatting online, offering photos of various degrees of revelation, a no thank you, a brief sexual encounter, or long-term engagement. I am assuming these GSNs are mere extensions of the human mind. While some could argue the GSNs are engineered to encourage fantasy, I feel it is safer to say human fantasies, sexual and otherwise, are ready to color the world when it comes to practically anything, but particularly so with partner seeking.

This time around, I am addressing the use of dating/hookup GSNs in the broad sense of people – male, female, gay, straight, bisexual, transsexual. Clinical experience has repeatedly demonstrated that while specific GSNs may cater to specific people, in search of a specific kind of person, the way all people engage is remarkably similar. In a more strident sense, I do not want to participate in the fantasy of the urban gay male as a prolific indulger of anonymous sex. Indeed, I have encountered heterosexual female and male patients who are as prolific consumers of sexual opportunities provided by these GSNs as my gay male patients. But we must not assume the sole aim is sexual union. Research as well as clinical observation confirms that searching, chatting, and flirting takes up far more time than a date or sexual encounter. And ongoing conversations that may lead to friendships are providing a psychological function as well.

One can also assert that dating/hookup GSNs are another manifestation of partner seeking in the long history of using media to facilitate human connections, be they brief, for a specific fetish, or for marriage. In the seventeenth century a proper young Ottoman woman would send her female servant to the man who caught her eye to obtain a copy of his Divan (a collection of poems authored by the man). In the case of male/male interest, one man might write a write a gazelle (poem) to the object of his affection. The so-called mail order brides common during the settlement of the western United States involved the use of what we would now call 'personal ads' that were quite common in many upstanding newspapers. The venerable personal ad in print media was gradually eclipsed by online media. With the advent of computer databases and search features came the promise of dating with a perfectly matched partner. GSNs allow for perusal of photos, details about the person in their own words, and in many cases geographical location (i.e. how close or how far).

Whether a marketing tool, or a veil over true intentions, GSNs are billed as either dating GSNs or hookup GSNs. Clinical experience indicates the way people use these GSNs is quite fluid. Experience also indicates *when* people use or perhaps *turn to* their GSNs is highly fluid but potentially understandable as well. What is also remarkable is the degree of ambivalence about these GSNs. Patients often complain bitterly about the people they engage, or the GSN itself; they worry they are spending way too much time perusing and engaging, and wonder if something is wrong. One patient bragged one week about how good he was at finding sane, interesting people, only to complain bitterly the following about a frustrating encounter with someone he thought was a "good guy". Many people worry that their app usage is a sign that they are "truly crazy". Social research tries to estimate actual numbers of users and successful relationships, and the popular media often offers up cautionary tales about the consequences of GSN usage.

As analysts we often encounter GSN use in the context of the broader clinical encounter. As such, we need a reasonable, broad, and deep clinical framework with which to think about GSN usage. In the broadest sense, what patients tell us, how, and when is under the sway of the transference–countertransference continuum. Our ability to successfully engage with patients around their GSN usage is facilitated or hindered by the relational dimension as well. The complexity of the personality and how partner seeking is pursued; when difficulties arise; repeating patterns of hope, frustration, and profound disappointment can all become useful clinical data.

My position in the 2002 paper continues: psychoanalysis offers us a plethora of terms and concepts to call dating GSN usage, but the ultimate issue is its clinical utility. When patients bring in their dating GSN usage, they are also bringing in many dimensions of their complex personalities. Essentially, we are offered a route to deeper engagement. To that I will add that frustration, not gratification, keeps some patients locked into the world of dating GSNs. To frame this exploration, we will explore some of the findings of social research, and psychoanalytic concepts that can provide a helpful framework. My clinical thoughts are primarily addressed to people who we might consider having 'regulatory problems or disorders'. I am by no means pathologizing GSN use; rather, these are the patients I tend to work with, and the GSN use is part of a larger personality/self-configuration. Additionally, the psychoanalytic concepts are derived from self psychology and its elaboration post Kohut.

Research and popular media

We have all heard the phrase "Everyone is on Tinder" [or Grinder or Scruff, etc.]. We could argue that these GSNs do create the illusion of plenty, a whole world of potential partners for surveying and engaging. Perhaps it is best to take a brief detour into the realm of social science research and popular media for a more complete sense of this new phenomenon. Space does not permit a thorough review of the mounting research literature on GSN use, but general trends do offer us a general sense of frequency, how people use GSNs, and the outcomes.

The Pew Research Center offers the following broad trends: in 2005, 44 percent of US adult respondents felt online dating was a good way to meet people. In 2015, this number had increased to 59 percent. In 2005, 29 percent of respondents felt people who used online dating sites were desperate. In 2015, this view had dropped to 23 percent. The use of online and dating GSNs among eighteen- to twenty-four-year-olds rose from 10 percent in 2013 to 27 percent in 2015. Among those aged fifty-five to sixty-four, usage rose from 6 percent in 2013 to 12 percent in 2015. When researchers looked at use versus actual engagement on a date, 44 percent of online daters had progressed to a date in 2005, and 66 percent had progressed to a date in 2015. This means that one third of users do not make the transition from online/GSN engagement to engagement in the 'real world'. Researchers also found that 5 percent of respondents in a marriage or committed relationships met their significant other online, while 88 percent say they met their partner offline, without the help of a dating site (Smith and Anderson, 2016).

In terms of gay men, most of the research, whether academic or marketing, tends to focus on patterns of usage, not percentages of men using the GSNs over the lifespan. In terms of gross numbers of users, Karlan, Feder, and Rial (2017) analyzed GSN downloads, GSN usage by country (truly international GSNs), and company usage claims. Grinder was the most popular among gay and bisexual men, with the company reporting over 2 million men in 196 countries using the GSN every day. Scruff claims 60 million messages exchanged every week. The reporters listed many other GSNs popular in other parts of the world.

Interesting findings about usage have emerged. A fairly rigorous study conducted by the website grabhim.net (2015) reveals a complex range of use: 83 percent of respondents sent pictures of their penises; 33 percent lied about their age, height, or weight; 44 percent of men who did meet did not hookup; and, most intriguing, of the 71 percent of the men who did meet up, the relationship resulted in some kind of relationship – although the authors acknowledge the wording of the question may have inflated numbers (they intended hookup, boyfriend, sex buddy, ongoing friendship). On a more onerous note, Beymer et al. (2014) found that men using location-based GSNs were 25 percent more likely to be diagnosed with gonorrhea and 37 percent more likely to be diagnosed with chlamydia than men who did not use GSNs.

We do not have to look far in the popular media to find an abundance of cautionary tales. Mikshe (2016), in an article published in *The Advocate*, asserts that GSN use can be a recipe for loneliness. Quoting academic Stephen Cole who compared GSN use to "empty calorie socialization" and studies that indicate loneliness is on the rise in America, he sounds a somber note about the hazards of GSN use. Another article (Gerard, 2017) in *The Advocate* decries the racism embedded in user profiles, and the previously mentioned grabhim.net survey indicates that 57 percent of HIV-negative men discriminated against HIV-positive men.

On the other team, Wong (2018) decries the fetishization of Asian women she encountered on Tinder, and Matchet (2017) describes five kinds of creepy guys you will meet on Tinder. Silver (2018) details why after ten years of frustration with online dating she is calling it quits. Her complaints include: bad dates that go nowhere; good dates that go nowhere; online dates are not dates, they are two strangers meeting up and talking; and that online dating is full of single women and single men, but nothing else. She also adds that for ten years she did not listen to her conscience, and that eventually she did and deleted her apps. For those frustrated with online dating, many online articles offering advice and tips for a more successful experience abound.

In summary, social science and media research paint a complex picture of GSN usage. We can conclude that the majority of people do not use GSNs regularly. Those who do report a mixed picture of communicating: some dating and some sexual encounters, some longer-term relationships, and several hours per day of GSN usage. There is clear evidence that indeed not everyone is on these GSNs, and that people spend more time perusing profiles and communicating with or without exchanging pictures than actually hooking up. And yes, people do report finding love and longer-term relations using GSNs. But as the popular media indicates, ambivalence, frustration, and disappointment for the majority of people is present along with a tendency to become highly engaged with the GSN apps despite poor results.

Towards a psychoanalytic perspective

Psychoanalysis has been hard-pressed to theoretically define 'normal' sexuality, let alone a model of enduring relationships. (A fully elaborated theory of sexual attraction, pleasure, and bonding is beyond the scope of this chapter.) Yet the tendency persists to valorize longevity and to be suspect of purely sexual (if there is such a thing) serial or short-term relationships. Freud's (1912b) "stereotype plate" (p. 100) for the condition of falling in love implies that the stereotype plate – the who, what, when, and how – a metaphor for the combination of hopes, wishes, appearance, and specific fantasies that evoke the wish to engage another with love or infatuation, is faulty, neurotically tinged, and in need of analysis, of sorting out. The hysterical stereotype needed to be projected onto the person of the analysist and straightened out to pave the way for more successful relationships (pp. 99–100).

A highly relevant view for our understanding of GSN usage is found in Tolpin (1997). In summary, she posed several broad principles: our clinical theories can blind us to the complexities of sexual life; childhood fantasies are naïve, not polymorphously perverse; the wide ranges of self states firm, or prone to disorganizing fragmentation effects the experience and expression of sexuality in long and short-term relationships. She offers:

> My main point about sexuality is that it reverberates with the very ways in which the self developed over the whole course of childhood. The reverberation lasts for a lifetime and is transiently reached into and reexperienced in connection with one's own sexual feelings and the sexual responsiveness of the other. Thus, with sexual maturation come two interrelated forms of intense pleasure – pleasure from sexuality, in and of itself, and pleasure from sexuality as a way of transiently re-accessing the deepest roots of self-experience in primary connections with responsive (selfobject) others.
>
> (p. 184)

Far from a neurotically tinged stereotype plate projected onto another person, in this model, people are seeking out others whose sexual fantasies 'line up' with theirs and they are able to 'go there together'. The multitude of sexually related activities in this framework reflect previous selfobject experiences and the 'naïve' expression of the drives. To some, the idea of adult sexuality as a reflection of history and naïve ideas about adults and the thrill of being able to realize them with another may seem a bit preposterous, that is until we stop and reflect. I remind the reader of Racker's (1968) assertion that fantasies of sexual acts are also routes to psychological union. To this we must add that sexual activity is an act of revelation – we are putting our fantasies 'out there' in the hopes for a response and engagement. For some people, the act of revelation is potentially mortifying, for fear of repulsion on the part of the other, or the fear of another person being aware of one's deepest longings. For others, the repeated revelations of desire and deep engagement and acceptance of fantasy is an ongoing and uncomplicated endeavor; it is just one part of living life as a couple.

We must also address the role of exhibitionism in sexuality in general and in GSNs. All the GSNs I have heard about (and in many cases been offered a glimpse of by patients) include the ability to offer up a range of personal photographs to others in a range of states of dress and undress, different body parts, and at times evidence of fetishes. For some users, 'unlocking pics' (many GSNs have public photographs and private photographs to be shared at the user's discretion) is part of the thrill, realizing that another person is intrigued, if not enthralled, and perhaps pursuing further engagement. We might even say it taps into private fantasies of being a porn star. Ultimately, people are looking for someone whose explicit or implicit fantasy life and relational longings 'line up' with those of another person. Of course, we do not have to look far for examples of rejection if not cruelty. The patient enthralled with another's attention one day is crushed and humiliated by coarse rejection another day. A seemingly successful engagement may be followed by 'ghosting' – ceasing communication, essentially disappearing. For some, placing a face photo on one's personal ad is a tortuous decision; for others, not a thought is given to public exposure, but rather to which photo to put out to the world.

The role of sexualization – broadly defined as the defensive use of sexuality (Goldberg, 1995) – also needs to be considered. Coen's (1981) argument that we should consider the psychological, not the behavioral, manifestations of sexualization has merit. We must also consider the considerable push, the energy the sexualization can impart to the pursuit of sexual union. One can say it can be a 'roaring' defense. Tolpin points to Kohut's 1996 observation of the almost addictive defense of sexualization, used in an unending effort to fill in a structural deficit, is the feeling of intense pleasure and enormous relief from the sudden reorganization or reconstitution of the self that may accompany sexual activity (Kohut, 1996). This perspective takes us beyond mere discharge and tension reduction. It can lead us into deeper inquiries and understanding about the qualities being sought in another, the deepest hopes for short- or long-term encounters, recurring patterns of frustration and disappointment. Perhaps most important is the ability to tolerate the inherent frustration of longer-term engagement –the ongoing revelation and comparison of the hoped-for person, with the 'real' person and how they live their life.

We run the risk of our own theoretical blindness (Tolpin, 1997) when we assume that the goal of driven sexuality is simply relief from sexual urges. To the contrary, self psychology poses that the relief is from the reorganization or reconstitution of the self, secondary to sexual union in real time or fantasized via masturbation. In the case of patients who are very good at finding highly satisfying sexual encounters via GSNs, but then are repeatedly frustrated by their lack of ability to engage someone long term, then we have a truly clinical question to explore.

Finally, we must consider disavowal and Kohut's concept of the vertical split. Kohut posited a vertical split held in place by disavowal versus the repression barrier or a horizontal split held in place by repression. Disavowal at its core is the separation of meaning. Goldberg (1995) has also implicated the defense in ignoring unpleasant reality. Basch (1983) asserted that disavowal allows for the wished-for reality when another reality is impinging. The expressions of disavowal are multitude, but in the clinical encounter it often comes down to people not paying attention to what they are feeling in the moment, or the depths. While the concepts may be derived from self psychology, I am advocating a position similar to Freud's (1916–17) assertion: " 'the phenomenon has a sense'. By 'sense', we understand 'meaning', 'intention,' 'purpose' and 'position in a continuous psychical context" (p. 61).

The clinical encounter

Theorists strive for clean, precise definitions of terms and concepts. However, we all know the clinical encounter is often far from clean, clear, and precise. It is messy, and at times bewildering, and our quest for premature clarity can lead to an overreliance on technical concepts rather than the interplay between analyst and analysand. In short, the clinical concepts just discussed are nothing more than guideposts or a sketch that is filled in by the richness of the individual mind.

I am advocating an interpretive stance towards the analysands' accounts of GSN usage, and their experience of people they meet via GSNs – to treat them as any other association. Freud's (1916–17) definition of interpretation as a process of finding the hidden meaning remains relevant. But the meanings are hidden from the analysand and the analyst. Concepts provide a blueprint or sketch to lead us to the strivings. Hence interpretation should be hard; it is hidden from both parties in the clinical encounter. The complex associations around GSN usage are complex, rich, and at times highly sexualized and exciting, which only increases the possibility for analytic distraction. A good interpretation is a revelation to both parties, or to quote Goldberg (2008, personal communication), "a good interpretation should change both parties"; essentially, the clinician's understanding is deepened, and the analysand is more aware of just what they are striving for, and hopefully less defensive about any deeply imbedded wishes or longings.

The transference–countertransference configuration has great influence on whether, how, and why GSN usage is brought into the analytic relationship. Details may be sketchy at first, given the state of resistances to deeper transferences. But a steady inquiring stance and interpreting any potentially threatening transference fears will help the process in general deepen.

Clinical vignette: I [1]

A thirty-something single gay male came into analysis due to what I would call extended virginity – a complete paralysis around sexuality and partner seeking. He gradually brought in his GSN usage and the deeply imbedded fantasy that his mother always knew what he was up to. Memories emerged of his mother reacting with great distress and hysteria at any sign of sexual interest in her son. He was able to relate that while he had been carefully "watching me" and aware that I was always curious and even-handed, he was also waiting for me to go off, to scold and moralize about the end of the world if I got wind of his sexual interests. He felt I knew what he was up to; he hoped I did not know, but deeply wished I could help him figure out how to be an adult sexually active gay man. The early accounts of his GSN usage and partner seeking and fantasies in general were so sketchy as to be maddening. I finally offered, "I really do not know what you are doing online or with the GSNs". Once said, I think we were both stunned – he that he indeed felt I knew his innermost thoughts, I that the depth of a negative transference was stunting his ability to associate and engage. He was also a man who desperately needed the regulating, modulating dimensions of the transference and analytic relationship to grow into his sexuality. Deepening the regulating and organizing transference required addressing prior overwhelming experiences with a parent determined to blot out any signs of developing sexual interests in her son.

Another phenomenon I have encountered with increasing frequency are young heterosexual women who as adolescents encountered older men or boys in Internet chatrooms. These stimulating conversations were hidden from the parents and became a kind of secret place they could go to for reassurance and in some cases 'dating' older boys, if not young men, that were a powerful counter to feeling excluded by peers and/or being bullied for their physical appearance. As young women, dating and hookup GSNs quickly grabbed their attention. While manifestly searching for love, they were prone to being used for quick hookups and perpetually disappointed that nothing enduring came of these encounters. Clearly something got laid down in adolescence that was now being replayed in the world of adults.

The foregoing comments show broad-stroke understanding. In actual practice, we need to be able to engage on a highly particular level that is accessed by deepening transferences and deepening understanding of the analysand. We do encounter analysands who, although quite inhibited and reticent in their day-to-day life, feel free and sexually potent while chatting on GSNs. This could be considered a kind of practicing, but we should not assume that practice will readily translate into personal lives.

Clinical vignette: 2

Early in the analysis the male analysand had a dream of seeing his father in his "tighty-whitey" underwear. He reported feeling grossed out; his father was pudgy and hairy and parading around the home. "Cover up for god's sake, cover up!", he shouted in the dream. At the time, he would tolerate no further exploration other than his reaction. No possibility of being intrigued but then overwhelmed by his desire to see, or exploring his reaction as a reflection of disrupted idealization of his father couched in the guise of an uninteresting male body. At the time, early in the analysis, it was a kind of paralysis of associations and possibilities. Many years later in the analysis he related that he had gone to the local bath house and was thrilled that he had had an exciting time; he allowed himself to be turned on by watching and doing, by letting himself be swept up in the 'masculine atmosphere' created by the many men that surrounded him. In sharp contrast to previous associations to his father's underwear that were acutely strangulated, his account was rich in imagery, feelings, and excitement.

A prominent feature was his sense of triumph. Eventually I offered that he was throwing off, overcoming the terrible inhibitions that were expressed in his dream about his father in his underwear. This time he agreed that the dream was about him, not his father, but added an additional concern, and perhaps a transference interpretation of his own: "Am I going off the rails? Would you tell me if I was, well, I know I am not, because when I talk to you, you never tell me what to do, but just being with you, I know I am not beyond redemption, and it all makes sense".

Clinical vignette: 3

A young woman who discovered chat rooms and dating 'older boys' to counter her sense of isolation and being bullied at school began to bring in her intense excitement with dating and hookup GSNs. Parallel to her relating of hookup GSNs, she revealed that there was a time in latency when she was enthralled with her father and she felt he with her. She was also enthralled by her uncles and looked forward to family reunions when she would hang out with the guys. But there was a sudden change; her father precipitously withdrew (she later asked him about this, and he replied along the lines that she needed to learn that affection was contingent on performing well in school; she needed to get that affection was not a given, that affection had to be earned). Her grades plummeted; she gained weight, was bullied at school, and eventually found Internet chatrooms. There she felt pretty and desirable. To her parents' horror, she wanted to take a twenty-year-old to the prom. Her parents could criticize, but not modulate, affirm, or respond to her evolving needs. Nor were they aware of her Internet life, until a twenty-year-old showed up for the prom.

Working with her associations (and often show-and-tell with her dating/hookup GSN) was difficult. She was on the lookout for a critical response. She also could say, "I know you won't get down on me the way my mother does, but I think you will". She herself felt out of control but dared me to say or do anything. Eventually, I was able to say that my concern was that she was not always paying attention to her feelings during her dates with men she met on the GSNs that often led to sexual encounters. This led to a profoundly moving account of a sexual assault in college, and a tendency to just 'get it over with', rather than say 'no thank you'.

Sometime later, she was quite pleased and excited about a man she had met. Pleased, because it happened "organically, not on a hookup GSN". But the same pattern emerged. She became overwhelmed with passionate and hopeful romantic fantasies, while at the same time relating worrisome details about how the man lived his life. Both expanded side by side while she worried that he would reject her. She also pointed out to me how well she was doing, limiting her texts to two or three per day. The culmination was a most unsatisfying sexual encounter for her, but she did not really pay attention to the mounting data that this guy was no catch. That is until he ghosted her. Still, her experience was half "I thought he loved me" and half, "what a loser he turned out to be". Even after the man wrote a quite reasonable note explaining his current situation and lack of availability, she remained locked in her divided world of "I thought he loved me" and "what a loser". Her grossly divided self was both stunning and disconcerting, but eventually she was able to relate how her mother repeatedly called her a "greedy child" and her confusion that perhaps she did want too much, "I always wanted more, more, more! More excitement, more foods, and more affection". This could also be understood as a reflection of her parents' profound inability to regulate and respond to the reasonable strivings of a child who was quite a bit more effusive than they. As evidence of regulatory problems continued to emerge in her development, their attempts to clamp down, to regulate with force, only made matters worse.

Both cases (superficially presented to protect identity) suffered from similar dynamics. Both wanted to find true love, enduring relationships, and children and a family of their own. Both were drawn to the excitement of the hookup GSN, and both were repeatedly disappointed. Both had florid romantic fantasies that were occasionally activated, but neither were able to find a partner with whom the sexual and the affectional could meld in a reasonably satisfactory way. Here again GSN usage can lead us into clinically useful material. Both cases involved many hours of listening to associations about GSN use, careful exploration, and occasional frustration on my part. For both parties, to be honest, there were times I wanted to scream, "Delete the damn GSN and go play in the real world!"

In the first case, the analysand kept his reasonable romantic fantasies off his GSN profile. As he complained about no one wanting to stick around, or only young men being into him, I would ask, "What is in your profile?" – not that I expected a profound change in his luck by changing a few words, but rather what might be the hidden motivation – what is the public statement about yourself that you are putting out there? Sexual fantasies? Ultimately looking for Mr. Right, but having fun along the way? He was struck by my question and a bit confused. Eventually he realized he was "putting himself out there, but not really".

Another dream led us perhaps to the heart of the matter. Working with the dream revealed there really was no room in his mind for anyone other than his parents. In the deepest sense he continued to participate in his parent's fantasy of "you and us against the world, and without us, you will have nothing". Again, the clinical encounter is rarely neat and tidy. Parallel to his bath house visits, he would invite men over for a movie or dinner or other activity. I am not saying one is preferable to the other, but being with people for an extended period in a variety of settings is what longer-term relationships are about. Sometime after the interpretation about room for other people, he planned and executed a party for his friends (gay and straight) in his parents' home. All parties were excited about the venture, and it did raise questions about how a way of thinking and being – that is, 'you and us against the world' – may have been from a time in the development of all parties but remained locked in my patient's mind.

In the second case, the parents' gross inability to regulate their daughter's affects and help her regulate her drives created a complex set of problems. My patient was ultimately confused as to whether she really was an out-of-control greedy child or if she had exuberant needs that could not be responded to. At times she did her best to convince me she was indeed out of control, hiding the facts that she was making straight As in college, holding down a responsible job, and was well liked by peers. Ultimately, we encountered her fear that if she did slow down, did feel more regulated, she would get in touch with a deep, deep sadness and profound sense of being an alien in her parents' home.

Both patients suffered from structural self-deficits. Regulatory problems and a disavowal or a vertical split played a central role in their difficulties in general and successful engagement of others. Both patients at various times showed me conversations or pictures of others on their GSNs. I tend to view the need to illustrate – to show pictures, to read texts or email – as an indicator of disavowal and listen for what is being ignored as I am being engaged in the need to demonstrate, rather than associate.

Summary and conclusion

Dating and hookup GSNs are the latest manifestations of the quest to find a partner, to mate for a few moments or for years. Many of our patients are using them, and as research indicates many are not. For some, the hope, the intrigue, the seeming bounty of available people, becomes a siren's song, too hard to resist. Popular media offers cautionary tales, and our patients often complain about the GSN, the people they meet, and the ongoing frustration. I do maintain that it is frustration, not gratification, that keeps some people deeply engaged with their GSNs and their quests – be they manifestly sexual or looking for love. Indeed, many patients report great ambivalence about their GSN use, but return time and time again. But then again, many patients have great ambivalence about their most private sexual fantasies, but here again, they return time and time again.

Frustration, if not tragedy, in the pursuit of love has informed poetry, operas, and the visual arts for centuries. Here is a sixteenth-century poem that addresses the heart of this chapter:

> *Words of love and constancy*
> *   are words spoken well*
> *A gazel on flirting and flightiness*
> *   is a torment to the tongue*

> *Praise him to the skies*
>   *when he is loving and true*
>   *'Ware Nişanı, write no gazels to him*
>   *whose favors are but few*
> (Nişanı, circa 1540, cited in
> Andrews and Kalpakli,
> 2005, p. 91)

Andrews and Kapalki (2005) are uncertain of Nişanı's exact identity, but they are certain he was a high-ranking court or religious official of the Ottoman Empire. Here was a man of great achievement, writing about his frustration with love, and cautioning others to not waste their time with frustrating others. This was most likely addressed to another male who did not respond to repeated overtures. While frustration and longing are often themes in love poetry, as analysts we are confronted with ascertaining the source of the frustration – a need for frustrating objects; a self-deficit that leaves people blinded and hampered in their quests; or, on a broader scale, as Tolpin (2002, p.c.) said, "a lot of people are just not as available as they think they are". This applies to both parties, our patients and the people they engage.

As an analyst, I do advocate listening to associations about GSN usage as any other area of inquiry, rather than a nasty habit that needs to be broken. The way our patients talk about GSN use, what they hold back, and what they willingly share are all potentially useful clinical material. My position echoes that of Corbett (2013), who advocates the promise of analytic listening to accounts of online encounters. The possibilities for a serious interest in associations to online experiences are myriad (see Essig, 2015, for an elaboration of possible dynamics and their resolution in treatment). Hopefully, they may lead us into a deeper engagement with the patient and their mind. The cases presented were indeed somewhat superficial to protect patients' identities. I do hope I conveyed how an interpretive stance took us into realms far beyond the excitement, hope, and frustration that are so often imbedded in GSN use. I can also assert that GSN use declined the more engaged these people became in their analysis; that is, the analysis was containing, regulating, and expanding relational capacities. But for that to happen, we must embrace the multitude of associations, defenses, hopes, dreams, and frustrations around the use of GSNs as clinically useful material.

Note

1 To protect confidentiality, I will offer composites of several cases.

Part III

Clinical realm

Chapter 8

Adult sexuality in clinical discourse

Louis Rothschild

Created and found in bodily tension and release, sexual intimacy can be culti-vated, manipulated, and dissociated. For some, a rigid consistency may typify an encounter, whereas others may experience a multitude of self states during a single orgasm. Study of lust finds that hallucinatory prone desire can foster or destroy links within and between individuals, and that a sense of sex as harm-less often persists against evidence of harm (Eigen, 2006). In a similar fashion, kissing has been considered not simply to be a communication of passion, but a compromise in which a fantasy of eating up and ingesting an Other is contained in an act of reciprocal taming (Phillips, 1993). Taming may require the develop-ment of "antihallucinogenic capacities" (Eigen, 2001, p. 5) such as curiosity and creativity (Schachtel, 1959/2001) that are found through toleration of and faith in an ebb and flow between joy and pain in and across contact and separation. In this chapter, actual, embodied sex is considered an event that may facilitate an intersubjective transitional space that allows mutual expressions of inner-being (Celenza, 2014), thereby co-creating a joy that may inscribe ethics in the body (cf. Eigen, 2001). However, sex may also fail to embody a loving gratitude and instead foster increasing fractures and alienation (Bion, 1970).

Catch as catch can

An ephemeral or mysterious quality that could be called mystical is often felt in human interaction. How this is felt and responded to can vary in and between people and in activities much the way Wilfred Bion (1991) considers alpha func-tioning to operate within individual psychology. Bion's cognitive concept of alpha functioning has been considered an intuitive and fluctuating capacity for modifi-cation and storage that shapes a thinker (cf. Eigen, 2004, 2011; Williams, 2010; Brown, 2012). One example of explicitly marking the existence of creative shap-ing capacities shared to varying degrees between people may be found in a prac-tice denoted by the French word *lagniappe* where something extra is intentionally given to mark and respect a pleasurable quality in social and business exchange (cf. Bataille, 1985). At the intersection of drive and relational theory, pleasure is complexly moderated by personality differences, health status as found in the presence or absence of mood disorders, moral reasoning, and cultural differences (Haslam and Rothschild, 1998). In regard to sex, when an intuitively felt, creative quality of play with extra-ordinary pleasure is absent, something has gone wrong. From an enigmatic perspective (Laplanche, 1999), sex begins internally and externally with excesses in seeing and being seen in a myriad of successes and failures that may be traced back to a mutuality expressed or not in any maternal gaze (cf. Celenza, 2014; Atlas, 2015; Benjamin, 2018) as the shared sensuality of nursing has been considered a primary sexual dyad (Freud, 1914). This developmental orientation requires a profound appreciation of a maturational process, as some adults are prone to mistake the play of children for the expression of desire by a mature person (Ferenczi, 1933/1980). When a developmentally attuned parent is able with some consistency to differentiate solitude from a distress signal (Winnicott, 1963), and an interpersonal developmental dance is maintained in a reasonable fashion, we may learn to mediate desire and encounter the excess of unmediated desire that, while marked symbolically by lagniappe, is *jouissance*, a pleasure that is too great to be contained (Lacan, 1966/2002). In deference to Oedipus, one hopes to appreciate that desire is excessive, and that we cannot have sex with everyone (Celenza, 2014) or contain all desire. Through such appreciation an opening is created that allows one to become increasingly attuned to the manner in which feelings are different in regard to social distance, and that this awareness can serve to moderate relationships (Eigen, 2006). Sex then can work to provide a rapprochement in adult development where feelings of loss and hope are repeated and may be reworked across the lifespan (cf. Atlas, 2015).

Oedipus and other tragic youth, like Icarus, also serve to illuminate the manner in which abandonment and mis-attunement alter relational capacities in manners that may fail to allow reworking. When a nurturing environment is absent, the shadow side of excess, lack, fosters unbearable conditions (Zeal, 2008) whereby dissociation (Stern, 2010), fragmentation (Benjamin, 2018), and rigidity (Shapiro, 1981) may govern a quality of relating considered a perverse (Celenza, 2014) hardening of the self that is a part of individuation as we twist ourselves out of shape in order to say alive (Eigen, 2009). Paradoxically, these very defenses may be considered to be adaptive in the manner in which any regressive interaction experienced as a consequence of coercion – that is, an enactment (McLaughlin, 1991) – is an attempt to find another chance against the pain of life (Rozmarin, 2011). My concern in this chapter is to flesh out and embody relational tensions between love and perversion as found in varying degrees in an intersection between a private boundedness and mutual contact between psyches and somas as mediated by capacities to enjoy a mutual mentalization that is able to play with embodied contact. This focus follows prior efforts (cf. Bass, 2000 for his reworking of Loewald, 1980) to integrate the instinctual into relational phenomena. However, instinctual and relational integration appear to encounter dialectical trouble as a fissure between sexual drive and other ego functions (Freud, 1914) continues to haunt a basic conceptualization of integration within psychoanalysis (Winnicott, 1961/1987). In contemporary practice, dialectal emphasis has flipped as an overemphasis on relational phenomena (other ego functions such as object relations) has successfully facilitated a return to trauma as a significant site of study while simultaneously losing an emphasis on sexuality that persists despite an integrative argument that sexuality is a central realm in which relational conflicts are played out (Mitchell, 1988).

Notwithstanding Stephen Mitchell's call to situate sexuality within relational theory almost thirty years ago, there exists a general sense that this integration remains a work in progress due to a professional naiveté that fails to situate erotic longing as a bedrock state to such a degree that at least some, if not many, clinicians are not prepared to deal with erotic material (Celenza, 2014). The persistence of difficulty situating the gap between relational and sexual aspects of the human condition into a preferable model is significant as reports of problems are found throughout the ample attention given to this Freudian knot. Attempting to unravel the knot, Norman O. Brown (1991) advocates remythologizing Freudian instinctual dualism with a Nietzscheian-infused instinctual dialects that maintains a Dionysian emphasis in creative transmutation (cf. Kaufmann, 1967). Additional critiques maintain that a Freudian focus on castration and competition has lost a relationship to pleasure (Harris, 2005), and that one may read Lacan to find that the sex drive is no where to be found as sexuality is always about something else (Eigen, 2006). Adam Phillips (1988) considers that while Donald Winnicott recovered from what Phillips playfully refers to as Freud's flight to sanity, that, in turn, Winnicott flew from the erotic. Neil Altman (1995) has provided a cogent review of the manner in which the Fromm–Marcuse debate relates to disagreement surrounding movement from drive theory to object relations. Adrienne Harris (2005) adds that relational theory ignores the body and that neoclassical accounts of femininity miss relational phenomena. Freud confesses that he separates ego instincts and sexual instincts "In the total absence of any theory of the instincts which would help us to find our bearings" (Freud, 1914, p. 78). Over one hundred years later, where are our bearings? Is contemporary dialectical trouble a tired adherence to a dichotomy we no longer believe in maintained by a confusion of tongues (Ferenczi, 1933/1980) in our discourse that arises out of a fear of conflating mental representations with real relationships and conflating talk and action, whereby avoiding sex as a conceptual end is an enactment of schizoid shyness related to the incest taboo (cf. Hoffman, 2009)? To that end we may wonder how far we have moved beyond an embryonic stage of development (cf. Bion, 1994) and if the intersubjectivity of sex is too much for our personal and professional psyches (Benjamin, 2018).

Still nothings

Halfway through a session I found myself saying, "Did you just say pizza in bed?" in response to my patient. He smiled, and with immense pleasure replied, "Yes!". Sex talk is fascinating. In this case two men in bed, one with HIV, the other on Truvada as a prophylactic to HIV exposure, eating pizza post-coitus becomes an evocative image. It would seem that pizza holds its own physiological intensity, especially when it is eaten naked in bed. The drama of foreplay itself warrants attention in regard to its activity. Pizza was ordered, and together appetite was situated so as to be delayed for culinary delight in apres coup. My patient was not only sharing joy about having had great sex and pizza, he also delighted in the dramatic interpersonal significance of being together in mutual relational capacities to organize and play. This delight found and shared in the bedroom came across the consulting room in a plurality of relational matrixes.

I wish to consider this clinical moment as a projective stimulus on the page in order to assess where we may be professionally. At this moment it is possible to consider two men as lovers within a model of health in psychoanalysis, and it is a quality of health that is intended to be situated in the provocative portrait described. Simply, that my patient's joy may be considered an end in itself. Against a backdrop of HIV, does it matter which of the two men is my patient? Does this impact what sort of mutuality is felt here? As a reader, what more about the case history would you want to know in order to consider my client's joy to be authentic as opposed to reactive? For example, what may have prompted his making an appointment? Is the need of pizza a defensive play in isolated withdrawal or a celebratory mutual process, as play may occur in either frame to make the horror of existence bearable (Green, 2005)? Or do such concerns not arise at all?

Here, an openness toward creative possibility is being advocated that allows one to stand in spaces (Bromberg, 1998) of experience in an uncertainty that tolerates, if not welcomes, the unknown (Phillips, 1988) whereby *bedrock envy* (Fairfield, 2002) can be felt. Through capacities that support such a tolerance of uncertainty, a core self may be viewed as existing in diversity that is not bounded to a static conception of authenticity. In having a security to tolerate uncertainty, a static and rigid conception of an authentic self may be outgrown, allowing intersubjectivity to become a site of fluidity where thought can become complex so as to adopt a playful attitude of paradox that thwarts dialectical and relational splitting (Rothschild and Haslam, 2003; Paras, 2006). Such openness to possibly has a psychosocial home in work by feminists and others who identify with queer theory to assert a poststructuralist idea that social variables (and thereby one's own position and assumptions) benefit from being situated within psychoanalysis (cf. Fairfield, Layton, and Stack, 2002). Within psychology, such an orientation may be traced back to John Dewey's 1899 argument that psychology cannot be independent from society (Sarason, 1981).

The subject of postmodernity has been considered to be one in which fracture and fragmentation is a norm (cf. Harris, 2005). Personal experience shows that not all body zones are erogenous zones for everyone, and clinical experience shows that not all fractures cleave in the same manner. Not all pain or pleasure is equally felt. In regard to sex, and in line with the above example of male penetrative sex, Michael Eigen (1993) has compared writings on anal sex by Marquis de Sade and William Burroughs to show that anal sex may vary in its sadistic and loving capacities. Here there is a call to remain open to the chosen experience of a subject, to hear a patient's particularity as opposed to foreclosing in regard to knowing. For me, this example rekindles an adolescent moment when after learning of two male friends having had sex, I began to wonder why this interesting knowledge created no erotic feeling for me. As I arrived in a level of acceptance and pleasure in my own heterosexuality, I noticed that for me, the thought of anal sex remains uncomfortable and is not a turn on. Yet, from that absence I appreciate that for others such contact is of as profound importance as my own erotic longings. Here I find work following Laplanche (de Kuyper, 1993) helpful in the idea that no identification is entirely discrete, and multifaceted dissociated residue remains in any orientation be it a heterosexual or homosexual resolution that is greater than the resolution itself. A position that considers otherness as arising in a shared developmental journey of identity formation is a focus of entering a shared vulnerability of mutual respect of divergent points of orientation and identification whereby one and another's hearts may open to an appreciation of difference.

> There will be instances where sexuality works out something about gender and instances where gender works out something about sexuality; or there will be instances when sex and sometimes gender are solutions to other psychic problems, like self regulation or safety.
>
> (Harris, 2005, p. 119)

These lines penned by Adrienne Harris may seem so obvious as to be taken for granted by our contemporary ears. Why would sexuality not work out something about gender and vice versa, and why would sex and gender not impact other aspects of character? To consider the radical quality in her writing benefits from a look into the middle of the last century. In his critique of the 1948 Kinsey Report, Lionel Trilling (1950/2008) observed that the very need of such a report was indicative of the atomization, isolation, and ignorance found in modern society where social affection could be considered a scarcity. An exemplar of a fragmented subject in the 1950s is found in Harry Harlow's (1958; 1971) rhesus monkey research that simultaneously illuminates Freud's separation of sexual and other ego instincts in addition to the ignorance found in a cultural isolation and atomization that continues to haunt clinical conceptualization.

Due to an artifact of learning research, attachment was discovered in the laboratory by Harry Harlow in the 1950s. In post–World War II bomb culture, Harlow startled a relatively stable rhesus monkey that had been placed in a forced-choice T-maze. On each side of the top of the T was a mannequin. One mannequin was made of bare wire with a sparse feeding tube from which the monkey could suckle. The other mannequin was covered in terry cloth, allowing a soft embrace. Harlow's finding that stressed monkeys preferred a soft mannequin that could be held onto over the mannequin that provided food shifted his focus to the study of attachment in relationships where he found that monkeys that did not have relational contact became reactive. While such a finding was considered a strike against drive theory, it was by no means a strike against Freud's work where hunger is considered involuntary and love is considered a voluntary choice (Freud, 1914). In this laboratory split that is consistent with Freudian theory, we find Harlow's monkey voluntarily choosing and hoping for love over an involuntary hunger that found in isolation of a loving context could well foster experiences of a helplessness that may kindle addiction. Without the luxury of full-blown reflexive human consciousness, this monkey looks like a wise monkey in its choosing the promise of curiosity and creativity found in love (cf. Schachtel, 1959/2001).

For Harlow's monkeys, disintegration (Winnicott, 1961/1987) is an artifact of the laboratory. Simply, in nature an integration exists whereby a nipple at the end of a feeding tube is attached to a body in which a soft mammalian touch also exists. Freud (1914) considered that the sex drive and other ego functions could also appear to be integrated in this manner. This is to say that eroticism may entail a profound integration in which the sex drive is contained in a mutually loving encounter in which one is simultaneously fed and securely held. However, Freud also observed that such integration was tentative at best. Humans appear to be able to disintegrate this pairing without the laboratory, and interestingly when this happens it is often the physicality of feeding on drives such as overeating, alcohol misuse, sexualizing sports (Celenza, 2014), or sex itself in which one may desire to feel like a "dummy stuffed with straw" in order to avoid pain found in relationally (Bion, 2015, p. 231). In such a state, there is not enough faith in the capacities of a felt intimacy to contain elements of risk found in encounters with *jouissance* and the unknown. One quality that exists for each of Harlow's mannequins holds a key to this relatively common human helplessness. Each mannequin is empty; so for the monkey any enigmatic emotional responsiveness of the other must be hallucinated. In contrast, for a reactive person who cannot tolerate fluctuations, emotional responsiveness may also be hallucinated or denied. In regards to this fractured breakdown of intimate potential, a living interactive other is both dissociated and hoped for in an absence or living death (Gerson, 2009) that is comparable to suffering from an I-thou deprivation (Eigen, 1998). In human relations where each member of a dyad is at least partially alive, disavowal maintains this deadly deprivation in the self and other (Bass, 2000). Winnicott (1963, 1971/2005) considers being traumatically dropped, which is to say not being recovered and received in a manner that feels like recovery, to be a position in which the loving dependency found in mutual holding may be replaced with radical self-sufficiency or a false self, and it is the celebration of such self-sufficiency by way of disavowal that Trilling considers to have created a need for Kinsey. Being alive – that is, developing and maintaining optimal tension between an emphasis on self and an emphasis on relational development and experience (Blatt, 2008) – is to cultivate states in which being off-balance may well be more common than maintaining balance. Welcoming that sort of movement requires a security that may well be uncommon.

A few years into treatment, a patient begins to speak about sex with her partner. She speaks of never having enough and enjoying what she is able to cultivate in a relationship in which planning appears to take great effort. As we make eye contact, I realize that I can only imagine what she enjoys, and that I really do not know what she is referring to when she speaks of a lack of satisfaction. I begin to consider speaking in regard to my not having a sense of her experience. Foreplay, holding, smiling, lubrication, penis size, clitoral contact. So many questions. I simultaneously see the face of a colleague. My reverie with my colleague entails having been asked if I feel generally safe enough to explore sexuality in session. Why not simply leave this? My patient is associating. I could sit quietly, and she might change the subject. I could then decide that she is not yet ready to go into greater detail; that any lack of greater engagement is only about where she is in treatment, and has nothing to do with my anxiety. Here as I consider speaking, I find a sincere question asked by my colleague regarding what goes on behind closed doors. Do I dare ask my patient what actually went on behind her closed doors? Is such a move a voyeuristic one masquerading as clinical care by both my colleague and myself? Can I trust that moving on without knowing what my patient is referring to runs the danger of conflating my own mental representations with her history? Further, such silence on my part may well facilitate a quiet but pervasive shame on the part of my patient who may feel that her vulnerable and personal experience should not be talked about. What is the point of treatment? I decided to enter the fray and go for it, doing my best to embrace my uncertainty and her presence as gently as I can.

She describes that in order to have an orgasm that she needs to be on top, and that her husband must remain completely still, that any movement on his part is too much. Sex is a relational encounter, and feeling safe and regulated within an interpersonal encounter is no small matter when risk and activation are felt. Over the course of treatment, a need for stillness was found in other relational contexts in which movement by another in speech or action activated excessive shame. Therein symmetry appears between the sexual instinct and other ego functions as attention and work in treatment began to foster an interest and awareness of capacities to mutually move. Sometimes treatment can work out something about sex, and sometimes talking about sex informs deep characterological work in treatment. Here I aim to underscore that we pay attention to our silences and consider when it is prudent to inquire into another's experience.

Shake my nerves, rattle my brain

In the 1957 song "Great Balls of Fire" (Hammer and Blackwell, 1957), Jerry Lee Lewis sings of a thrill in having a broken will. Another line from this song informs that too much love will drive a man insane. What of women? James Thurber and E. B. White (1929/2004) consider that men were concerned World War I would never end, and that once it did end, that stranded men transferred a preoccupation with endless war to a preoccupation with never-ending sex. A conflation of excess and timelessness in sexual intimacy with the shaken nerves and rattled brain of war trauma exists in a manner that is also found in the bikini swimsuit named after the atoll where atomic tests were conducted (Nuttall, 1968). Others (e.g. Moss,

2010) have noted that a pleasure exists in listening and hearing in a manner that may blow the mind apart due to an inability to distinguish pleasure from harm. It is striking that such difficulty in separating qualities of vulnerability in activated states exists. In this regard, an ability to feel secure while feeling passive is significant as conscious or not, feeling helpless during experiences of passivity in being struck is considered to be a limiting factor working against the function of cognitive capacities to integrate experience (Schachtel, 1966/2001). Cultivated in battlefields or early childhood, an insecurity that cannot yield to subjective passive experience is a marker of traumatic damage (cf. Eigen, 2004). Through narratives of kids being kids and honor and pride in war, a sensitivity to traumatic violence may be obfuscated which in turn aids the cultivation of hallucinatory capacities that replace the uncertainty of spontaneous feeling with rigid certainty.

In concert with cultural trauma, the conflation of sex and war serves to maintain a confusing cultural landscape that not only degrades war veterans' experience with traumatic symptoms, but degrades the value of love in sexual encounters. Here I wish to emphasize that the manner in which vulnerability is dissociated and reified culturally has a significant bearing on sex. While a clinical orientation may emphasize a treatment goal found in a postmodern epistemology that "holds polarities lightly" (Celenza, 2014, p. 3), whereby the terms feminine and masculine are utilized only for psychic clarity, reactive and anxious qualities found in rigid clinical presentations find gendered binaries in which being passive is coded feminine and activity is considered a sign of masculinity in an essentialist manner that thwarts dynamic intimacy (Benjamin, 1988; Ducat, 2004; Ducat, Metzl, and Rothschild, 2008) in a manner that is far from a postmodern clinical model.

In accord with such splitting, war has been depicted as a hyper-masculine activity trading in an invulnerable ideal that denies bodily experience (Rothschild, 2003) and is an exceptionalism considered part of a social defense of disavowal that exhibits the relational failures of retaliation and withdrawal that occur when vulnerability cannot be sustained and in which rape becomes ritual sport (Harris and Botticelli, 2010). The behavior of some popular and political figures reveals that an attitude that sex is part of the spoils of war is also found off the military battlefield. The consequences of viewing sex through a lens of 'exploits' is at least something that appears to trickle down from the highest levels of celebrated alienation, as institutional difficulty in finding cogent and coherent narratives to situate and contain if not prevent acts such as date rape in supposedly safe places as college dormitories may leave one noticing that sexual violence, like the trauma of war, appears to be rediscovered for the first time whenever a new conflict occurs (cf. Davoine and Gaudilliere, 2004). Simply, collusion with the denial of trauma is significant as trauma can facilitate feelings of holding or being held in a grave, while through attuned witnessing capacities, such a container may become a womb where new growth can occur (cf. Williams, 2010). That Lewis's singing and the bikini swimsuit are typically celebrated without an avowal of traumatic links reveals that the link between sex and war remains a troubled one. Is it worth considering that the charge of sensuality found in a bikini-clad human could be retained if the bikini were disconnected from a nuclear holocaust? With rape, kissing is an eating of the other, as faith in a taming that can delight in the mutuality of uncertainty has been lost. A key to the disentanglement of kosher love and cannibalism may be found in critique of Freud's specific use of not simply the sex drive, but the death drive which may well have been motivated by Freud's own disavowal of sexual trauma (Bonomi, 2018). Disagreement exists regarding Freud's understanding of love. This is to say that disagreement exists regarding the problem of relations between the ego and external objects. In addition to fractures in motivation found in the existence of Freud's sex drive, there is the problem of fantasy in which imaginary objects may take the place of a real object whereby one may move from introversion to regression (Freud, 1914). On one hand, Freud has been considered a discursive thinker whose own work on problems such as this anticipates all the gallons of ink that have come after it (Foucault, 1977). Alternatively, critiques of Freudian theory as mechanistic and therefore prone to problems such as rigid encapsulation exist among a multitude, dating back to the origins of psychoanalysis with later examples such as W. R. D. Fairbairn's romantic conflict shyness and Harry Guntrip's use of schizoid withdrawal of libido from lived relations to rework drive theory (see Greenberg and Mitchell, 1983). In some fashion the mechanistic critique may be understood as locating Freud on the hunger side of Harlow's experiment. Additionally, mechanistic critique may also be understood as one in which Freud's theory misses the enigmatic and is as empty as each of Harlow's mannequins. Although critique is warranted, limitations are readily found as psychoanalysis also finds a meaning-making need at the core of the human condition that works against dehumanizing tendencies even when coexisting with what may be considered perverted tendencies (Knafo and Lo Bosco, 2017). The next section will explore this problem in part through exploration of uses and abuses of conceptual thinking about perversion.

Of organ location and dislocation

Freud's (1917) general theory of neurosis reflects an insistence on the importance of innate instincts due to the abandonment of his earlier focus on trauma. Favoring heterosexual vanilla sexuality in which integration between pleasure and reproduction means that orgasms should occur when a penis is inside of a vagina, Freud considers departures to other flavors of sexuality a disintegration that may occur as hysterical neurosis can produce itself in any system of organs whereby desire may become a perverse impulse which seeks to replace genital function in another location. With Freud, perversion is a case in which other organs behave like substitute genitals. This is to say that, for Freud, a gap between a functional and sexual significance of bodily organs is shown by hysteria, and that there are multiple ways of reading Freud on his account of psychopathology in human functioning as he considers any sex other than reproductive sex to be perverse, while simultaneously acknowledging that perversity is a central part of the human condition. Freud writes that all childhood sexuality is perverse because it is not linked to the sexual function, and considers the belief that children are asexual to be a repudiation that exists as a function of child rearing whereby infantile sexuality is culturally forbidden.

The importance of social function and genital integration is sadly and mostly clearly stated in Freud's treatment of the clitoris. Freud writes that in childhood a girl's clitoris takes on the role of the penis, and that through normative development women pass clitoral sensitivity on to the vagina. For Freud, retaining clitoral sensitivity is viewed as a perversion of development. This misogynist view has been attacked (Horney, 1967) on an interpersonal ground that to renounce clitoral pleasure requires a previously formed masochistic identity. With masochism, sexualization may be seen as a hyper-autonomous masquerade (Riviere, 1929; Yates, 2015) sending a distress signal to express vulnerabilities that cannot be tolerated such as the experience of infinite exploitation (Winnicott, 1963; Celenza, 2014). Following the work of Josine Muller (1932, in Harris, 2005), Adrienne Harris situates integration in a pluralistic register whereby a centrality of clitoral pleasure for girls is sought in an active and passive movement deemed essential for the dissolution of anyone's castration complex. Such reworking is essential for an ethical embodiment of pleasure be it penile or clitoral. Concern with pleasure, castration, hyper-autonomy, and clitoral renunciation are central problems holding the Freudian knot of discrete drives together, and one way into and through this knot is the examination of reactive violence that perpetuates trauma.

One key to situating Freud's view that sexual specificity and organ location is a problem is found in Carlo Bonomi's thesis that actual castration had been central to the founding of psychoanalysis (Bonomi, 2015, 2018). Bonomi writes that Freud encountered a belief that masturbatory play in infancy was a plague related to hysteria in the neurological department of Vienna's Public Institute for Children's Diseases between 1886 and 1896 where procedures such as eliminating a boy's foreskin and a girl's clitoris could be a cure. Remarkable here is that Freud, aware of genital mutilation, began to view castration as a fantasy only regarding the male genitals that were uprooted and placed "beyond time, history, and culture" (Bonomi, 2015, p. 77). Bonomi further argues that Freud created the death drive in order to fill the gap left by the absence of this actual trauma, and here we may see that Ferenczi's comment that hysterics were quite possibly responding to violence from adults who mistook the play of children for the expression of desire by a mature person as a critique of Freud. Bonomi's analysis then suggests that Freud's need of discrete drives that should be integrated along normative social lines is an obsessional attempt on the part of Freud to situate his own hysteria in response to his witnessing medically induced trauma in the service of a Victorian social program attempting to eradicate childhood sexuality.

Inhabiting an intersubjective body

Developmental insults may not always be as dire as rape or clitoridectomy, yet in a world that is frequently violent, maintaining faith in life-affirming, creative, and nourishing capacities is no simple manner (cf. Eigen, 2010). In this regard, experiencing physiologically heightened sexual states may entail being unable to tolerate the uncertainty of a full emotional responsiveness in another, and such vulnerability may be denied or defended against in a sadistic or masochistic fashion. Phillips (1988) reads Winnicott to suggest that the central task of living is to facilitate self-development so as to inhabit one's body. In this regard, inhabiting one's body entails existing in a mutually cooperative framework that is experientially different than a sadomasochistic frame. Such an account problematizes, but does not wholly discount, the idea that consensual sex could be rough and mutually enjoyed while not foreclosing on the uncertainty of emotional responsiveness. How we conceptualize a lovingly rough-and-tumble relationship to the body requires particular attention. Help may be found in a reworking of the death drive as a need for tension reduction as opposed to a drive bound in annihilation (Schachtel, 1959/2001). Relatedly, Winnicott breaks with Melanie Klein (1958/1975) in considering the death instinct of little value as, according to Winnicott, a child is not engaged in a paranoid schizoid struggle between life and death instincts but between integration and disintegration. Potentialities for integration continue into adulthood, and like Bion's sense of working with feelings of catastrophe and faith, Winnicott writes of continual transitional movement in becoming (Eigen, 1999). Here we may ask if a sexual act facilitates integration, and paradoxically if the shattering qualities of penetration and or an orgasm facilitate a greater sense of connection and cohesion or traumatic disconnection and disintegration.

Becoming in transitional space then is a way of working with developmental stuck points, also called trauma clots (Eigen, 2007), in order to more fully inhabit one's body so as to find joy in a loving contact. Yet, the very existence of trauma clots may eclipse the faith required to be in such work. The focus on trauma clots later in this chapter aims to situate sex and sexuality as a potentially loving frame through attention to the coercive quality of masochistic relations to satisfaction and the clinched fist found in the heart of dissociation whereby links between rigidity, dissociation, and fragmentation may be noticed and possibly felt as forces that preclude mutual intimacy. Here focus is drawn to what is wrong in order to find what is right (Eigen, 2009).

Despite historical controversy found in institutional sexism and low base rates, male hysterics do exist alongside frigid men (Thurber and White, 1929/2004; Ellenberger, 1970). One argument in support of low base rates is that through body envy or womb envy (Ducat, 2004) men disavow a feminine identity and transfer their envy to women's subjective desire, so that attitudes become gendered and polarized. For disavowing men, the reified attitude that remains is one of being strong, steady, and certain (Kupers, 1993) in a manner consistent with the culture of war discussed earlier. Remarkably, in a sexist binary, uncertainty may be seen not as a source of intimate curiosity, much less a position for a creative and feminine identity, but as a sign of weakness whereby some women may favor the reactive certainty found in an idealization of men's social roles whereby performative certainty is sought (Layton, 2004a, 2004b). A danger here is that what is privileged as a correct attitude or zeitgeist may be one in which both men and women are dysregulated due to an inability to avow the body and attendant curiosity as an uncertain and intimate site. In place of curiosity is a perverse hubris echoed in a neoliberal culture of thinking that we know exactly what we desire to an extent that to feel love becomes potentially humiliating as one is able to anticipate needs that might be greater than what one is able to respond to (Green, 1999). In this regard, masochism and sadism are but two sides of an alienated coin where the body of the doer is hidden or dissociated and the body of the done to is devalued (cf. Benjamin, 1988, 2018). To that end, both masochism and the Victorian surgical alteration of the clitoris may be understood as the negation of embodiment that is a contempt of a lived relationship to pleasure and vulnerability that has implications for humanity in general.

In keeping with the observation that style in neurosis is exaggeration (Shapiro, 1965), Freud (1924b) comments that it is a masochist who holds a cheek out when there is a chance of receiving a blow. For Freud (1919), a masochist seeks punishment in order to purge feelings of guilt and anxiety. The death instinct (Freud, 1924b) was offered to explain why a masochist turns the libido against the self, and such thinking was supported by Marie Bonaparte who funded Geza Roheim's anthropological research which concluded that surgical alteration of the clitoris "fosters the right attitude of women" (Roheim, 1932, p. 232, cited in Bonomi, 2018, p. 187). The perverse idea that masochism is only but a slight exaggeration of normal female development fostered by trauma has been critiqued along lines that there is a distinction to be made between enjoying and enduring subjugation (Horney, 1967; Blum, 1977; Caplan, 1984), and that the wish for humiliation does not belong to normal woman (Reik, 1941). I would add that in a culture of war, a macho reactivity to real or perceived humiliation is normalized and that disavowing the threat of humiliation is a fear of uncertainty in emotional engagement that need not belong to normal humans be they male, female, gay, straight, bi, or trans.

Abnormality in regard to autonomy that cannot find a shared faith in interpersonal mutuality then is a disintegration reflecting a trauma history that has congealed into a clot standing in the way of a joyful sexuality. In this regard, fragmentation and dissociation warp character into an actively maintained rigidity. One view of masochism posits a breakdown due to an inability to modulate the tension needed for mutual recognition caused in part by fragmentation of aggression in earlier developmental (typically pre-Oedipal) stages whereby one despairs of never being able to hold another's attention (Benjamin, 1988). Another view emphasizes the active function of pride in placing the cheek in line for a blow, and sees not breakdown but instead finds that subjective experience and active autonomy have been distorted to an extent that rigidity is found that enables alienation from one's feelings in order to avoid vulnerability to threat (Shapiro, 1965, 1981). Each of these views allows consideration of the idea that the ends sought are something other than pleasure in pain, and that we are not working so much with a sex problem but with an ego problem in which pain and alienated sex is but a detour (Reik, 1941), whereby a sadistic or masochistic individual may be estranged from their desire for mutual recognition (Benjamin, 2018) due to a failure of alpha functioning or the capacity to remain intimately connected. This reactivity appears driven by an urgent need to isolate a sense of what is not me in the other (Stern, 2010), and such a tortured dynamic may be maintained by relentless hope and despair (Stark, 2017a, 2017b).

Some concluding thoughts

The center of my argument is that situating trauma alters the Freudian knot so that sexuality is returned to relationally and relationally is returned to sexuality. The body then, as a shared intersubjective container, is an uncanny site, which is to say a site that may be at once foreign and strange (Freud, 1919) and is simultaneously embedded with home and familiarity (Harris, 2010). Feeling over time in mutual sexual encounters with the uncanny is to reawaken aspects of self and other in transitional experiencing that have previously been considered 'not me'. Work with dissociation and enactment is to relax what has previously been clenched, and to the degree that one may be able to tolerate and enjoy previously repudiated and conflicting aspects of self has a great bearing on intimacy whereby one may need to experience cycles of enactment with an analyst who is lovingly patient or a lover who may tenderly embrace until conflict can be tolerated so that emotional intimacy may be enjoyed (cf. Stern, 2010). Such work aims to increase capacities to tolerate the idea that inhibition is an envy of growth-stimulating objects (Bion, 1991) which loses the faith needed to work with a felt sense of mutual recognition. Thus, mutual recognition is not a static achievement, but one of breakdown and recovery (cf. Eigen, 1999, 2012; Kieffer, 2014). This thinking is consistent with a view (Fajardo, 2001, in Kieffer, 2014) of analyst and patient as coupled oscillators who begin to operate regularly and rhythmically in response to each other, thus being able to discern moments of harmony and difference.

An appreciation of harmony and difference that allows one to develop in their own way is a point of contact that recognizes that mutated aspects have something to offer. This line of thinking about working with strange aspects of self has been extended to the self as a whole, to consider that we may develop not only mutated aspects, but as mutants, and that loving appreciation of mutant qualities allows intensities to resound in enriching contributions (Eigen, 2004; Fetting, 2015). Relating in such a manner to strangeness, absence, or uncertainty is challenging, and with an attitude of a Zen master commenting on Wilfred Bion's writing, Francesca Bion (2014) suggests that answers will only be found through one's own intuition and understanding. She (Bion, 1981) considers in an introduction of her late husband's that he had written for an unpublished collection of poetry that it is easy to lose the capacity for awe. One can indeed have sex without awe, and some report having hot sex without awe, but often with drugs and alcohol. As clinicians, we may consider the importance of tuning into the warp of such differences. Herein is a bias: for sex to be hotter, a faith in the richness of an emotional encounter that co-creates mutual awe appears to be essential with or without tequila.

Chapter 9

Voyeurism

Salman Akhtar

Fred Pine's (1988) reminder that psychoanalysis subsumes 'four psychologies' (involving drives, ego, object relations, and self) is commonly overlooked in the current enthusiasm about relational models of theory and technique. The 'movement' especially neglects, if not derides, drive psychology. This is a pity since such body-oriented 'primal' perspective retains validity and usefulness in clinical work, being especially instructive in understanding matters pertaining to human sexuality. To be sure, the nature of object-relations, the expressive and defensive devices of the ego, and the coherence and efficacy-seeking agendas of the self all play important roles in the narratives that underlie an individual's erotic life. But this does not exclude the silent – and sometimes not-too-silent – operation of what Freud (1905a) called the 'component instincts'. Sexual life in general and the interactional unit of a sexual encounter in specific are replete with the pleasures of looking, showing, smelling, shedding one's shame and gently overcoming the partner's shame, sucking, licking, biting, inflicting small amounts of pain, teasing, withholding, and so on (Kernberg, 1991). Even though the ego, self, and object relations regulate its cadence and volume, the symphony of sexual foreplay is largely composed of 'pre-genital' instincts.

It is with such heuristic pluralism that I approach the topic of voyeurism here. For didactic ease, I will divide my comments into four sections: (1) words and phenomena, (2) the evolutionary foundations and cultural facilitations of voyeurism, (3) its individual psychodynamics, and (4) the clinical setting, which will highlight the manifestations and management of voyeuristic impulses and behaviors during the treatment hours. I will conclude by summarizing what I have offered and by touching up what might have been left unaddressed and where we might go from there.

Words and phenomena

Words

Many overlapping words and phrases are found in the early literature on the topic of our concern. These include "scopophilic instinct" and "scopophilic perversions"

(Freud, 1905a, pp. 166, 192), "scopophilia" (Abraham, 1913, p. 169; Ferenczi, 1922, p. 363), and "scoptophilia" and "scoptophilic fantasies" (Fenichel, 1945, p. 71). The tendency in subsequent writings is to deploy 'scopophilia' for pleasure derived from the component instinct of looking (Eidelberg, 1968; Almansi, 1979; Mahony, 1989; Moore and Fine, 1990), and 'voyeurism' (Rosen, 1964; Bak and Stewart, 1975; Akhtar, 2009) for a specific form of sexual perversion involving looking. Curiously, the venerable psychoanalytic glossary by Laplanche and Pontalis (1973) does not mention any of these terms – scopophilia, scoptophilia, or voyeurism – even it its discussion of "component instincts" (pp. 74–75).

Another interesting feature of word usage in this context pertains to the 'scopophilia' versus 'scoptophilia' conundrum. It is generally believed that Freud's (1905a) original expression, *Schaulust*, or 'pleasure in looking', was translated by Strachey as 'scopophilia' and by Fenichel as 'scoptophilia'. A careful scrutiny, however, reveals a far more complex picture:

- The fact is that it was Strachey himself and not Fenichel who originated the term 'scoptophilia', although he rectified this error in the *Standard Edition* of Freud's work. Strachey (1963) later gave a detailed explanation of how this happened: "Greek terminology was all the rage and the word 'scoptophilia' was suggested and accepted with acclamation. It certainly looked a little odd but nevertheless passed into all the four volumes of the *Collected Papers* [of Freud] uncriticised. You might have imagined that we should have remembered telescopes and microscopes and so have suspected that the Greek root for 'looking' was something like 'scop'. Actually, there is a Greek root, 'scopt', but what it means is 'to make fun of'. And so to this day, you may still come upon references to the component sexual instinct of pleasure in derision" (p. 229).
- The three major psychoanalytic dictionaries that address this matter do so somewhat differently. Eidelberg (1968) cites a personal communication from Strachey declaring that 'scoptophilia' was the original translation but has been replaced by its "correct form" (p. 392), 'scopophilia'. Moore and Fine (1990) go a step further and state that "scoptophilia would refer to a pleasure in derision, a meaning never intended" (p. 173). De Mijolla (2005) avoids taking positions and instead offers historical details regarding this lexical ambiguity, some of which I have cited.
- Yet another position is taken by Bettleheim (1983), who regards the language of 'scopophilia' and 'scoptophilia' as a "monstrosity contrived by Freud's translators" (p. 91). In his view, both these terms fail to convey the passion contained in Freud's *Schaulust*. At the minimum, Bettleheim contends, 'sexual pleasure is looking' should be substituted for the sanitized 'pleasure is looking' that is currently used to convey Freud's intent.
- An entirely different take on the 't' in 'scoptophilia' is that of Cliff Robinson, a Philadelphia-based Professor of Classics. He says that the first unit in this compound word comes from the Greek, *skopos*, which stands "most basically

for an aim or mark, but it came to be used for scouts and spies, and then more generally for watching and viewing. The prefix 'scopto' seems like a fusion of *skopos* or *scopus* (a Latin calque from the Greek) with *optiké*, the science of visual phenomena and the eye's faculties" (personal communication, September 11, 2018).

- As if the 'scopophilia–scoptophilia' conflation was not confusing enough, there also exists the term 'scotophilia'. Though the term actually means 'love of darkness' (Mahony, 1989), many early analysts (e.g. Lorand, 1933; Willard, 1934; Weissman, 1960) used it as a synonym for scopophilia.

All this can be discarded as hermeneutic hair-splitting. I submit, however, that there is something of significance hidden here. The superficial aspect of the 'scopophilia' versus 'scoptophilia' mystery involves Strachey's vague comment that the term 'scoptophilia' was "suggested and accepted with acclamation" (1961, p. 229) without revealing *who* suggested it and *why* it was so uncritically accepted. We know that the 'informal glossary committee' (Ornston, 1985) in charge of translating Freud's terminology for the *Collected Papers* and the *Standard Edition* included Ernest Jones, Joan Riviere, James Strachey, and Alix Strachey, so it seems fair to conclude that it was one of these four who 'suggested' the term. But this is trivial compared to why such educated and informed folk would readily confuse 'pleasure in derision' for 'pleasure in looking'. Was it a simple and meaningless error? Or, could it be that this "important mistake" (Jones, 1936, p. 247) betrayed the unconscious knowledge on the group's part that the ordinary pleasure in looking can readily be enlisted for sadistic purposes? And this brings us to the voyeuristic perversion, but before delving into it, it seems warranted to elaborate upon the 'primary' and 'secondary' manifestations of the scopophilic instinct.

Primary phenomena

A curious aspect of psychoanalytic writings upon voyeurism is the relative inattention to the actual phenomenon of looking and the quick transition to search for 'meaning'. To avoid this pitfall, let us take a close look (pun unintended) at what is involved in the sexually exciting form of looking. Freud (1905a) declared that ordinary scopophilia turns into voyeurism when the focus of looking is upon genitals, when disgust is totally eradicated, and when looking is not preparatory to sexual intercourse but supplants it as the end in itself. This covers ample terrain. Still it seems useful to consider *what* is it that the voyeur wants to see, *how* does he go about it, *what* role does the unwitting participant play in this psychic drama, and *why* is the voyeur doing what he is doing. Leaving the last question for later, let us consider the 'what' question first.

The voyeur derives pleasure mostly from looking at sexual scenes (e.g. where a couple is involved in foreplay or actual intercourse, or someone alone is masturbating). At other times, the voyeur can find watching non-sexual scenes (e.g.

changing clothes, bathing, taking a shower) also sexually stimulating. Total or partial nudity turns him on but he possesses an uncanny ability to transform the mere glimpse of a bare ankle or calf or an exposed midriff or the slight protuberance of nipples through a silky blouse into total body nudity in his imagination. Such acts of looking usually lead to the release of sexual tension by masturbation and orgasm. No sexual partner is needed for this; Freud's statement that a voyeuristic perversion results when the scopophilic instinct has supplanted mature, dyadic sexuality is thus upheld. Freud's proposal of eradication of disgust is also 'confirmed' in the case of voyeurs who derive sexual pleasure from watching others urinate or defecate. Freud's third proposal that the voyeur's focus is exclusively upon genitals is a bit shaky since most voyeurs, while deeply fascinated by sexual acts, actually avoid looking intently upon genitals; this seems especially true of men (Almansi, 1970; Arango, 1989).

The next question is *how* does the voyeur go about his activities? The most typical scenario is that of someone lurking in darkness, maybe in unlit alleys, and peeping through the windows of other people's homes. This does happen. However, more frequently, the voyeur operates in public places (e.g. hotels, restrooms, elevators, parking lots, even streets), carrying on his visual thefts surreptitiously and remaining content with only partial gratification of his erotic desire. Yet another avenue is the enlistment of modern appliances such as one-way mirrors,[1] miniature cameras, and other sophisticated video- and audio-monitoring devices for observing unsuspecting individuals' nudity and sexual acts.

The implication of hostility in the forgoing expression, 'visual theft', becomes unmasked when one considers the role of observed 'victim' in the voyeur's psychology. On surface, the persons being looked at are 'objectified'; such 'dehumanization' disregards their subjectivity, robs them of any choice in what is being done to them, and breaks the barriers they might have erected to protect their privacy. Let us put it bluntly: sadism is an integral component of voyeuristic perversion. So maybe the 'scotophilia' error was not so bad after all!

Secondary phenomena

The scopophilic instinct can undergo manifold alterations. These can occur as a result of the fluidity of libidinal cathexis in the system Ucs (Freud, 1915b), the imperatives of a strict superego, or the exhortations of an ego ideal. The following five outcomes are commonly seen.

1   *Repression*: the origin and consequence of the scopophilic instinct getting repressed were first enunciated by Freud (1910) in the following terms:

> If the sexual component-instinct which makes use of sight – the sexual 'lust of the eye' – has drawn down upon itself, through its exorbitant demands, some retaliatory measure from the side of the ego instincts, so that the ideas which represent the content of its strivings are subjected to repression and

withheld from consciousness, the general relation of the eye and the faculty of vision to the ego and to consciousness is radically disturbed. The
ego has lost control of the organ, which now becomes solely the instrument
of the repressed sexual impulse. It would appear as though repression on
the part of the ego had gone too far and poured away the baby with the bath
water, for the ego now flatly refuses to see anything at all, since the sexual
interests in looking have so deeply evolved the faculty of vision.

(p. 216)

Besides 'hysterical' blindness, which is now rarely encountered in clinical
practice, there are many other manifestations of repression of scopophilia.
These include 'neurotic photophobia' (Abraham, 1913), that is, an exaggerated aversion to light and undue protection of one's eyes from any source of
light (e.g. by wearing sunglasses all the time); complaints of blurred vision;
intense dislike of illustrations in a book; compulsive blinking; and a constant
fear of going blind.

2   *Condensation*: this causes scopophilia to merge with other instinctual aims.
Pleasure in looking can thus become pleasure in hearing, making 'eavesdrop-
ping' a disguised form of voyeurism. Klein (1925) reported a case of a man
who had been repeatedly exposed to the primal scene as a child and later
developed a hatred for cinema; he loved music and had an "intensified interest in sound [that] was partly the result of repression in the visual sphere"
(p. 111). Looking can also become merged or equated with knowing. Thus
heightened or 'instinctualized curiosity' (Akhtar, 2017) can arise and if this
undergoes repression, "the consequent 'stupidity' may represent simultaneously an obedience to or rebellion against the parents from whom the patient
had suffered frustrations of his curiosity" (Fenichel, 1945, p. 181). Also, lascivious looking can change into lascivious speaking, giving rise to a love of
'dirty talk' or what Ferenczi (1911) termed 'corporophemia'.[2]

3   *Reaction formation:* the use of this defense against scopophilia results in an
inhibited and shy personality (Fenichel, 1945; Rosen, 1964); the type of character called the 'shy narcissist' (Akhtar, 2000) especially gives testimony to
such psychodynamics. "Keeping a tight rein on his wishes to be noticed, the
shy narcissist feels especially uncomfortable upon being photographed, the
attention of a camera suddenly floods his ego with primitive exhibitionism
and causes him much anxiety" (p. 116).[3]

4   *Sublimation*: this mechanism diverts scopophilic instinct "in the direction
of art, if its interest can be shifted away from this genitals on to the shape
of the body as a whole" (Freud, 1905a, p. 156). In a related vein, Ferenczi
(1916) spoke of the "optic aesthetic sphere" (p. 300) and regarded the pleasure in travel and sightseeing to be a sublimated form of scopophilia. Fenichel (1945) added "interest in research" (p. 72) and Moore and Fine (1990)
included "curiosity, learning ability and creativity" (p. 173) among the character traits resulting from the sublimation of scopophilia.

5   *Reversal of object*: from the earliest tackling of this issue, Freud (1905a) had underscored that scopophilia and exhibitionism are intricately linked, active and passive aims of the same component instinct; one propels looking, the other demands to be looked at. Famously, he declared that "in scopophilia and exhibitionism, the eye corresponds to an erotogenic zone" (p. 169). Not surprisingly then, a modicum of exhibitionism always accompanies voyeurism; this can be at an unconscious level whereby the voyeur identifies with the person being watched (Freud, 1905a, 1915a; Fenichel, 1935) or at a conscious level whereby the voyeur occasionally turns into an exhibitionist, displaying his own genitals or at least making others witness his nudity or toilet acts.[4]

In addition to these defensive distortions and disguised versions of voyeurism, there exist deeper dynamics involving oral hunger, phallic-Oedipal anxieties, and the vicissitudes of rage and revenge. Before delving into these configurations though we must consider the 'envelope of voyeurism' which is constructed on the one side by an evolutionary bedrock which puts premium on certain visual cues for sexual attraction and on the other side by a panoply of cultural avenues that stimulate and gratify voyeuristic desires.

Evolutionary basis and cultural variables

To be sure, voyeurism, especially in its intense and sexually perverse form, originates from psychodynamic constellations that vary from individual to individual. Such forces, however, exploit what is hardwired in the brain (e.g. the propensity of certain objects or part objects to appear sexually alluring) and what is offered by the culture-at-large (e.g. Internet pornography). It is therefore useful to consider, even if briefly, these two variables before entering into a discussion of the deeper and more individualized psychodynamics of voyeurism.

Evolutionary foundations

The rapidly developing field of evolutionary psychology is grounded in the ideas proposed by Darwin in his seminal work, *The Origin of the Species* (1900). It suggests that what is found erotically appealing is only so because it assures the propagation of our species. Beauty and sexual allure are mere billboards for reproductive health. This premise bifurcates when it comes to the two genders. And, this bifurcation rests upon the concept of 'parental investment' (Trivers, 1972); that is, "any investment by the parent in an individual offspring that increases the offspring's chance of surviving at the cost of parent's ability to invest in another offspring" (p. 55). Elaborating on this line of thinking, Baselice and Thomson (2018) write:

> The female of our species must produce a nutrient-rich egg, build an expensive placenta, gestate the fetus for nine months, endure the hazards of

childbirth, and burn countless calories to produce milk and breastfeed a child after birth. Even though the modern woman may choose not to breastfeed, the basic minimal physiologic investment is massive. Men's baseline physiologic contribution is sperm and two-and-a-half minutes.

(p. 85)

This difference is responsible for the bifurcation of sexual object choice and mating strategies. Women can produce fewer children, and at that, too, at higher costs to themselves; therefore, they look for evidences of power and protectiveness in their male partners. These evidences are not necessarily dependent upon the males' physical appearance. Men, in contrast, can father more offspring and, unbeknownst to themselves, look in their female partners for signs of fertility and the potential for safely carrying a pregnancy to term. Across cultures, men prefer the childlike features of big eyes and relatively small nose in women, features that are indicative of youth (Cunningham, Druen, and Barbee, 1997). They like women with bigger breasts and slender bodies and with low waist-to-hip ratio, which are felt to be evidences of good child-carrying and child-rearing capacities.

The relevance of all this to voyeurism lies in the fact that the signs women look for in mate selection are less visually dependent than those sought by men.[5] The capacity to read visual signals (of fertility and hence attractiveness) is a silent but powerful legacy of male evolutionary history. This preference is 'hardwired' in the male brain, operates outside of conscious awareness, and is enlisted in the service of libidinal aims arising out of regression and/or traumatic experiences. Voyeurism thus becomes a male, and not female, 'sport', so to speak. As a counterpart to the psychoanalytic concept of 'somatic compliance' (Freud, 1905b), one might call this evolutionary propensity to lend itself for psychogenic uses an instance of 'phylogenetic compliance'.

Cultural overlay

Societal containers of voyeurism range from the softer, aim-inhibited beauty contests, fashion runways, and erotic painting and sculpture to the massive, id-oriented porn industry. The former permits gratification of voyeuristic impulses in relatively 'civilized' ways. The latter relies upon numbing of empathy, objectification of human partners, and devaluation of women; elements of rage and revenge also contribute, even if unconsciously, to the pleasure derived from watching pornography.

Such demarcation between the 'civilized' and 'uncivilized' forms of erotic art, literature, and film, is, however, not always easy to make. And, a quick review of how ancient such invitations to the lust-driven eye are and what transformations such creativity has undergone over time lends support to this assertion. Artistic depictions of sexuality are centuries old. They go back to a statue of a man and woman having sexual intercourse sculpted by German hunter-gatherers (circa

5200 BCE) through the sexually explicit frescoes found in the ruins of Pompeii (79 CE) to the sculptures of myriad sexual acts (often with multiple participants) in central India's Khajuraho Temples (circa 950 CE). The first sexually explicit novel, *Memoirs of a Woman of Pleasure* (Cleland, 1748), made its appearance over 250 years ago, and the English word 'pornography' was originated in 1857 by conflating the Greek *porni* ('prostitute') with *graphein* ('writing'). It originally referred to any work of art or literature depicting the life and activities of prostitutes but soon gained acceptance as a general term for sexually explicit material. In 1969, Denmark became the first country to legalize pornography, and in 1973 the US Supreme Court defined it as comprising of three features: (1) appeals to prurient interests, (2) is patently offensive in its depiction of sexual conduct, and (3) lacks serious literary, artistic, political, or scientific value.

What this breathless survey does not make explicit is how cultural forces have shaped the form of pornography and forever opened new windows to people's access to it. The old 'peeping-tom' felt little need, as time passed, to prowl darkened alleys and stand on tiptoes to peer into others' bedrooms and bathrooms. He could use high-powered binoculars, visit 'peep-shows' in the back rooms of adult book stores, and spend stolen hours at 'Gentlemen's Clubs'. He was further comforted by the invention of one-way mirrors that permitted him to surreptitiously watch others in the course of undressing, masturbating, or having sex. The early twentieth-century appearance of 'blue movies'[6] (low-cost, short films showing sexual acts) gradually paved the way for the golden age of porn during the 1970s. Initially, pornographic films were only shown at adult movie theaters, brothels, and stag parties. By the 1980s, however, the voyeur could satisfy his desire to watch such movies using home video appliances.[7] Another decade or so later, the rise of the Internet made pornography readily and globally accessible to any and all who wanted to replace the intimacy and mutuality of human relationships by an omnipotently controlled and magical pathway to masturbatory excitement. But the pleasure was not all libidinal. Hostility invariably lurked in the porn addict's mind. Pertinent in this context is Stoller's (1975) reminder that "there is always a victim [in pornography], no matter how disguised: no victim, no pornography" (p. 32).

Referring to pornography as "the stealer of dreams", Khan (1983, p. 222) emphasized that what masquerades as mutual intimacy in it is actually a sterile mental concoction. Pornography alienates its user from himself and from the Other. Khan also noted that the capacity of pornography to transmute latent rage into omnipotently controlling erotic events

lends it three potent functions: subversion, therapeutics, and instruction. It is subversive in so far as it negates the *person* through its somatic expertise. The accomplice/reader can reach and participate in this type of *écriture* only in vary specific states of depersonalization and association. It is therapeutic in so far as it transmutes the threat of total violence and destruction from latent rage in the individual and the culture into manageably distributed, dosed, and eroticized language. . . . Its instruction lies in that it has to *teach* the tricks to its accomplice/reader for its peculiar reality to be participated in.

(p. 223, italics in the original)

Khan's insightful passage about the functions of pornography brings us to the threshold of considering the ontogenetically determined psychodynamics of the voyeur.

Individual psychodynamics

Like any and all psychological phenomena, voyeurism is subject to the principles of 'overdetermination' (Freud, 1895a) and 'multiple function' (Waelder, 1936). It originates from myriad sources and has diverse consequences. Three outstanding dynamic configurations include (1) the oral–visual link, (2) the Oedipal fig leaf, and (3) vision and violence. Let us take one of these at a time.

The oral–visual link

Early on in the history of psychoanalysis, Fenichel (1935) noted that the fantasy of incorporating the object through the eye often underlies voyeurism. A few years later, he stated that "observation of a child who is looking for libidinous purposes readily shows what the accompanying features or prerequisites of pleasurable looking are: he wants to look at an object in order to 'feel along with him'" (1945, p. 71). Fenichel went on to note that a historically important incident in childhood (e.g. watching a sibling being breastfed) can lead to the conflation of looking and eating. Arising out of such experience is "voracious looking that can be recognized as a substitute for gluttony" (1945, p. 491).

Four prominent analysts advanced this idea, giving it further developmental nuance. Greenacre (1953) noted that the shift from tactile to the visual modality for contact with the mother originates in experiences of separation; children who are not sufficiently held and cuddled by their mothers display an "uncanny reaching out with eyes" (p. 90) to her. Spitz (1965) refined this line of thinking even more by stating that:

When the infant loses the nipple and recovers it, contact with the need-gratifying percept is lost and recovered, again and again. During the interval between loss and recovery of *contact*, the other element of the total perceptual unit, *distance perception* of the face, remains unchanged. In the course of these repetitive experiences, visual perception comes to be relied upon, for it is not lost; it proves to be the more constant and more constant and therefore the more rewarding of the two.

(p. 65, italics in the original)

While Spitz (1965) underscored the solace-giving role of the child's visual contact with the mother's face, Winnicott (1971) declared that the mother's face is "the precursor of the mirror" (p. 130). In other words, "the mother's looking at the baby and what she looks like is related to what she sees there" (p. 131). Such mirroring relationships can undergo pathological distortions. In the extreme case, the baby looks at the mother and sees nothing of himself; the mother's face is then not a mirror. In the milder case, "the baby will study the object intensively in the hope of finding something there" (p. 132). Some of these children become experts at reading the mother's mood in her face. Visual modality of replenishing ego resources becomes hypertrophied under such circumstances.

In the developmentally later context of toddlerhood, a similar observation was made by Mahler (1974):

> Despite the children's apparent obliviousness to their mothers during the early practicing period, most of them seemed to go through a brief period of increased separation anxiety. The fact that they were able to move away independently, yet remain connected with their mother – not physically, but by way of their *seeing* and hearing her – made the successful use of these distance modalities extraordinarily important.
>
> (pp. 157–158)

Common to all these observations is the 'oral use' of the eyes and the caressing, touching, and incorporative aspect of vision. More recently, Wright (1991) has elaborated upon this theme in his monograph titled *Vision and Separation*. In an especially eloquent passage, Wright states:

> vision gives depth and clarity to separation, and comes to show at the same time the means that I must employ to overcome that separation. If I am a baby, it places my mother 'out there' where I can touch her or not touch her, reach her or not reach her, crawl to her, walk to her, call to her, smile at her. It shows me her comings and goings, the door she walks through, the places I can find her or not find her. It shows me the space that not only separates me from her, but joins me to her – for looking, it must not be forgotten, is still anticipatory touching.
>
> (p. 63)

Pooling together these various observations and hypotheses leads one to conclude that object hunger consequent upon separation traumas (subtle and chronic or shocking and acute) often plays an important role in the genesis of voyeurism.[8]

The Oedipal fig leaf

Childhood development during the phallic-Oedipal phase also contributes to intensification of visual function. Though outdated in their gender-determining influence, Freud's (1925) observations in his paper titled *Some Psychical Consequences of the Anatomical Distinction Between the Sexes* are not entirely without merit. The paper's phallocentrism, mindless devaluation of the female genitalia, and claim to ubiquitousness of its proposals are certainly misplaced and incorrect. But, it is plausible that in certain familial configurations, and in certain well-timed associations with other traumas (e.g. a broken bone), a male child might become traumatized by the sight of female genitalia and then evolve a counterphobic attitude to looking at them. Usually, this occurs in displaced forms (e.g. looking at breasts, legs), or with a concomitant inclination towards fetishism which assigns an imaginary penis to the woman (Freud, 1927).

More common than such 'phallic-phase' fixations are the Oedipal anxieties consequent upon exposure to (or curiosity about) the primal scene. Imagining (or seeing) parents in sexual intercourse fuels curiosity on both sublimated (e.g. scientific inquisitiveness) and instinctualized (e.g. peeping, watching pornography) fronts. The humbling experience of exclusion from parental privacy is thus reversed; one intrudes into a couple's sexual activity by surreptitiously watching it.[9] Painful triangulation that is integral to the Oedipal situation is eliminated, since in such witnessing one becomes (via identification) one or the other partner in coitus.

In this context, a link to Freud's (1905a) proposal that sexualized looking (voyeurism) and being looked at (exhibitionism) constitute the active and passive aims of the scopophilic instinct becomes evident when we come across the following passage by Arlow (1980):

> In some instances, the individual brings about a repetition of the primal scene in which he casts himself in the role of witness, often enough interrupting and causing distress to a couple making love. Relatively underemphasized, however, are those vengeful repetitions of the primal scene in which the individual causes others to be witness to his sexual activities. The unconscious impact of this behaviour is to make the betraying parents experience the sense of humiliation, exclusion, and betrayal that the child experienced at the time of the original trauma, except that in this repetition the role of the parent may be assigned to somebody else – spouse, child, lover, etc.
>
> (p. 523)

The mention of such revenge motif brings up the consideration of violation and violence that is integral to voyeurism.

Vision and violence

As the foregoing passage by Arlow demonstrates, voyeurism can also contain a thick streak of rage and sadism. However, this does not have to be restricted to the angry intrusion (or mocking invitation) into a couple's personal activity (that proxies the primal scene). Such sadism can have pre-Oedipal roots as well.

Thus Fenichel (1945) spoke of "aggressive looking" (p. 201) as a displacement of oral sadistic tendencies. Since the voyeur is aiming simultaneously to achieve too many goals – for example, deny genital differences (phallic), intrude on primal scene (Oedipal), control an object (anal), or cannibalize and merge with it (oral) – a modicum of failure is guaranteed. The resulting inconsolability fuels rage, and the desire to look acquires a more and more sadistic significance. 'Scopophilia' transforms itself into 'scoptophilia' and a 'piercing gaze' comes into existence.[10]

Though masochistic links between vision and violence are better known (e.g. the blinding of eponymous protagonist in Sophocles' *Oedipus*, and that of Gloucester in Shakespeare's *King Lear*), the fact that eyes, looks, and looking can carry contempt, commit violation, and become tools of violence has also been recorded. One powerful illustration of this comes from the intrusive look of Medusa in the well-known Gorgon myth. This is a catastrophic form of looking which distances, separates, objectifies, and empties out the observed one. In clinical practice, one occasionally comes across the devastating recollection by a patient of being looked at with contempt by their mother; this childhood experience often leaves an indelible mark on the psyche. In voyeurism, such objectification and derision is reversed. Voyeurism, within the context of pornography or outside of it, is based upon the linkage between dehumanization, omnipotent control, and erotic defilement of the object.

The clinical setting

Individuals with full-scale voyeuristic perversions are infrequently seen in psychoanalytic practices; most end up in judicial systems and in court-ordered behavioral counseling settings. Indeed, psychoanalytic literature contains very few detailed reports of voyeurs being analyzed (Speilrein, 1923; Nierenberg, 1950; Fain, 1954; Müller-Eckhard, 1955; Bergler, 1957). At the same time, it seems reasonable to conclude that due to the easily accessible pornography on the Internet, today's voyeur does not have to prowl the streets; he can indulge in his dark passion in the privacy of his own home. Thus the dearth of actual 'voyeurs' in psychoanalytic practice might be balanced by the glut of 'porn-addicts' in sex addiction therapies of various types. For the psychoanalyst, it is more common to encounter 'non-perverse scopophilia' (Mahony, 1989) in the course of an otherwise ordinary analysis.

When the analyst does find a real voyeur in his practice, he finds himself faced with the triad of (1) early oral frustration, and consequent upon it, intensified object hunger; (2) childhood visual trauma (e.g. seeing a sibling being breastfed, primal scene exposure, parental nudity), and the resultant rage; and (3) great castration anxiety and the need to reinforce masculinity through visual reassurance that the female body and sexual intercourse are not dangerous. Working with such patients requires the analyst to explore the patient's great neediness for attachment and love, as well as his dread of 'resourceless dependence' (Khan, 1972). Paranoid fears in transference also need to be unmasked; some of these are displacement based (i.e. recreations of insults and desertion by parents), while others are projection based (i.e. attributions to the analyst of the patient's own hostile intentions). As such work proceeds, there is a considerable risk of 'emotional flooding' (Volkan, 1976), severe sadomasochistic enactments within the clinical situation, and violent acting out in relationships outside of it. The analyst needs to remain receptive and tolerant of such developments while willing to depart from neutrality and set limits (Hoffer, 1985). A firm anchoring of the analyst's mind on the principles of 'overdetermination' (Freud, 1895a) and 'multiple function' (Waelder, 1936) is of great assistance under such circumstances since it permits the analyst to hold on to the complexity of the clinical picture; need for love is warded off by dread, hate defends against love and guilt, shame prevents expression of anaclitic longing, and so on. Much can be accomplished, in a piecemeal fashion to be sure, when the analyst succeeds in 'holding' the patient well and in empathizing with the pathos of the patient's life.

This is also true of cases where voyeurism is 'non-perverse', though the rage and hate in such circumstances might be milder. The pain of object loss, often actually experienced during childhood, exerts a greater pressure on the transference–countertransference axis. The patient desperately longs for 'actual' closeness with and belonging to the analyst. The analyst oscillates between 'role-responsive' (Sandler, 1976) fantasies to adopt or marry the patient and burdened psychic states of anaclitic fatigue.

Clinical vignette: 1

Orrin Anderson, a fifty-seven-year-old successful attorney, entered treatment as his chronically unhappy marriage was coming to an end. His principal symptom was dread of aloneness and shame at nor having a partner, even though he had already decided upon getting a divorce. He felt that he was dying in this marriage and, since his only child, a daughter, had left for college, it was time to end his marital suffering.

As I gathered more information, it became apparent that he had married his wife to 'rescue her'. She had arrived at his door some twenty years ago in connection with a legal case involving her deceased father. This had resulted in a serious downward economic turn for her family. Never prone to mixing work and pleasure, Orrin somehow became romantically involved with his client and, upon the completion of legal proceedings, quickly married her. The considerable socioeconomic and intellectual difference between then (he was far more educated and affluent than she) did not bother him at that time. Bit by bit though, this became a source of irritation. The fact that Orrin himself had come from a humble background rendered his wife a suitable container for the projection of his own shame-laden parts. The situation was worsened by the fact that his wife was not given to physical displays of affection and was very often sexually unresponsive to him. Orrin led a life of chronic frustration, forever thinking of getting divorced, but staying in the marriage due to his great concern for his daughter.

The theme of voyeurism appeared in analysis when he began talking of his childhood. Orrin had grown up on a remote farm in the Midwest and recalled with shy trepidation that he watched various animals (e.g. dogs, mules) copulating with great fascination. (The screen function of such affects in defending against the angst of primal scene exposure was handled much later in his treatment). Unrelated (in his mind) to this was his exposure to the farmhands' (mostly men but occasionally women also) genitals and/or buttocks and their urine and feces in the farm's outhouse. He remembered feeling ashamed about the pleasure he drew from secretly watching all this, even during his childhood. A third source of visual excitement was the fact that his uncle, who lived with the family, had a leg that had been severely affected by polio; it was very thin. As a result, the uncle walked with prominent limp but no one was supposed to notice it. Above all, the fixating factor was the long hospitalization of his mother who suffered from cancer, was frequently bed-ridden, and died when little Orrin was only seven years old. He was then raised by the trio of his father, his polio-affected uncle, and the latter's wife; their children became his near-siblings, though he often witnessed with great envy their being hugged and kissed by their mother, a comfort that she never offered him.

Within the clinical situation, Orrin never looked at me while entering or leaving the office and never commented upon any of its accoutrements (e.g. paintings, a big red vase, little knickknacks, and a profusion of books). It was as if he were blind. Gradually, however, he began to reveal his love of looking – at buildings, paintings, sculpture – but above all, at women. He was fascinated by breasts and could almost feel their texture by looking at them from a distance. Still later, he told me that he was fascinated by pornography and, upon investigation, revealed that the most important thing to watch were the expressions on women's faces. One had to make sure that they were enjoying what was going on (in fact, he said, "what was being done to them"), which betrayed his primal scene trauma as well as his wish to dominate and control the object of his desire, most likely the aunt and lurking behind her, his sick mother.

Interpretations along these lines led to Orrin revealing yet another aspect of his voyeurism: he loved seeing women who were at some distance – across the street, behind a glass pane, encountered during a misty night. All such instances created a vagueness about their silhouette which excited Orrin very much and which he felt compelled to sort out by exercising what he called 'visual logic'. This remained deeply private and did not lead to any overt action on Orrin's part. On one occasion though, he walked up two floors of a building across the street from the hotel room where he was staying to see a woman up close. Thankfully, no adverse consequences for this risky behavior happened but Orrin himself was quite shaken up and never repeated it.

As the treatment deepened, two themes pertaining to looking became central: (1) the appeal of sorting out the full picture of a 'foggy' woman and (2) not seeing me or anything in my office. Reconstruction of the 'fogginess' led to many painful memories of mother's hospitalizations and of the ambulance, with her in it, driving off in a distance. Memories of her funeral and internment also emerged with much sobbing and weeping. Reconstruction of 'not seeing' led to the family collusion around the uncle's limp and his fragile thin leg. Throughout this work, the affect in the office was thick with sadness and vague dread. Orrin's desire was to never end analysis but to continue without paying any money: I was to be his mother forever. Orrin's fear was that if he looked at me (or at things in my office), he might see something he disliked (the polio-affected leg) and get frightened about expressing that emotion. Linkages of sadness, exclusion, and dread to the primal scene response of his early childhood were also gradually made.

In contrast to this case where looking was partly sexual and partly sexualized, there are still milder encounters with scopophilia during clinical work. Mahony (1989) reports the case of a female analysand who was prone to all sorts of "optical acting-in" (p. 373).

Looking, prolonged or darting, was one. And she was ingenious in concocting countless pretexts to lengthen a glance into a gaze – sometimes verbalizations about the monthly statement or her check or a change of hour, sometimes delays in putting on her sweater or shoes after the end of the hour, and so on, endlessly; there was also constant looking back from the couch. . . . I reveal no secret in saying that I found her penchant for visual monitoring quite trying.

(p. 372)

The mother of this patient had 'visibly' preferred her siblings over her, and often refused to kiss her with "averted face and eyes" (p. 368). Fascinatingly, in relation to my patient reported above, Mahoney's patient has also been exposed not only to primal scene but to an aunt who "limped because of a large thigh wound" (p. 367).

In contrast to such 'blatant' cases are those where scopophilic tendencies came to surface transiently when the patient gives up sitting and begins to lie on the couch. The analyst then has to be mindful of the effects of this upon the patient's feeling states and ego capacities, as well as of the defensive strategies mobilized by the patient to compensate for this increased distance. Talking rapidly and incessantly to seek contact with the analyst, curling up in a frightened ball to hold on to oneself, asking provocative questions and mumbling inaudibly to evoke activity from the analyst, and focusing on the details of the office as a derivative of the wish to maintain visual contact with the analyst, are all manifestations that betray anxiety over this increased distance and should be interpreted as such. Unusual manifestations of anxieties pertaining to this sudden increase in distance should also be kept in mind.

Clinical vignette: 2

Susan Rosenbaum began to lie on the couch so that a significant portion of her face was visible to me and I found myself repeatedly looking at her. My subjective experience was quite conflicted: I wanted to look but felt uncomfortable, even quite anxious by this desire. The interpretation of this situation appeared multidetermined and included Susan's childhood overstimulation by parental nudity. Her mother habitually walked around the house naked, never shut the bathroom door, and often walked in when Susan was using the toilet or taking a shower. This chronic visual trauma led to the development of both an anxious scopophilia and a teasing exhibitionism. With the loosening of ego boundaries in the clinical situation, both were deposited, via projective identification, into me. At the same time, her reversal of voyeurism into exhibitionism also seemed also linked to her distress at losing visual contact with me upon beginning to use the couch.

Many questions arise here. Do patients who have sat up for long periods before using the couch react more or less intensely, similarly, or differently to lying down? Are there patients who should not be kept sitting up for long because the distance might become socially too close or, conversely, fixated in a more than optimal apartness from their deepest inner lives? Should some patients be seen at first sitting up, even four or five sessions a week, for a long period of time so that they can establish a "reality base" (Volkan, 1987, p. 85) about the analyst's personality necessary for them to avoid dangerous transference regressions? Finally, can the analyst undertake active measures, besides the usual empathic remarks and clarifications, to minimize the patient's distress on beginning to sue the couch? Some analysts do report an early 'noisy phase" (Boyer, 1967; Volkan, 1987) when they grunt more than usual to assure their sicker patients of their continued involvement. Could this grunting be a form of showing their face to the patient? What do we think of this? Or of Winnicott's remark at the end of the first session of Guntrip's analysis with him? Winnicott remained totally silent throughout the session and said at the end, "I've nothing particular to say yet, but if I don't say something, you may begin to feel I'm not here" (Guntrip, 1975, p. 152).

All in all, the technical stance in dealing with intensified scopophilia (within the clinical setting) and perverse voyeurism (in the life outside) varies with whether it is perverse and sexual, oral and sexualized, acted out or acting-in, or persistent or transitory. In perverse, sexual, acted out, and persistent types, greater confrontation, departures from neutrality, and limit-setting might be necessary. In non-perverse, sexualized, acted-in, and transitory forms, more customary interventions might be sufficient. In either case, the analyst must oscillate between affirmative and interpretive interventions, between empathy and unmasking, and between reconstruction and transference interpretation. The capacity on the analyst's part to bear intense affects arriving out of the patient's dependent longing, real or imagined boundary violations, rage and hate, also goes a long way in healing the primal wound of the voyeur's eye.

Concluding remarks

In this chapter, I have surveyed the vast phenomenological and etiological terrain associated with sexual pleasure in looking and with the specific sexual perversion involving looking. I have elucidated the nosological conundrum resulting from the deployment of overlapping terms such as 'scopophilia', 'scoptophilia', and 'voyeurism'. I have then discussed the biopsychosocial substrate of these entities, paying attention to the evolutionary, sociocultural, and ontogenetic tributaries to the causation of voyeurism. Finally, I have delineated the nuances of psychoanalytic technique in dealing with erotic, eroticized, and perverse forms of looking.

Despite casting my net wide, I have not been able to address certain important variables in this realm. This is largely because of my lack of knowledge pertaining to these areas but also owing to the dearth of existing literature on them. The three areas I have in mind are (1) gender differences, (2) the homosexual experience, and (3) life-span-related unfolding of voyeuristic tendencies. I shall now enter brief comments on each of these areas, knowing fully well their tentative and limited scope.

As far as the gender difference in the prevalence, form, and intensity of scopophilic instinct in general and voyeurism in particular are concerned, there exists a consensus in the literature that (1) significantly more men than women watch internet pornography (Schneider, 2007; Metzl, 2004), (2) the 'old style' prowling and peeping individuals are almost exclusively men (Eidelberg, 1968; DSM-5, 2017), and (3) while sexual voyeurism does exist in women (Garza, 2007), the 'non-perverse' (Mahony, 1989) form is perhaps more common among them. Explanations for such differences lie in both 'hardwired' evolutionary proclivities whereby the visual modality of erotic attraction and bonding holds less sway for women and in cultural pressures that enforce 'visual modesty' on them.

Regarding the homosexual–heterosexual difference in the prevalence and nature of voyeurism, there is little data available. Scattered clinical reports (Joannadis, 2004; Parsons et al., 2008; McAfee and Schwing, 2012; Corbett, 2013) of porn addiction among gay men reveal psychodynamic antecedents of childhood neglect, adulthood loss, loneliness, and object hunger; these variables could readily be discernible in similarly afflicted straight men. Thus, the nature of reliance upon cyber-voyeurism seems to be little different in the two groups.

Finally, there is the issue of age at which voyeuristic phenomena manifest and/ or intensify. Generally speaking, the seed of voyeurism is sowed by the early breeches in the infant's relationship with his mother and the ensuing plant is nurtured by the anxiety of fecal loss and the curiosities of the phallic-Oedipal phase. It's not until adolescence or young adulthood, however, that a well-consolidated voyeuristic perversion makes its appearance; the DSM-5 (2017) stipulates eighteen years as the minimum age for the diagnosis of this 'paraphilia'. This makes sense since the sexually exciting hormonal levels are at their peak and succumbing to 'component instincts' is frequent around this time. Similarly, it is expected that the pressures of sexual instinct diminish with age and are mostly eclipsed by existential concerns during late midlife and old age. While true, this is not always the case. In the setting of narcissistic character pathology, especially the inhibited or 'shy' type, there is at times a fresh emergence of promiscuity and perversions in the latter phases of life (Kernberg, 1980; Akhtar, 2000). What these recent 'discoveries' have overlooked that nearly a hundred years ago, Ferenczi (1921) had noted that:

> The old become narcissistic again – like children; much of their interest in family and social matters fades away, and they lose a great deal of their former capacity for sublimation, particularly in the sphere of shame and disgust. They become cynical, malicious and mean; that is to say, their libido regresses to the 'pregenital stages of development', and sometimes expresses itself in undisguised anal and urethral eroticism, voyeurism, exhibitionism, and a tendency to masturbation.
>
> (p. 205)

Conservative postures regard such emergence of alluring 'pre-genital' sexuality in old age as regressive and 'childish'. And this stance has validity. At the same time, using Silberer's (1914) 'anagogic' perspective on interpreting clinical material, a modicum of healthy holding on to life (and its pleasures) can also be discerned in this development, a 'last hurrah' so to speak.[11] What then is wrong if the elderly, robbed of sexual prowess by the ravages of time, seek one final bit of erotic excitement and try to establish at least a robust visual tie to a love object? In the words of the renowned Urdo poet, Mirza Asad-Ullah Khan Ghalib (1785–1869):

Go haath ko jumbish nahiN, aaNkhoN meiN to dum hai/
Rehne do abhi saaghar-o-meena mere aage/[12]

Notes

1 An international scandal involving the renowned British osteopath Stephen Ward (1912–1963) broke open in 1963. Ward, who had treated Gandhi, the US Ambassador Averell Harriman, and Duncan Sandys, the son-in-law of Winston Churchill, frequently threw stag parties and watched sexual acts of celebrities from across a one-way mirror. The scandal involved Lord John Profumo, England's Secretary of State for War, Yevgeny Ivanov, a naval attaché at the Soviet Embassy, and a charming teenager, Christine Keeler. It led to the resignation of Lord Profumo and contributed to the defeat of the Conservative government a year later (Knightley and Kennedy, 1987).
2 See also Sharpe (1940) for how the act of speaking can acquire sexual and aggressive functions.
3 Allen's (1974) term, 'scopophobia', which somehow did not gain popularity, refers to this type of situation.
4 Sabbadini (2000) has recently coined the term 'collusive voyeurism' for the situation where the observed one is aware of being looked at so that the perpetrator's voyeurism gratifies the victim's exhibitionism.
5 Not surprisingly, women show less interest in watching male nudity and pornography in general. The women's magazine *Viva* began offering nude male centerfolds à la *Playboy*, but soon discontinued it. Its readers did not seem terribly interested in such material.
6 The designation 'blue movies' has unclear origins. Prominent among the hypotheses to explain it are (1) the cheap production values resulted in a blue tint to the film, (2) they were sold in blue packages, and (3) such films broke 'blue laws' that perpetuated seventeenth-century Puritan standards and existed in many US states until the mid-twentieth century.
7 The distinction between 'soft-core' and 'hard-core' porn also appeared around this time. The former was merely suggestive of sexual acts while the latter included frontal nudity, genitalia, and acts of penetration.
8 In a lighthearted but persuasive manner, Irwin Shaw's (1939) short story, *The Girls in Their Summer Dresses*, conveys the same point. Its protagonist, a young happily married man, is criticized by his wife for ogling at other women during a pleasant Sunday morning walk. He admits doing this, which further infuriates the wife. Fascinatingly, when she moves emotionally and physically away from him, he finds himself leering at her legs!
9 The pleasure in this case is derived from the defiant overcoming of a prohibition. No better example of such curiosity can be given than that of the man in the nudist colony who desired to see what is under the Band-Aid on the arm of a fellow female nudist.
10 Gediman (2017) has recently explored the sadomasochistic aspects of voyeuristic stalking in detail, using some well-known movies (e.g. Hitchcock's *Rear Window*, Eastwood's *Play Misty for Me*, and Powell's *Peeping Tom*) as her 'subjects'.

11 The 2006 British movie *Venus* (directed by Roger Michell) poignantly portrays the relationship of an aging actor (played by Peter O'Toole) with the grandniece of a friend. The connection begins with sexual lust on his part which goes unrequited and is transformed into voyeuristic pleasure which, in turn, leads to a warm, if chronologically mismatched friendship.

12 Literally translated, this verse means: "True, my hand is frail but my vision retains its reach/Please do not remove the wine glass and the bottle from my sight./

Clinical lessons learnt from eight important papers on erotic and erotized transferences

Lorrie Chopra

While attending a panel presentation at the American Psychoanalytic Association Annual Meetings in New York, I realized I had never read an article of Freud's that had been referred to in the presentation – *Observations on Transference Love* (1915c). I was nearing the end of my candidacy, ready to graduate, and had somehow managed to never have read this important paper. I don't think it had ever been assigned in any of the courses I had taken; I had never sought it out.

I don't have much of a recollection of studying, talking about, or reading papers about erotic transference during my analytic training years. I can't recall that it came up in supervision either. How could this be, especially since I had a total of six control cases during my training as an adult, adolescent, and child analyst? Why would this be? Was I unable to talk about it? Was it being avoided by myself, my teachers, or all of us? I know I was regularly exposed to many other types of transference throughout my years of study, and of course countertransference as well. My teachers and supervisors were so helpful in teaching, sharing, and expanding my understanding and thinking about all things transference and countertransference. But, it feels to me that anything erotic transference–countertransference were woefully missing.

I clearly recall very important classes on boundary violations in which articles on the topic were read and discussed in thoughtful ways. However, I am struck on how there was an absence in learning about erotic transference and how to listen for it in material, understand the dynamics at play, and technically work with this transference. And, what about the missing discussions on an analyst's countertransference experiences of a growing erotic transference in the analysis? Is this topic being addressed as fully as it should be, considering the potential transgressions that can come about in the closed quarters of the analytic consulting room when a heated erotic or erotized transference is exploding? And if not, why not? The desire to find answers to such questions forms the basis of this chapter.

Eight major contributions in this realm

A search of the PEP web resulted in a total of fifty-two papers on erotic transference and thirteen more on eroticized transference. Clearly, there are papers that have been written, but not as many as I might have anticipated on this extremely important clinical topic over a span of a hundred years. This chapter will review eight of these papers, all significant in their own right, to glean clinical lessons learned around this very important, but not widely written on transference.

Sigmund Freud (1915)

In his paper, "Observations on Transference-Love", Freud (1915c) gives us a starting point to help us to see the importance of understanding and being able to work with the erotic transference. His focus in this paper is on women patients who fall in love with their male analyst, a situation which he states is almost to be expected. In the paper, Freud grounds us in the importance of understanding this very strong transference, and why it must be understood to have many antecedents, unique for each patient, and then analyzed if we are to help the patient. He also reminds the reader that the falling in love is a byproduct of the analytic situation rather than the result of the charms of the analyst. In other words, we invite our patients to come five times a week and tell us all their uncensored thoughts and feelings, resulting in a regression allowing infantile/early childhood origins to enter the treatment. We set things up in the hopes that transference (of whatever kinds necessary for each individual patient) will develop so we then may help our patients.

Freud lays out the case why we cannot just stop the treatment when a patient falls in love with us, despite the discomfort that may arise in the analyst. If stopped, the patient will attempt a second analysis and will yet again fall in love with her doctor. She must return to treatment, because she needs an analysis, so she will continue to start a treatment, fall in love, and then feel she has no option other than to leave the treatment. The analyst must help the patient stay in treatment if her neurosis is to be worked through. Freud is teaching us about the power of working in the transference and what psychoanalysis has to offer our patients. The experience of love for the analyst must be expressed in words and analyzed, only then will there be any possibility of contributing to the patient's recovery.

Freud instructs us that transference-love can be a very problematic involvement for an analyst when they experience this for the first time, making it difficult to be ones best analytic self. Being on the receiving end of a declaration of love, offers of sex in the consulting room, and idealization of all that you are as a person could result in anyone feeling very challenged in the work. It will only be with the help of one's reflective abilities as an analyst that a foothold can be achieved in the treatment. Freud instructs that we must remain suspicious of why this demand for love is happening at this particular time in the treatment and consider the possibility that this may be a resistance put forth to avoid some difficult work that is beginning to surface.

To work with these intense feelings and demands the patient is putting forth, Freud helps us understand how explaining the moral and social improprieties of acting on these feelings would be unhelpful to the patient. He is aware of the shame and humiliation a patient would experience if the analyst pointed this out to her. Additionally, the result from this technique could be a total repression of these feelings the patient was honest enough to share, closing off any future exploration and understanding of this aspect of a person's mind. He also warns against stating our feelings of affection for the patient, as it may lead down a path where we one day cross a line that we had not intended to – the start of a slippery slope.

Wisely, Freud reminds us we are analysts who have the tools of analysis at our disposal to best help the patient. We can understand this erotic transference as a repetition of earlier interactions, including those of the patient's early life, and know that it must be explored fully. The patient must be left with this need and longing to keep them engaged in their treatment and continue to want to work to understand what these powerful feelings might be about. To either act on the patient's offer for sex or to profess love and admiration for the patient would do nothing to alleviate internal struggles. Rather, we are guided to not steer away from the patient's feelings or respond to them as problematic, but instead invite the patient to tell us more, to express all they are able to about what they are experiencing, including their thoughts and fantasies. As analysts, we will help the patient begin to understand we can hear all they have to say without acting. The end goal, Freud tells us, is to help the patient analyze the erotic transference so that she may love fully in her world outside of the analysis instead of using the transference-love as a surrogate.

From the beginnings of psychoanalytic theory, it seems that Freud was telling us: *this is big! You must pay attention to this, as it is something that will come up in your work as analysts, it can be very difficult to work with, and treatments may be lost over this, or boundary violations may occur, and our very vulnerable patients will be retraumatized by analysts.* He was in a sense letting us all know we must realize that when we invite individuals into analytic treatment, we will become very important to them, both consciously and unconsciously. That is both what makes this work different from other avenues of treatment, but also incredibly demanding on us as analysts. To have individuals need us, become dependent on us, fall in love with us in all the many ways that might be expressed is something that can be a challenge on the analyst during each session.

The paper has limitations, of course. It didn't seem to occur to Freud that transference-love might also happen with male patients, or that the women he described as having such an intractable need for love who could not accept denial of a love relationship with the analyst might actually be very traumatized or narcissistic patients we would now be working with in our offices. But, his comparison of what is happening in the erotic transference to the dangerous work of a chemist indicates he was giving us something very important in this work:

> The lay public, about whose attitude to psycho-analysis I spoke at the outset, will doubtless seize upon this discussion of transference-love as another opportunity for directing the attention of the world to the serious danger of this therapeutic method. The psycho-analyst knows that he is working with

highly explosive forces and that he needs to proceed with as much caution and conscientiousness as a chemist. But when have chemists ever been forbidden, because of danger, from handling explosive substances, which are indispensable, on account of their effects?

(pp. 170–171)

Leon Saul (1962)

"The Erotic Transference" by Leon J. Saul (1962) is the next paper written on this subject, forty-seven years after Freud's contribution. Saul himself notes how little there has been on the subject since Freud's paper, and even suggests it is neither taught or studied enough considering the importance of the subject to both analyst and patient. He reminds us how the analytic situation is highly charged emotionally as it deals with all the deepest and strongest feelings of the patients, which could lead to inappropriate action. He states: "But extreme transference feelings sometimes arouse less modulated countertransference feelings sometimes arouse less modulated countertransference responses" (p. 55).

Saul introduces a short vignette where he describes a young woman who had parents who were emotionally distant, leaving her unconsciously hostile, frustrated, and longing for closeness and love. She had a pattern of falling in love with older men, and these affairs always ended disappointingly. She sexualized her feelings, and when entering analysis with an older male analyst, her hostile and libidinal feelings led her to demand love and sex from the analyst to manage intolerable affect. In this short paper, Saul points out four psychodynamic reasons why it is against good analytic judgment to respond to the demand for love and sex from a patient.

First, Saul points out that the patient must not be gratified because she is trying to create a coupling relationship that she has not been able to manage in life due to internal difficulties. The analytic work will need to focus on helping the patient remove these inner blocks so she can be successful in a relationship in her life outside the office. Warmth and love given by the therapist is not the route to removing these internal problems for the patient. Rather, the frustrated feelings that arise toward the analyst will need to be analyzed to help the patient see the pattern she is recreating from childhood. He puts forth:

> For the needs of the adult to be loved are based upon the needs of the child toward his parents, the original dependent love needs of the child from his mother, which groove the channel through which the adult's needs for love and sexual satisfaction flow.

(p. 57)

Saul goes on to tell us the second reason why giving in to the patient's demand for love will fail is because the "transference is a repetition to the analyst of the emotional patterns toward the parents, especial of those parts of the pattern that persist and cause the patients present difficulties" (p. 57). We are indeed working with the unconscious child living in our adult patient, wishing for a good, loving parent who is emotionally available. This is the work we do in the transference. Acting in a sexual way with the patient would be a great injury to the child within and would result in overstimulation. I find this point very helpful in thinking about the powerful demand coming from the patient-child that can be relentless at times in attempting to get their need met by an analyst-parent. Children need parental love in order to survive, and the patient is expressing this desperately in their request for the analysts love and/or sex.

Thirdly, Saul points out that any expression of love toward the patient will harm the treatment by intensifying the transference without regard to analyzing it. This will lead to the patient essentially living within the analysis rather than in life. To not help the patient understand what the feelings are linked to would be a disservice.

The final reason Saul speaks of lies in the deeply repressed hostility and guilt, which are probably always hidden behind, but intrinsic to, the sexual desires toward the analyst. He reminds us that what is expressed as sexual desires and love needs will also have a flip side of hostility and guilt. A child would be frustrated and angry when they did not feel loved or emotionally connected to the parent, and the relational pattern would have been laid down at a young age only to repeat itself in the transference. The frustration turns into anger and resentment, resulting in guilt and masochism. Saul explains that the repressed hostility leads to the guilt, causing the masochism to unconsciously keep the patient frustrated in life. Upon reading this paper, a patient of mine came to mind.

Clinical vignette: I

Susie was a twelve-year-old patient who continually wanted physical contact from me. She would want to sit very close, put her hands on me, and eventually wanted me to hug her. She said, "If you really cared about me, and I really mattered to you, you would hug me". At other times she would yell and scream at me how I didn't love her, and she had no idea how I even felt about her. Her demands for physical contact or a declaration of my love for her were growing. She would try and control what I had to say and insist that I would say it exactly as she requested if I cared about her. I was often aware of feeling very angry and controlled when with Susie, and at times dreaded her sessions.

Susie had a mother who was very intrusive and would use Susie as a confidant and discuss marital problems with her daughter when she and her husband were not getting along. Susie's father was very depressed and though home every evening after work, he would isolate himself in his room from Susie and his wife.

Though it was not easy, I did not allow physical contact or answer Susie's pleas to tell her my feelings for her. I talked about how disappointed she was in me, how frustrated she was with me, and how angry she was. Susie would at times agree to the frustrated, but not the disappointed or angry. She told me she never got angry (often moments after screaming at me), that she only had good feelings.

After many, many months of this, Susie was able to tell me that she had no idea how you would know if anyone cared about you unless they hugged you. When I tried to explore this with Susie, she seemed unable to think with me about other ways you may know someone was interested or cared. Susie's mom, who also was very uncomfortable with her own anger, would often hug Susie and snuggle with her for very long periods of time. Her mother was either doing too much for Susie, or unavailable emotionally. I experienced her in the same way during our parent guidance sessions; she was either intensely engaged, or felt miles away. When I spoke with the mother about the extended physical contact, she assured me it was very special, and both loved that time together very much. She was unable to hear my thoughts, and I believe the hugging was filling some emotional need of her own.

Susie and I continued our work together over several years, and she eventually came to know additional ways you could tell other people were thinking about you, and that you mattered to them. She no longer asked to touch me, hug me, or demand I say specific things to prove she mattered. She now seemed to know additional ways that people expressed feelings about one another. She put this into words in the following way: I had experienced a death in my family and was out of the office for several of Susie's sessions. On my return, she had asked me about the death, and we talked together. She let me know some things that she thought would help me when I was sad. Susie was kind, empathic, and expressed her condolences. The following session her mom came in with her to the waiting room and said she just needed to give me a big hug (which she did) and brought me a small gift to help with my grief. When we went into session, Susie said "yeah, that's my mom. She doesn't really get how we do things here. She asked me yesterday if I remembered to give you a hug. She doesn't get how you can talk about stuff and be really close".

Harold Blum (1973)

In his paper, "The Concept of Erotized Transference", Harold Blum (1973) makes an important distinction between erotic and erotized transference and delineates the pathogenesis, dynamics, and analytic significance of the erotized transference. Blum explains that the concept of erotized transference has been used to describe demands for physical contact, desire for sex under the guise of love or antagonism, unrelenting demands for admiration, and dependent clinging with fear of object loss. Blum considers the hallmark of erotized transference to be "a patient flooded with erotic transference preoccupations and fantasies about the analyst and hopes or expectations that the analyst shares in these feelings" (p. 63). He goes on to explain that the "erotized transference is a particular species of erotic transference, an extreme sector of a spectrum. It is an intense, vivid, irrational, erotic preoccupation with the analyst, characterized by overt, seemingly ego-syntonic demands for love and sexual fulfillment from the analyst" (p. 63). There are endless attempts to seduce the analyst into a shared acting out, or alternately, the patient may act out with a stand-in for the analyst. The transference is "passionate, insistent, and urgent" (p. 64).

Blum includes clinical descriptions that paint a picture of how difficult working with the erotized transference is. He helps us to see some of the common early life experiences in cases of erotized transference, including childhood sexual seduction (often in the Oedipal phase), parental overstimulation and deprivation, lack of protection and support, family tolerance of incestuous behavior, and repetition of precocious sexual behavior in adolescence. The erotization often masks the trauma of repeated seduction and overstimulation and has elements of suspicion and sadomasochism. The patient may repeat the seduction in similar detail to what had occurred in childhood, using the erotized transference as an effort to master trauma through active repetition.

Blum clarifies how erotized transference is different from transference-love.

> It would appear that erotized transference has multiple determinants and a variable course. It resembles a vehemently exaggerated, distorted form of expectable erotic transference. Erotic transference is a relatively universal, though variable intense and recurrent phase of analysis. There is a continuum from feelings of affection to strong sexual attraction, from ubiquitous unconscious sexual transference wishes to conscious ego-syntonic, erotic transference preoccupation. It is this insistent, conscious, erotic, transference demand that is "erotized transference" proper. The erotization would serve resistance and defend against hostility, homosexuality, loss, and a host of other unconscious conflicts, while representing a revival of infantile love.
>
> (p. 69)

Clearly, these patients, when in the throes of an erotized transference, will be very difficult to work with and evoke strong countertransference feelings in the analyst. The alliance will be tested, as the patient may have extreme regression and acting out. The analysis itself can be experienced by the patient as a seduction, or a danger that must be warded off by seduction. Blum offers hope when he states that the patients he wrote about did not leave treatment. Over time, and with great effort, their demands were quieted, and they could verbalize and integrate their longings into their adult mind. They could hear "no" from the analyst. This resonates with many of us who have worked with patients who were seduced, overstimulated, and unprotected during their early years.

Clinical vignette: 2

Mr. W. was a patient of mine with just such an early history. There was a wide occurrence of sexual abuse and incest throughout his immediate and extended family. Mr. W had been exposed to nudity and pornography as a child. He was excited and felt special as a result of the private conversations his mother would have with him about adult topics, but also recalls feeling angry and overlooked when she would exclude him from other adult conversations. Additionally, he had female relatives who would comment and touch his body in sexual ways when they greeted him, even as a very young boy.

Mr. W entered treatment because he was having nightmares and severe panic attacks as a result of remembering some terrible childhood abuse he experienced. He was very distressed and appreciative to be in treatment. Early on, Mr. W was guarded and not sure if he could trust me. He was clearly unsure if he was safe with me and was always cautious. Slowly, he seemed to have a little more trust, as a result of my remembering things he had told me. This seemed to have great meaning to Mr. W., and he often commented on how touched he was that I remembered something he had shared.

Over time, he began sharing much more about his life, and his difficult experiences as a young boy. As he shared more, and I remained attentive and interested, Mr. W began to ask things of me. He thought we should do longer sessions and meet seven days a week, but at times he wanted to talk with me. He began telling me about the women he was able to easily pick up and take home for sex, never to call them again. He also was calling me often outside of our sessions. He began asking if we could meet somewhere else for sessions, like at a coffee shop. He became more and more insistent, and at times very demanding that our agreed-upon frame needed to change. He felt it was completely unfair that everything was on my terms. He began to tell me that I had tricked him into the analysis, that I got him to come knowing that he would want more, and that I was using him for my own purposes.

Mr. W's demands were strong, and I felt a great deal of pressure to do something about them. I also questioned my own motives and wondered if I had tricked him in some way. Though I did not have any intention to meet him outside my office, the persistence of the demands along with his not being able to talk about what he was asking in terms of fantasy or what we might learn if he said what comes to mind was agonizing for me to sit with. During this period, he would miss sessions, or call and ask for a phone session and tell me this wasn't like a normal relationship, and that I should tell him more about myself and my life.

At some point, after months of this very heated transference, Mr. W called and left me a voice mail indicating he would no longer come to sessions unless I agreed to meet him at a local restaurant at a time he would designate. Part of me was relieved at the thought the treatment may end, and it took a while for me to begin to think about how I might to speak with Mr. W about this. Eventually, I was able to call him back and explain to him that I would not meet him outside of my office as I felt it would be a repetition of what had occurred when he was a young boy. I explained that if I saw him outside of the office, outside of the way we agreed to work together – in my office at regularly scheduled appointment times – I would be transgressing the boundaries without thinking of what impact my actions would have on him, and I recognized I would become like all the other adults he had experienced in his life. I let him know that the choice was his, and I would always be available to see him as we had agreed to, but that I would not change the parameters because it was not in his best interest. Mr. W began to sob as I said this and chose to come back into his sessions with me.

We talked about this for many months, but it was now being expressed in words rather than all the action. Throughout the analysis, there would be periods of regression and this erotized transference would surface, but not as intensely as this initial phase, and together we seemed to be able to work to understand why it was happening at any particular time, and he was able to remain in the room with me even while he expressed his new demands of me.

Ethel Person (1985)

In her paper, "The Erotic Transference in Women and Men: Differences and Consequences", Ethel Person (1985) brings forth what had been absent in the literature – how the transference love is manifested in men and women, and in each of the four dyads (male analyst–female patient, female analyst–male patient, and male–male, female–female). She puts forth the proposal that "in general, the erotic transference utilized as resistance is more common in women in analysis – and, more particularly, women in treatment with men – while resistance to the awareness of the erotic transference is more common among male patients" (p. 160).

Person suggests that that there are differences in how the erotic transference takes form in analysis. Contributing factors to how it is expressed include the patient's unconscious conflicts and personality structure, the sex of the patient, and in part, the sex of the patient in relation to that of the analyst. Additionally, she points to the fact that although we have since Freud stated that the erotic transference is universal, it was only thought of as something seen in women who were in analysis with men. This limits our ability to think about erotic transference and suggests that it is purely a problem of the female psychology, and not one of importance for all patients. "Analytic problems related to the erotic transference can occur depending on whether it develops fully within the analytic situation, is enacted extratherapeutically, or remains undeveloped and is neither fully experienced or expressed" (p. 164).

As she discusses the female patient–male analyst dyad, Person reminds us that there is variation in this group, as of course there will be with all the dyads. Some women will develop pronounced erotic transferences, others will not, and others of these will act out the erotic feelings outside the analysis by starting affairs at critical analytic points. If the erotic transference is suspect, the male analyst must interpret and analyze the resistance to the awareness of the transference. If it is not fully analyzed, it will become the resistance to the analysis, and other important dynamics and conflicts will be concealed. If analyzed well, there is potential for significant extra-analytic change. If left unanalyzed, it will be a barrier for the patient and growth potential.

In the female–female dyad, Pearson states that if the patient is heterosexual, the erotic transference tends to appear as tender, affectionate feelings rather than sexual. There is a strong wish for intimacy and feeling understood and cared about. If they are sexual in nature, they often appear in the context of an idealizing transference which may be defending against a competitive transference. She indicates that in homosexual women, very intense erotic transferences develop with 'some regularity' but does not expand on this. Pearson tells us that the most intense maternal transference seen in this dyad are not erotic but rather come with the emergence of envy, rivalry, and fear of loss of love, starvation, and annihilation.

There is very little written about the male patient–female analyst dyad (at the time of the paper, 1985). What has been reported indicates a more muted and short-lived erotic transference that appears in dreams, triangular preoccupations, is seldomly consciously experienced in affect, and frequently placed onto a woman other than the analyst. If it does appear, it takes on the desire for sex rather than a longing for love. Sexual fantasies may be many, though not with erotic longing. Many of the thoughts are aggressive in nature, as a defense against the unconscious affectionate longings. "Frequently, one witnesses defenses against the erotic transference rather than the transference itself" (p. 171). Person discerns that there of course will be dangers in suppressing or repressing the experience of the erotic transference. Sexual and dependency issues that are not integrated will result in uncertainty in the man's capacity to form lasting love relationships.

Finally, with the male–male dyad, Person has just one short paragraph written. For both heterosexual and homosexual male patients, the erotic transference is seen as muted, so much so that when an erotic thought or dream occurs, the patient dissociates. She ends with, "It is the relative paucity of homosexual erotic transferences, even among homosexual patients, that confirms the underlying male resistance to the experience of the erotic transference" (p. 174).

The overarching idea is that the erotic transference is used by women as resistance to the analysis and in men, resistance to the erotic transference is more often seen. The difference "parallels an extratherapeutic difference. In general, women achieve their self-identity as women by virtue of certain defining relationships, whereas men achieve their self-identity as men through achievement and autonomy" (p. 177).

Stefano Bolognini (1994)

In "Transference: Erotised, Erotic, Loving, Affectionate", Stefano Bolognini (1994) describes four types of erotic transference: erotized, erotic, loving, and affectionate. He reiterates that erotized transference is based mostly on psychotic modalities, and erotic transferences on the neurotic modalities. With this paper, he newly adds the loving and affectionate transference, which are felt to fall in the arena of normal development, and differ from each other based on the level of maturation in the Oedipus complex. Lastly, he formulates a list for analysts that includes "guarantee factors" (p. 73) which allow them to work with the "highly explosive forces" (p. 73) of the erotic transference and maintain a "useful, rigorous, sensitive and sufficiently creative framework" (p. 73).

Bolognini describes the loving transference as consisting of two components, the neurotic part which is a defensive repetition of negative internal and external relational attitudes used to repress the positive aspects of the relationship with the love object. These defenses and resistances are born of guilts and fears of various types. This neurotic portion fights to hold prisoner the other portion of the loving transference: a healthy capacity for love, which is struggling to manifest itself and exist. As this second portion can be experienced, "understanding, trust, intimacy, contact, sexual specificity and complementarity, gradually come to be acknowledged and appreciated, albeit conflictually. Openness, warmth and trust are the natural result of the understanding encouraged by these factors" (p. 78).

Bolognini uses a detailed clinical example to help the reader follow along as he demonstrates a loving transference in which his patient can allow contact with a part of her that had been excluded for so long, and with good analytic help, she can now reintegrate.

When working with the loving transference in the analytic setting, the patient's development must be considered from to differing aspects. First, the defensive erotization must be acknowledged and interpreted. At the same time, the genuine loving aspect must be received by the analyst with respect and greeted with joy and used in the best possible way to help encourage the development of the capacity to love. As I read this, I thought of a brief and tender moment in my own analysis. I was expressing a wish of how it would be wonderful if I knew my analyst in another capacity, perhaps girlfriend, and we could go out for lunch, enjoy each other's company. I painted a picture, and when I was done, she concurred that that would indeed be lovely. I recall her voice being filled with warmth, and feeling content, even as I knew we both knew this would never happen. She was encouraging my capacity to love.

We are instructed to note that loving transferences can be difficult to work with because patients are often ashamed. They are not comfortable being involved in a one-sided relationship and fear that the analyst does not reciprocate, and they are often hesitant to indulge in their loving feelings because of all their inner fears. He traces this back to Oedipal disappointment when the disenchantment of not having the adored parent as a partner results in an unwillingness to risk any possibility of again being deeply disappointed.

Bolognini describes the affectionate transference as one that is not often seen. He defines it as "the transposition in the analysis of an ameliorated internal object relationship involving sexual specificity, gratitude, and quite free appreciation of the objects and subjects own relational potential, while at the same time respecting reality, and the relevant limits" (p. 83). He goes on to say that internally, the person has been able to move to the depressive position and work through the process of being a separate individual. The affectionate transference does not contain the same level of excitement found in the other erotic transference experiences. Rather, there is a phase of growth due to having 'good-enough' internal objects. It is often seen at the end of a very productive analysis, when the patient can resupply himself with a capacity for love.

Bolognini discusses some factors he believes will provide the analyst with a sufficient and rigorous attitude to cope with the 'highly explosive forces' of erotic transference, including a good psychoanalytic superego that has internalized boundary violations that are incompatible with the analytic situation. Identifying with our own analyst and supervisors help with this. Having a private life that is fulfilling in pursued activities and love relationships will be important. Being aware of your patient population, and consulting about countertransference experiences will prove helpful. A strong interest in pursuing psychoanalytic literature that encourages development of the person is needed. And lastly, an interest in establishing and guiding those younger than us and experiencing the pleasure in this type of giving. This is what Erikson (1950) refers to as 'generativity'. A good enough analysis and maturational experience will help us to move toward this advanced stage of personal development.

Jody Messler Davies (1998)

"Between the Disclosure and Foreclosure of Erotic Transference-Countertransference: Can Psychoanalysis Find a Place for Adult Sexuality?" by Jody Messler Davies (1998a) expands psychoanalytic understanding of the erotic transference as she puts forth questions about how we think about post-Oedipal adult sexuality in the erotic transference–countertransference process. She asks us to consider if there might ever be a time when the analyst is in a role other than the Oedipal parent when the erotic transference surfaces, and wonders if our current model offers room for the analytic couple to recognize important developmental changes that may take place during treatment.

She begins by speaking to the difficulty's psychoanalysts have had in managing the erotic countertransference. Some of us believe that such feelings do not exist, others feel any sexual or erotic response to a patient indicate pathology on the part of the analyst, indicating unresolved Oedipal or pre-Oedipal issues that require a return to analysis for further work. At the same time, there are others who would see it as important information to be understood and processed, but never to be shared with the patient. She goes on to say some, like her, have put forth the idea that:

> Judicious and tactful disclosure of the analysts sexual response in particular clinical situations can facilitate a demystification of infantile conflicts and a deepening of analytic inquiry particularly where the patient's disavowal of his or her own or the analysts sexuality becomes a substantive resistance to unraveling the transference-countertransference situation.
>
> (p. 748)

Davies shines a light on the fact that regardless of how we work with the erotic transference–countertransference, as a profession we have felt the need to do something with it: hide it, show it, think about whether to show or hide it. She points out the uncharacteristic need to want to act rather than to "understand its intrapsychic, interpersonal and developmental significance; what it means, in the first place when such erotic experiences infuses the analytic space" (p. 749). The idea that there are 'should's' and 'shouldn'ts' closes down our thinking, where the 'why we could' and the 'when we couldn't' may help us open and think about meaning of the countertransference experience.

Davies looks at developmental issues structuring countertransference experiences that become infused with sexual feelings. She asks where in developmental path are erotic issues entering the transference–countertransference process. She points to the absence of any theoretical presumptions about normal adult sexuality and how it manifests in clinical practice. She addresses a specific form of eroticism that may be encountered:

> It is a form of sexual aliveness that most often (though not exclusively) marks the termination phase of analysis- that form of sexual aliveness that exists in an inextricably intertwined state of dialectic tension with the deepening intimacy and potential interpersonal space of successful analytic work. It is that form of sexual vitality that suggests that maybe the analytic work is nearing an end, that the patient is ready for the world, and that it is time for us to let go.
>
> (p. 752)

Davies walks us through her thinking as she describes the 'post-Oedipal parent' that is necessary to be available to help the child-patient shift from the Oedipal stage into adolescent development where the erotic replaces perfect, magical, and unavailable objects. She sees the Oedipus complex as not something that is resolved and ending, but rather the beginning of what will be "a lifelong postoedipal process of recognizing, containing, enhancing, elaborating, and ultimately enjoying one's sexual subjectivity in myriad situations despite the formidable obstacles that tend to disrupt and impede this journey" (p. 758). It stands to reason that such a significant developmental shift will be felt within the patient and analyst's transference–countertransference experience. Davies demonstrates this developmental postulate with a detailed case example.

Her patient, David, states: "Forgive me if I'm wrong, but I think you're flirting with me". Though caught off-guard, Davies can think through what has been said and sees the patient is accurate. She carefully shares her thoughts and feelings, allowing us to be part of her experience:

> If I believe in what I have said here – that the individual's capacity to leave behind the fantasied world of oedipal circularity for the more reality based experiences of intimate sexual mutuality is predicated on the growing capacity to clearly distinguish between the real and imaginary – I would be hardput to legitimize anything but the most direct, self-reflective, nondefensive response. To the extent that seduction involved disowning sexuality, a direct, self-reflective, nondefensive response would embody the most rational counterpoint to the sexually aggressive, predatory 'anti-transference' mother – replacing her with a mother who could safely recognize her son's sexual appeal while managing her own erotic response and accompanying sense of loss. He would no longer be hers. She would set him free, she would allow herself to be "seen".
>
> (p. 761)

Davies reminds us we all have sexual desires, and that often we do not act on them. Part of being an adult includes having desires that won't be fulfilled; wanting without possessing. As analysts, she suggests that it is when we can release the role of adored other and allow our patients to see us as real, flawed humans that we can free them to seek a substitute in their own world. Being able to think about our own erotic countertransference, rather than deny or banishing them, will allow for deeper and more intimate work with our patients.

Sidney Philips (2001)

In his paper, "The Overstimulating of Everyday Life: I. New Aspects of Male Homosexuality", Sidney Philips (2001) presents the idea of how being a homo-sexually inclined boy raised in a Western heterosexual culture can lead to con-tinual erotic overstimulation and impact his adult sexual life. He examines the often-seen phenomena of adolescent homosexual boys' one-sided love affairs with adolescent heterosexual boys, and also proposes the overstimulation of eve-ryday life as a new model for understanding aspects of male homosexuality, and the analyst's countertransference when patients re-experience everyday overstim-ulation in the analytic work.

In the Western culture, many common childrearing practices and school activi-ties are implicitly set to heterosexual norms. Children may share a bedroom with same-sex siblings, and locker-rooms at schools are organized by gender (there has been some movement on this in our current cultural climate, but it remains, overall, the norm). Phillips helps us to think about how life being set up in terms of heterosexual norms may be surrounding a homosexually inclined boy in an environment of sexual overstimulation that affects his development, symptom formation, and adult sexual adaptation. A young boy showering with his father, sharing a room with his brother where they are in various stages of undress, or in locker rooms undressed with many other boys could be very overstimulating to a homosexually inclined young boy.

Phillips began thinking about this everyday overstimulation that surrounds homosexually inclined boys as a result of analyzing several adult gay men who had reported falling in love with a heterosexual boy during mid-adolescence. These patients all described being sexually attracted to boys and or men from the age of four or older. All the patients share stories of having fallen deeply in love with a heterosexual boy during mid-adolescence, though the declaration of love was never made. A boundary was kept in all the cases keeping any erotic behav-ior and discussion off limits allowing a mutual, close friendship to ensue. All the friendship/love affairs between the homosexual and heterosexual boys ended when the heterosexual boy turned his attention to a heterosexual girl.

Phillips refers to a paper by Isay (1989) where he suggested a developmental pathway specific to homosexual men that involves an early homosexual orienta-tion. Gay men report having early homoerotic fantasies from as young as age four or five, a period that lines up with the Oedipal stage in heterosexual boys. However, for homosexually inclined boys, their father would be the object of desire. Isay (1989) then revises theory to state that absent fathers do not create homosexual sons, but rather the homosexually inclined boy exhibiting Oedipal attraction to a conflicted father precipitates the latter's withdrawal.

Phillips explains this is a way to understand these unrequited love affairs. The homosexual boy is falling in love with a father replacement in the heterosexual boy to 'rework' his first childhood love affair. These friendships were "deeply felt on both sides: the love was mutual, even if the erotic attraction was not" (p. 1240). This was an essential component for the homosexual adolescent when seeking these friendships/loves. This was a way to repair the shame that was experienced when the father withdrew during the intense Oedipal desire. It is a way to experience love of another man without crossing the erotic boundary and risking yet another retreat of a loved man.

Phillips delineates the interplay between shame and overstimulation experienced by homosexual adolescent boys in everyday life. They live with fear of being exposed of their sexually aroused state that results from these close quarters with other adolescent boys. Phillips gives a touching example of a patient who shared a bed with his brother for years and felt aroused as they lay next to each other in bed and spoke with great shame as he told the analyst of touching his brother's chest long ago. The patient's sexuality remained hidden. This nightly overstimulation evoked the dynamics of shame and the need to hide. Without any internal defense against the shame, the only form of protection for the patient against his sexual arousal was avoidance of any exposure of the secret.

Phillips defines the 'overstimulation of everyday life' as:

> The frequent experiences, for example, of homosexually inclined children and adolescents who are placed again and again in the company of same-gendered parents, siblings and peers in various degrees of undress or nakedness and the subjective states generated by those experiences. It is a wholly different experience for a homosexually inclined boy to take a shower with his father or to sleep in the same bed with his brother than it is for a heterosexually inclined boy to do so. The homosexually inclined child or adolescent may be repeatedly overstimulated by gender pairings that paradoxically were meant to protect against just such a risk.
>
> (p. 1254)

When patients re-experience this type of everyday overstimulation in the transference, analysts may find themselves reacting in a dissociative way, similar to the hiding the patient had to do as a youngster to make sure no one was aware of his sexual arousal. The countertransference feelings may be distracted, bored, or sleepy as the patient talks in mind-numbing details of things that hide the burgeoning erotic transference. Alternately, the analyst may experience a countertransference of mild sexual arousal and associated fantasies followed by experiences of shame and/or guilt as if the reactions were indicative of a moral and professional failure. If the analyst can use these feelings in a self-analyzing fashion, they can shed light on the patient's early "warded off experiences of everyday overstimulation that resulted in shame" (p. 1261).

Phillips concludes this paper with an effort to keep open our continued psychoanalytic thinking when stating that we must also consider the impact on overstimulation in the lives of homosexual females. He asks what of the everyday overstimulation for heterosexual individuals? This, too, is an area that we have not yet addressed to understand the impact on heterosexual development.

Andrea Celenza (2006)

In "Threat of Male-to-Female Erotic Transference", Andrea Celenza (2006) looks at the female analyst's countertransference response and how it may either inhibit or foster the development of an erotic transference. Power, expression of aggression, sociocultural gender stereotypes, and maternal/containing transference are all considered in thinking about how female analysts may be impacted when working with difficult erotic transferences.

Celenza begins by discussing the idea that facilitation or inhibition of an erotic transference involves ideas about power: empowerment, the patient's experience with the empowered other, and the therapist's experience of the self as empowered. The treatment setting has a power structure, and this will be part of the context in which transferences and countertransferences develop. There is a differential of power because of the unequal distribution of attention between the analyst and patient, similar to the power differential between parent and child. The structure of the analytic setting

> provides the template for activation of the full spectrum of unresolved conflicts associated with early parent–child relationships and the ways these experiences were organized by gender. For some analysands, both aggressive and erotized strivings will be activated and experienced specifically in relation to this power differential.
>
> (pp. 1209–1210)

The analyst's comfort level with this power will influence countertransference responses and play a major role in what transferences are facilitated or shut out.

There is a significantly lower frequency of reports of erotic transferences in the female analyst–male patient dyad, and gender differences may explain some of this. Unconscious roots of gender development in relation to power and aggression along with sociocultural determinants may impact what occurs in this dyad in terms of transference development. The female analyst must accept the empowered analytic role and how that impacts both her and her patient. The analyst will have both conscious and unconscious determinants influencing how she reacts to being in this empowered role, which will influence her work with patients.

Celenza goes on to say that female analysts who are uncomfortable with this empowered role will deal with this by resisting, minimizing, or closing off their awareness of the power differential in the psychoanalytic setting. Currently, there is a sociocultural movement to dismantle traditional gender stereotypes and power imbalances attributed to gender. "In addition, for female analysts the resistance to power coincides with the traditional stereotypes themselves, especially those that have held an empowered male as sexually desirable while empowered females are more ambivalently portrayed" (p. 1211).

Some psychoanalytic writers have brought forth the idea that the female analyst's psychology and culturally determined countertransferences may prevent the development of a full erotic transference. The maternal/containing transference may be used defensively by the analyst patient pair if they unconsciously want to avoid more threatening affect, such as aggression or murderous wishes aroused along with sexual desire. The analyst may use the maternal/containing transference to stave off awareness and exploration of the emerging erotic transference and aggressive desires. It could also be used by the female analyst to escape conflict-laden ideas about the phallic power inherent in her role as analyst.

In discussing the aggressivization of the erotic transference, Celenza turns to Kernberg (1994), who attributes absent or muted erotic transferences in the female analyst–male patient dyad to narcissistic resistances against dependency and envy where sexualized longings for the analyst are experienced as humiliating or degrading. She further expands with Kernberg's thoughts on an intense form of transference love in which the transference is used to defend against an "aggressive sexualized seductiveness reflecting transference resistance against feeling dependent on an idealized analyst and an effort to reproduce a conventional cultural situation which the powerful, seductive male relates to the passive and idealizing female" (p. 1140). For some male patients, this aggressivization may activate murderous, envious and vengeful feelings that are an attempt to regain power and stave off feelings of dependency and humiliation that have surfaced due to the power discrepancy.

In the discussion section, Celenza notes that when either the analyst or patient insist on some form of total secrecy as a treatment condition, this is a red flag. The absence of any type of consultation during a treatment is considered a risk factor in cases of sexual boundary violations between therapists and patients. If a patient insists that the analyst never discuss the case in any way as a condition of treatment, what does an analyst do? Celenza considers what might happen if the analyst incorporates the idea of 'thirds' as part of the treatment frame from the beginning. In other words, the analyst may need to put into words to another trusted colleague, in confidence, the patient's story as they are hearing it. This reminded me of something a supervisor said to me when I was a candidate: 'we should consult or present every patient at some point during the treatment throughout our careers'. This is someone that I consult with on a regular basis.

In her paper, Celenza presented a case in which there was an erotic transference with extreme hostility and aggression toward her as the analyst. She points out that her case has similarities and differences with cases that involved sexual intimacy between analyst and patient. Both involve the erotic transference with the unmanageable hostility and aggression toward the analyst. With both, there is a motivation on the part of the analyst and patient to deny the existence of the aggression. In cases of female patients, the aggressivization of the transference is expressed as suicidality or other forms of aggression toward the self. Over 50 percent of male analyst–female patient sexual misconduct cases involve acute suicidality in the patient. Grandiose rescue fantasies may surface, and the analyst may resist seeking outside assistance in a fantasy of specialness and believing they are the only one who can help. Alternately, the grandiosity may mask intense shame and feelings of helplessness in the analyst.

Celenza shares that when she felt threatened by her patient's murderous fantasy toward her, she sought out and welcomed help. This is a crucial difference with cases of sexual intimacy between analyst and patient, where things are kept secret in the "treatment bubble" (p. 1226). Celenza asks where it becomes more acceptable to seek help if an analyst is threatened. Is there a gender difference? Does the disempowered, threatened one seek help to limit the power of the dominant one to find a way out of the situation? She thus implores us to further explore such matters if we are to deepen our understanding about these sexual transgressions.

Synthesis and conclusion

Freud (1915c) begins our understanding of the erotic transference with his important paper, "Observations on Transference Love". He explains we should expect this transference, stay with it by analyzing it, and never act on the patient's demands for love and/or sex. He teaches us to think about why it is surfacing at a particular time in the analysis and to be suspect of resistance on its arrival. Freud also shows the importance of being considerate of the patient by not shaming them for sharing these powerful feelings, but rather encouraging them to say all they can about them in an effort to help relieve them of their difficulties. He explains that the erotic transference comes from problematic early parts of the patient's life that are being repeated with the analyst.

Saul's (1962) paper, "The Erotic Transference", moves us forward by helping us understand the dynamic reasons why it is against good analytic judgment to respond to patients' demands for sex and/or love as expressed in the erotic transference. He tells us that if gratified, there will be no help for the patient's internal conflict, we would in essence be abusing the child part of our patient that is attempting to elicit a wish for parental love in the erotic transference, the patient would live in the surrogate love of the analyst rather than find a love in their own life, and the hostility and guilt of the erotic transference that must be analyzed could not be addressed if the patient's demands are fulfilled.

Blum's (1973) paper, "The Concept of Erotized Transference", focuses in on the erotized transference as a particular species of the erotic transference. It is on the extreme end of a spectrum, and is intense, vivid, and irrational. The erotized transference is passionate, insistent, and urgent. It is quite difficult to work with, evoking strong countertransference feelings in the analyst, greatly testing the alliance, with the patient having severe regressions and acting-out. Blum shares that progress will be slow and require great effort and demands on the part of the analyst, but if one stays the course, the patient will eventually be able to hear the analyst's *no* to the demands of the erotic transference.

Person (1985) discusses variances of the erotic transference based on gender and the makeup of the dyad in her paper, "The Erotic Transference in Women and Men: Differences and Consequences". Overall, she states that in women the erotic transference is a resistance to some other material that cannot yet be addressed, whereas men resist knowing of the erotic transference to avoid feelings of shame and humiliation for longing and dependency feelings. Exploration of all the four dyads (female patient–male analyst, male patient–female analyst, female–female, and male–male) are looked at, though there is limited information on the same-sex dyads, due to what is described as a paucity of information having been written about such erotic transferences. She felt this lack of reporting confirmed the idea that the transference in men is muted and verifies that men resist the erotic transference. I found myself wondering, based on the fact that this paper was written in 1985, if an additional reason might simply be fear of the psychoanalytic perspective that had been held that homosexuality was pathological, and any such feelings were indication that there were problems for both individuals in the dyad. Could it have been simply that it may have been problematic for an analyst to report or even privately discuss such erotic transferences at that time?

Two new additions to transference are added by Bolognini (1994) in "Transference: Erotised, Erotic, Loving, Affectionate". He adds to our understanding the loving transference and the affectionate transference. These transferences fall in the range of normal development and differ from each other based on the level of maturation in the Oedipus complex. In the loving transference, patients must hide any good, warm, loving feelings from the analyst, which must be interpreted to allow the patient to eventually be able to enjoy loving feelings. Bolognini also offers analysts important guidelines to work successfully with the erotic transference and not transgress.

Davies (1998a) asks us to consider furthering our understanding of sexual development theory in the paper "Between the Disclosure and Foreclosure of Erotic Transference-Countertransference: Can Psychoanalysis Find a Place for Adult Sexuality?". She expands thinking on post-Oedipal adult sexuality and speaks directly to all the turmoil that has been present when thinking and talking about the erotic countertransference through the psychoanalytic lens. She asks if we can think about this form of countertransference, as we do other types, and use it to further and deepen the treatment and potentially recognize growth that may be leading toward healthy termination for the patient.

Philips (2001) expands our understanding of developmental theory of homosexually inclined boys in his paper, "The Overstimulating of Everyday Life: I. New Aspects of Male Homosexuality". We can understand life through the daily experiences of a homosexually inclined boy living in a heterosexually normed Western culture. The daily overstimulation experienced by the homosexually

inclined boy and the resulting ways it may impact his adult sexuality is important knowledge for all analysts as a way to further understand of aspects of male
homosexuality. He expands developmental theory of homosexually inclined boys
using the frequently seen adolescent love affair of homosexual boys with heterosexual boys. He traces this back to the heterosexually inclined boy's Oedipal
love, the father. However, the adolescent is now attempting to rework the earlier
experience by constructing a situation where he may receive a man's love without
the earlier rejection that had been felt.

Celenza (2006) furthers our understanding of female analyst's countertransference response to male patients' erotic transference in her work, "Threat of
Male-to-Female Erotic Transference". She introduces the importance of power,
empowerment, and the power differential in the analytic setting, and how a female
analyst's response to this power position will influence the development or inhibition of the erotic transference. Additionally, she brings forth in a clear and educa-
tive way how hostility and aggression can be a very integrated part of the erotic
transference presentation. The idea of including a 'third' is presented as one of the
differences seen when erotic transferences are not acted on versus when sexual
transgressions occur because there can no longer be an insular bubble of only
analyst–patient, which leaves room for the analyst to think with another/others.

Each of these eight papers, spanning a hundred-year period, this survey of the
literature shows how psychoanalytic theory has presented the idea of 'transference-
love' and has continued to evolve in thinking about erotic transferences. The
paper also demonstrates how the literature has advised to work clinically with
erotic transferences and countertransferences and offer our patients relief from
their internal fixations. We have moved from Freud's idea that could only consider
women falling in love with their male doctors as inevitable to allowing room to
think about erotic transference in all four analytic dyads, countertransference feelings to be understood and made use of in helpful ways in to further the treatment,
looking at the hostility and aggression in the erotic transference, the role of power
and its impact on erotic transference, an awareness of the loving transference
and the affectionate transference, considering post-Oedipal adult sexuality and
developmental theory, and everyday overstimulation and its role in the development of the homosexually inclined boy. Clinical work has been helped and moved
advanced with each of these contributions.

Clearly, there is plenty to teach and discuss with what has been written thus
far. Hopefully, the writing, talking about, and furthering our understanding of
the erotic and erotized transferees will continue, resulting in a greater capacity to
work clinically with our patients in an attempt to offer them richer lives with a
great capacity for love.

Chapter 11

Erotic countertransference revelations

Andrea Celenza

In this contribution, I wrestle with the question of the analyst's verbal disclosure of erotic countertransference.[1] Is it ever clinically indicated? How far can we allow our participation and emotional engagement with the patient to be explicitly articulated? And most importantly, under what conditions might the disclosure of erotic countertransference be permissible and even warranted?

The need for this chapter is prompted by my work consulting on the problem of sexual boundary transgressions, but also my awareness (from supervisory settings, academic contexts, and other professional contexts) that analysts and analytically-oriented therapists do communicate their loving and/or erotic feelings more than is formally reported. This clinical reality needs to be brought under the umbrella of transparent clinical discourse so that the questions and conundrums attendant to these moments can be examined and discussed.

Further, it is also prompted by the current debates, mostly within the relational literature, on the challenge of self-disclosure of such feelings. I firmly believe it is not enough to have a mandate that clinicians refrain from directly expressing all modes of feeling. Clinicians do not abide this and are not helped by such a blanket prohibition.

There are now a few (counted on one hand) examples in the clinical literature on the explicit revelation of erotic countertransference, beginning with Jody Davies' (1994) paper, "Love in the Afternoon: A Relational Reconsideration of Desire and Dread in the Countertransference," where she revealed a courageous and controversial disclosure that she had made to her patient, where she told him that she "has had sexual fantasies about [him], many times" (p. 166).[2] In response to much of the debate that her paper generated, Davies (1998b) observed a phobic dread of erotic transference and countertransference due to the absence of theory. To this, I add the absence of clear guidelines for technique and this chapter is an attempt to address this gap.

Almost immediately after publication, Davies' (1994) paper instigated a torrent of authors weighing in on the use and misuse of disclosure of erotic countertransference with most advising against it except in unusual circumstances. Gabbard (1994) warned of unduly burdening the patient and foreclosing mourning. Benjamin (1994) wondered about the role of power and hate in the interaction. Cooper

(1998) advised "virtual disclosure", a statement that implies the analyst is willing to explore the patient's perceptions [of the analyst as a desiring other] while not definitively affirming the analyst's perspective. Both Gabbard (1994, 1996) and Benjamin (1997) emphasized the role of the analyst in protecting transitionality. Gabbard also cites Modell's (1991) writings that the asymmetry in the analytic setting is not an asymmetry of desire but an asymmetry of *the communication* of desire. Mann (1994) argues that erotic countertransference disclosure would only serve to stimulate incestuous wishes. Cornell (2009) believes direct disclosure of the analyst's personal, sexual interest or disinterest trivializes the erotic space. Hirsch (1994) directs us to the relational-conflict model of psychoanalytic theory for guidance in making use of the analyst's private countertransference feelings.

On the other side are those analysts who argue that judicious and tactful disclosure of erotic countertransference can facilitate the treatment (see Lijtmaer, 2004, for a helpful review). Knoblauch (1995) observes other affects that often go unexplored and unarticulated due to 'something else that occurred' in the moment of erotic disclosure, such as anxiety and fear of the analyst's actions. Slavin, Rahmani, and Pollock (1998) believe erotic countertransference disclosures can facilitate the demystification of infantile conflicts. Hoffman (2009) suggests that, while no single standardized mode of expression is generalizable, the "challenge for each of us is . . . to express that passionate response in a manner that is usable by each patient" (p. 635).

A more recent example is, ironically, embedded in a paper written as a celebratory discussion of Davies' 1994 paper twenty years later, by Jill Gentile (2013), entitled, "From *Truth or Dare* to *Show and Tell*: Reflections on Childhood Ritual, Play and the Evolution of Symbolic Life". In this discussion, Gentile describes a moment in her treatment of a patient, Mr. G, where she holds his beloved wooden baseball bat from childhood, offered to her during a session. Gentile's musings at the time included her awareness of multiple symbolic meanings for the patient, including the phallic imagery. At one point, she put the bat across her chair like a barrier and acknowledged to him that perhaps she is afraid she may get a little too excited for her comfort, if not for his, and for their work together. Despite the negation and future tense (i.e. "she may get" as opposed to "she is"), she presents Mr. G with the possibility of her embodied arousal. The use of physical objects (toys) had been frequent in the treatment with Mr. G and Gentile has a lovely way of likening the process to play therapy, defining the various dynamics in terms of structured games, including *Hide and Seek, Truth or Dare, Show and Tell* as well as *Lost and Found*. I have no problem with these analogies nor with the presentation of physical objects and their use, a common enough occurrence in many treatments, usually in the form of gifts. Most importantly, Gentile keeps her eye and analytic discipline intact by exploring the meanings of the various toys at every turn, including the implied erotic messages in many.

One factor that is important to note embedded in both Davies (1994) and Gentile's (2013) vignettes is that both authors acknowledged *a context wherein some important therapeutic work needed to be accomplished.* For Davies, it was a final moment of impasse, during the termination phase of a successful treatment that had, nevertheless, left a crucial piece of work undone. For Gentile, the moment in the treatment that led to the disclosure revolved around the patient's experience of himself as a potent man, perhaps wanting to test and claim his prowess through offering various symbolic props to his analyst. The issue I aim to highlight here is that the disclosures were made with the hope and intent (at least consciously) to perform some therapeutic piece of work. We might surmise that the analyst's countertransference experience was likely to be layered, with some measure of anxiety, confusion, and/or frustration, however these are not made explicit and we cannot definitively know. Necessity being the mother of invention, the rationale for the disclosure followed salutary lines, and in Davies' case, include disclaimers that all other possible analytic responses had been tried and failed. In Gentile's case, the erotic countertransference disclosure seems to occur organically, as a moment in an otherwise playful, even flirtatious process aimed at expanding the symbolic play space. For Gentile, holding the bat created a "markedness" that served to hold the line between the concrete and the symbolic.[3] Perhaps the placement of the bat (across her lap) symbolized a similar marking and Gentile trusted her patient to interpret these markings without confusion or overstimulation. I do not doubt the descriptions of either process material and in the spirit of collaboration and furthering our thinking about these crucial therapeutic choice points, I offer the following thoughts.

In contemporary theoretical discourse, including the colloquium conducted on the IARPP list-serve (May, 2013) on Irwin Hoffman's paper, "Therapeutic Passion in the Countertransference" (2009), there is, in my point of view, a tendency to justify analyst self-disclosure, especially when the content is positive, affectionate, loving, or even erotic, by making reference to the *mutual* dimension of the analytic relationship and adducing (I think, mistakenly) that the disclosure is encompassed entirely from within this dimension. I believe understanding disclosures in this way overemphasizes the mutuality inherent in the analytic process while minimizing or even ignoring the equally persistent, continual, and simultaneous dimension of asymmetry.

Clearly, we are still quaking from (and recovering from the trauma of) the classical depriving stance of abstinence, neutrality, and anonymity, whether occurring in our own personal treatments, supervisions, or other aspects of training. We can be tempted to overcorrect by emphasizing the mutual dimension of the analytic frame. This is, I believe, an oversimplification of the analytic process and contract. Hoffman (2009) himself asserts the complex dialectic between mutuality and asymmetry (see also Aron, 1996; Hoffer, 1996) that defines the analytic process *at all times*, whether or not we consistently adhere to this mandate. Maintaining the tension of this dialectic is our ethical responsibility and it defines a complex set of imbalances.

The undisclaimable analytic frame

In order to fully address the implications, context, and theoretical implications of analyst personal disclosure (and erotic countertransference in particular), it is important to review the intricacies and contradictions of the analytic frame. Aside from the important need to be mindful of the context in which any disclosure is made, it is imperative to keep in mind that the very dimensions that define the analytic frame (those of *mutuality and asymmetry*) also intensify the patient's experience and longing for intimate, sexual union in this context. Before entertaining the possibility of a verbal, personal disclosure by the analyst, a brief description of the complexity of the analytic frame is presented.

First, there is the background experience of *mutual, authentic engagement*. This dimension is bi-directional in the sense that there are two persons committed to working together, engaging in a relation that will involve emotional experiences on both sides, and withstanding whatever emerges. This commitment holds out the hope for and promise of continued acceptance and understanding for the patient of even the most loathsome aspects of the self. Since the analysand is invited and encouraged to reveal areas of self-contempt and self-hatred, the promise of continued engagement in the face of these aspects of the self is simultaneously dangerous and highly seductive. The danger is inherent in the risk of rejection or withdrawal, despite the (sometimes overt) promise of sustained commitment. The seductive aspect coincides with the universal wish to be loved totally, without judgment or merit. Though rarely actualized, the wish to be loved totally without having to give anything in return remains a lifelong wish (see, for example, S. Smith's [1977] discussion of *The Golden Fantasy*). These longings are never given up but can be set aside as life fails to fulfill them. One aim of analysis is to fail the patient in tolerable ways so that the analysand may mourn these wishes and get on with her or his life.

The seductiveness of unconditional acceptance and commitment is fueled and intensified by other fundamental, universal wishes as well. These include: (a) the desire for *unity* (to be loved totally and without separateness), (b) the desire for *purity* (to be loved without hate and unreservedly), (c) the desire for *reciprocity* (to love and be loved in return), and finally, (d) the desire for *omnipotence* (to be so powerful that one is loved by everyone everywhere at all times). All of these universals figure prominently in fantasies of romantic perfection and are stimulated in the treatment setting since the treatment contract partly instantiates their gratification. It can be said that the treatment frame both stimulates and frustrates these universal wishes which will be freighted with the analysand's historical meanings and unresolved developmental trauma.

The analytic context is stimulating, seductive, and frustrating for the analyst as well. The frustration for the analyst is inherent in the second dimension of the treatment context, defined by the *asymmetric distribution of attention*. This comprises the analyst's professional and disciplined commitment to the analysand. In the psychotherapeutic and psychoanalytic setting, the treatment context is defined by the asymmetric distribution of attention paid to the patient.

We are used to thinking of the power imbalance between analyst and patient as one-way, i.e., the analyst has it and the patient does not. But this oversimplifies the structure of the analytic set-up. The axis of asymmetry is hierarchical in that it is constituted by several power relations, yet it is not straightforward or simple. It is an asymmetry that frames several power imbalances at once, each of which is ambivalently held by both patient and analyst. On the one hand, the analysand is in a desiring or needful state (thereby vulnerable and disempowered) while the analyst, in contrast, is relatively contained in his/her need of the analysand (and is thereby empowered). This is the aspect of asymmetry that we usually refer to as the structured power imbalance in the analytic set-up. Simultaneously, however, the analysand is positioned as special (and thereby of elevated status) while the analyst is discounted in terms of the distribution of attention paid (and thereby dismissed, in terms of his/her personal needs). We know the long-term effects on the analyst of this arrangement if s/he is not mindful of self-care (Celenza, 2010). Both types of asymmetry deepen and are concretized as the treatment progresses in the sense that the analyst continues to learn more about the patient while the reverse (relatively speaking) is not true. As noted previously, the asymmetry in the analytic relationship is not an asymmetry of desire, but an asymmetry of the *communication of* desire (Modell, 1991). The emotional process is mutually involving but the content of the discourse is asymmetric. Further, the mutuality inherent in the analytic matrix is ineluctable; in contrast, the asymmetry is a matter of discipline and must be maintained continuously by the analyst.

With regard to the relationship between mutuality and asymmetry, these two axes function in dialectical relation. For example, the asymmetry deepens the analysand's need for mutual, affective engagement as a way to ameliorate the humiliating, disempowering aspects of being the continuous focus of attention. In this way, it is the facilitation and encouragement of the analysand's openness and vulnerability that makes the analyst's love and acceptance all the more important (Hoffman, 1998). Likewise, it is the extent to which the analysand reveals him/herself, especially areas of self-hatred and self-loathing, that intensifies the analyst's power in relation to the analysand. In other words, it is the analysand's self-revelations that empowers the analyst and intensifies the desire for a mutual, authentic engagement (deriving from the analysand's disempowerment).

In these ways, the treatment setting is a complex structure that uniquely instantiates several contradictions. Especially interesting is the way in which the treatment setting combines these two contradictory axes: the axis of equality and mutuality (a 'we're in this together' type of experience) along with the contradictory and imbalanced focus on the analysand (a 'you are in this alone' type of experience). The treatment setting is the point at which these two axes converge, creating the paradox of a simultaneous feeling of mutuality and asymmetry, of intimacy and aloneness, and of equality and hierarchy. These are tensions that the analysand is persistently moved to resolve, to disequilibrate or level the hierarchy, so to speak, and to make contact with the authentic person behind the professional role.

Maintaining the frame in the heat of the moment

All of these structural dimensions of the analytic set-up define the boundaries of the process and cannot be disclaimed, i.e., when we accept payment for services, we symbolically accept responsibility to maintain the various power imbalances while mutually participating in the enterprise. A question I often find myself asking when presented with clinical material that involves what I consider to be either gratuitous countertransference disclosure or a countertransference disclosure (especially erotic) borne of frustration in the context of impasse is, What happened to the focus on the patient's experience? This does not mean sidestepping the 'elephant in the room' but it does mean expressing the significance of the patient's erotic conveyance (in whatever form, e.g., a toy, a gift, a gesture, a question) *in terms of the patient's desire(s)*.

A related issue to erotic countertransference disclosure that is often raised as a rationale in favor of disclosure, especially in cases of sexual boundary transgressions, is the extent to which the patient may be viewed as a responsible adult and the corollary issue, how the analyst should take responsibility for his/her participation. How one views the assumptions inferred in these questions will bear on the technical decisions and their rationales regarding erotic countertransference disclosure. Hoffman (2009) asserts that the patient is a separate person with a will and is "not putty in the analyst's hands" with the capacity to agree, differ, and collaborate in meaningful ways (p. 619). I do not disagree with this assertion, however I believe the quality and extent of psychological autonomy and self-control, even experience of separateness for all of the above-named capacities fluctuates during the course of treatment and, especially under the sway of an intense erotic transference, can be markedly reduced for a protracted period of time.

Further, I suggest that the development of an erotic transference and the capacity to be under its spell for a period of time is a strength, a capacity to be fully receptive to the analytic process and the intensity of affects it evokes. This capacity to give oneself over to the process in a more or less complete way is parallel to the classical notion of a transference neurosis, once believed to be a *sine qua non* of analyzability. So I do not intend to imply that the patient is any less of an adult under the sway of an intense erotic transference but rather, has cultivated the capacity to become fully receptive to a set of emotional reactions that he/she may not have control over for a period of time.

Because the analytic process is mutual and because we participate in it, we have varying stakes in what we want or need at any one time. This means there is the possibility of defensively disclaiming one aspect or another of this complex interchange and our capacity for self-deception should never be underestimated, even for the highly sophisticated theoretician and experienced, seasoned analyst. For example, we can exclusively focus on our own personal meanings or intentions while denying the patients'. Often I have heard, "That phrase was not erotic, I had no intention of crossing that line," or, "I am very clear on the boundaries . . . I told her I loved her and I meant it in a Platonic way". In these statements, the analyst selectively disattends to the patient's experience or intent, including how he or she might attribute a different meaning to the very same words. It is not enough to be clear about one's own intent and there is a responsibility to refrain from engaging in actions that might be misconstrued. When we focus on the patient's experience, we engage our capacity to appreciate and monitor the asymmetry in the analytic relationship.

Further, there is frequently a minimization of the erotic potential in otherwise seemingly non-erotic language. We may desexualize, in the moment, words that at some later point may represent a highly charged conveyance. Language itself is elastic; surface and depth easily overlap manifest and latent meanings. More importantly, the treatment setting is rife with sexual metaphor – as noted in earlier chapters, the penetrating gaze and interpretative activity of the analyst can be experienced as 'coming inside'. Similarly, the background all enveloping support of the analyst's affirmative attitude and concrete office (including the couch itself) can engender feelings of sensual erotic longings.[4]

Comfort and clarity with erotic language

Especially for those patients whose presenting areas of distress involve sexual inhibitions, defensively eroticized activity, or compulsions, the analytic setting will provide ample opportunity to demonstrate erotic longings in metaphorized, displaced and hopefully directly expressed modes. Conversely, sexualized material presented as pervasive or intensely preoccupying may be revealed as masking non-erotic longings. In any case, attunement to sexual metaphor and *comfort with erotic language* will be essential in aiding a patient's self-understanding and the ability to explore his/her erotic life. For many patients, the language of the treatment becomes more direct, shame-free, and thereby more intimate as the treatment progresses. This does not imply the need or therapeutic value of disclosing the analyst's erotic feelings for the patient, however, though it may be more tempting to do so with greater comfort in the discourse. I am emphasizing here a comfort with erotic language that is used to explicate and directly clarify *the patient's longings and experience*, on conscious and unconscious levels, as they arise in either disguised or direct forms. Hoffman (2009) asks, "Why, in fact, do we favor implicit over explicit forms of affirmation, indeed, implicit over explicit expressions of love?" My response is simple: We always favor explicit forms of expressions of affirmation and love, including erotic longings *from the patient's point of view, but not from the analyst's* because love is a four letter word.

At the same time, the appreciation of the stimulating potential of direct expressions of the analyst's erotic longing or love must always be balanced with the need to be comfortable, explicit, and non-euphemistic in expressing erotic themes. Galit Atlis (2012) recounts a moment in a treatment with a female patient where the analyst repeated, exactly in the way her patient had expressed it, an erotic phrase about a man she had been dating:

> "In the dream you give him a blowjob," [Atlis says]. Ella giggles, "Oh no, it sounds terrible coming out of your mouth". [Atlis] get[s] confused for a moment and wonder[s] whether this was not the term that she had used. "Did I phrase it differently?" [she asks]. "No, not at all," she replies, "That's exactly what I said, it's just so strange to hear it . . . it's easier to say it . . . maybe even easier to do it," she jokes.
>
> (p. 4)

The analyst should speak about sex in plain language, as Atlis demonstrates, especially in ways the patient is familiar and the process should proceed to expand the discourse in this direction. I mention this vignette here, however, to highlight how powerful and saturated with meaning our words are to our patients. When *we* say something, it is not the same thing as when our *patient's do*.[5] It is not symmetrical nor is it predictable, but at the same time, we need to cultivate a measure of ease in speaking about sexuality and erotic life. One way to 'break the ice' in cultivating ease is to do what Atlis did, to repeat our patient's words exactly as they express their desires in order to facilitate a mutual comfort and hopefully advance the discourse as the work proceeds. But again, this is always from the perspective of the patient's point of view.

One supervisee was uncomfortable repeating her male patient's desire to be "fucked up the ass" (his words) yet knew she had to refer to his erotic desires in some way in order to explore them. I suggested to her that she repeatedly say the phrase out loud in her car (windows closed) to acquire more comfort with his way of putting it. She did this and became more comfortable using his phrase in their work.

The delicate balance that I aim to put forth, *ease with erotic discourse while maintaining the focus on the patient's desires* is illustrated in another clinical vignette. A patient was in the midst of an intense erotic transference for many months. He was explicitly fixated on the need to know if I was erotically attracted to him. He stated that he did not care whether I liked him or even loved him, but wanted to know what my sexual feelings were for him. This quality of the transference arose in the context of his uncertainty of his desirability toward women in general and whether they wanted to have sex with him. Questions about his potency and doubts about his 'masculine' attributes were lifelong struggles and had a severely inhibiting effect on his ability to perform sexually.

At this particular time in the treatment, this patient and I were in the midst of a heated transference/countertransference dance where his longings and my desires were relatively in sync and I had hoped my attraction to him would be palpably apparent to him. To be simple and direct, I was aware of being sexually attracted to him and hoped he could feel this though I had not directly articulated my feelings to him nor did I intend to do so. He consistently stated that he was unsure how I felt about him and that he needed to know, at times he insisted he would be cured if I would only say yea or nay to this crucial question. (Believe me, it was tempting.)

One day, this patient came to our session and offered me a gift, a rectangular box covered with beautiful Asian silk. Inside were two Chinese Health Balls. (I think these used to be called *Worry Balls* and yes, they were about the size of two testicles.) He asked me to take them out of the box and gestured how they are held "in order to release stress". I couldn't help but chuckle a bit and I probably also blushed, but what I said was, "You want me to see and feel your potency . . . to touch your balls". Before the reader cringes with embarrassment and dismisses this interchange as one that could not possibly be uttered with either seriousness or therapeutic intent, I must add that this patient and I had cultivated a way of speaking about his sexual desires, his body, and his sexual functioning that by now was an organic part of our discourse. This was the fourth year of a moving analysis and I knew I could speak to him using such blunt language. (This is not particularly unique to this patient and me; I try to cultivate similar plain speak with all of my patients, especially those with sexual symptoms or inhibitions. Not all patients develop an ease with such language, but I do see the development of some measure of comfort as part of the analytic work.)

At the time of this vignette and after I had expressed the above statement, this patient seemed immediately struck, not by my language, but by how he had unconsciously displayed his desires. Because he had already directly, in words, expressed these desires to me, he was not shocked or ashamed by the unconscious meaning of his gift. He also was able to experience some pleasure in my interpretation of the possible unconscious meaning, chuckling at the stark simplicity and almost innocence of his conscious intent. It was a moment of truth (Slavin, 2013) that acknowledged in words what we each already knew he felt. Ultimately, we were both amused by his unconscious selection.

Verbal disclosure of erotic countertransference

In all of the vignettes I have read involving a disclosure of erotic countertransference, I am always left with a lingering question. Why didn't the analyst maintain her/his focus on the patient's experience rather than respond to the patient's expressed wish (at least on the surface) to be told what the analyst feels toward him/her? It is my experience that the wish to *know the analyst sexually* is invariably complicated and usually highly conflicted. And if it is not, *it should be*, given the inherent power imbalances and (oedipal) transference structure from where the desire likely arises. Herein lies another responsibility of the analyst – to explicate the various levels of meaning in the patient's erotic desire for the analyst as someone who is virtually or at least explicitly unknown.

I realize all of our patients have a sense of our being, personality, and style; I do not engage nor endorse some impossible objectivist striving toward anonymity. But the analytic contract involves the conscious asymmetric distribution of attention and focus to remain on the patient's experience, so why is there a push, in some extraordinary moments, to shine the spotlight on the analyst's experience? I also realize we use our awareness of our feelingful engagement at all times to receive unconscious communications and to inform our affective responses to the patient, but the responsive focus remains on the patient's experience, even if we explicitly verbalize some of the ways in which we have metabolized, processed, or experienced the patient (see Renik, 1999).

I have nothing against passion in the countertransference and in the treatment as a whole (compare, for example, Hoffman, 2009). Despite the unusual power distributions and uneven focus of attention in the analytic relationship, it is still a human interaction with ongoing mutual, bi-directional passionate engagement. In addition, our patients come to us for help with affect regulation and desires for transformation by advancing their understanding of their emotional and erotic desires. Emotional constriction in the analyst would hardly help in this enterprise. However, too often the defensive uses of erotic feelings can mask corrupting influences in the treatment and our capacity for self-deception must always sound a cautionary note.

Necessary conditions of erotic countertransference disclosure

I will directly address the conditions under which verbal erotic countertransference disclosure may be permissible and perhaps even warranted by introducing an extended vignette and then offering explicit guidelines. The context for the way in which this verbal disclosure by the analyst came about was indirect and circuitous, but it is an example of an explicit, verbal disclosure of erotic countertransference that I believe meets the conditions for which such an intervention is permissible.

A supervisee was putting together a write-up to present a case at a clinical conference, a vignette and corresponding discussion that contained a description, privately held by her, of her loving, affectionate, and erotic countertransference with a patient. In preparing for the conference, she had obtained the patient's consent to write about an interchange that had occurred during the late phase of a successful analysis and in writing about this interchange, she described her passionate, affectionate, and erotic feelings for him in preparation for the presentation. When he gave his permission for the presentation, she invited him to read what she would be presenting with the intention that she would redact the dicey parts about her own feelings toward him. Interestingly, he refused the invitation to read her write-up, getting her off the hook for the moment. He said, "I don't want to interrupt what's going on between us right now". She prepared the write-up and presented the case at the clinical conference.

A year later, during the termination phase of the treatment, the patient asked to read what she had written. With some mixture of curiosity and trepidation, she printed out the write-up, *purposefully unredacted*, and handed it to him. He read it then and there, during the session. As I mentioned, the write-up included a description of her erotic countertransference toward him. Though it was not detailed, she explicitly said that she returned the sexual attraction that he had felt towards her. Her acknowledgments in the write-up were embedded in descriptions of love and affection for him and appreciation of his various personality attributes.

As part of the background in this case, it should be mentioned that periodically during the treatment, this patient had expressed his longing and attraction toward his analyst. He was happily married and the treatment had solidified his bond with his wife as well. Though the analyst never explicitly told him she found him sexually attractive, she did sense that he knew how she felt, given how safe he felt he was with her and how obvious her enjoyment of him was. Several times, he stated directly that he thought he knew how she felt about him and understood she could not express her feelings directly. In short, he could *feel* their mutual attraction.[6]

After reading the write-up, which included at least two instances where she spelled out her affection for him, her enjoyment of his sense of humor and her erotic attraction to him, he said, "I am so touched". He went on to say, "I already knew this was how you felt. In fact, I've told you how you feel about me many times! But it's nice to have it returned in an explicit way. I will keep this tucked away in my heart forever". She teared up when he said this and there was a palpable mutual appreciation for each other.

You might think this vignette and my approval of the way my supervisee handled this interchange contradicts all I have discussed thus far about verbal disclosure of erotic countertransference. To my mind, it does not, for the following reasons, all of which are interrelated. *First*, and most importantly, the patient already had surmised, sensed, thought about, and 'knew' his analyst returned his erotic feelings. How did he sense this? My supervisee is a passionate woman and does not withhold her *nonverbal responsivity* and passionate involvement in her relationships. That is different from explicitly revealing her feelings, putting them into words, and making them the focus in the session.[7] *Second,* the treatment had helped this patient hone his antennae for detecting his impact on others, in particular strengthening his ability and confidence in his capacity to erotically arouse another person. Thus, he did not need a verbal confirmation and, most importantly, the revelation of the analyst's feelings was not necessary to effect these advances in the therapeutic action. His capacity to surmise her attraction to him is a strength that partially grew out of the treatment and her disclosure was not aimed to fill a gap in his capacity to detect this. *Third*, the disclosure occurred in the termination phase of a successful analysis where the communication of the analyst's feelings was not used to perform a therapeutic function. The revelations did not occur in the context of a treatment impasse or the analyst's frustration with unrealized gains. I believe it is acceptable to reverse the asymmetry at the end of a treatment when doing so for affectionate reasons and when the therapeutic work is largely completed. One indication that this condition is met revolves around the awareness that the disclosure is not meant to move the patient in some unfinished therapeutic direction. Nor is it meant to sidestep or circumvent important mourning. This is a difficult judgment call but one that will revolve around the analyst's awareness that the patient has demonstrated his/her acceptance of the limitations in the analytic relationship. It is crucial that this work has already been done. *Fourth*, this patient was high functioning and especially so by the end of the analysis. He was capable (in the analyst's and my judgment) of receiving this communication without confusion and without becoming overstimulated. In other words, we surmised that he would be able to retain the 'I would if I could' sentiment (see Chapter 4), transitionality, or the 'as if' context, the persistently containing frame around her feelings for him. *Fifth*, this supervisee was aware of the performative nature of words, i.e., words *do*, they are not passive, they are actions, and the revelation of erotic feelings, especially when mutual, is a form of foreplay. This was a reason for her disciplined restraint throughout the analysis and is linked to her assessment of the patient's ability to receive this communication without becoming confused now. *Sixth*, all of these issues were being discussed in an ongoing and detailed way with a trusted supervisor, consultant, or peer group. The presence of supportive yet potentially correcting 'thirds' is a must as our capacity for self-deception is an ever-present corrupting potential. *Seventh*, and finally, the analyst and supervisor(s)/consultant(s) agreed that the analyst was contained in terms of her personal needs. Monitoring our own personal needs for self-care is an ongoing responsibility, much like the need for musicians to have finely tuned instruments.

Final thoughts

I have had many patients who want to know how I feel about them. Sometimes this revolves specifically around my erotic feelings for them. They want me to 'touch' them with words as a symbol that I care for them in a personal way, beyond my professional role and beyond their being my patient. "I need something concrete to let me know you really care for me," they might say in one way or another. The fantasy about the spoken word is that it is objectified, a *thing* that will *touch* them in a more palpable and lasting way than their silent speculations might.[8] But words have their own ambiguity and often do not last beyond the moment they are uttered.

I usually do not reciprocate a request for such signs of my caring, whether it be a loving or desiring phrase, a hug, or a meeting outside the office, but instead make it the very subject of a detailed analysis. Why do they need such an overt sign of my affection? Why is their ability to detect what I feel for them, in a personal, authentic way (not beyond my professional role but embedded within it) not speaking to them? Our focus becomes their overreliance on the concrete level of experience, overt expressions that indeed include words, in an effort to obtain an illusorily permanent reassurance that they are loved, wanted, or appreciated in a lasting way. I remind them that any concrete sign or gesture will fall flat in the absence of a resonance with what they experience within our relationship on a feeling level.

I remind my patients that words are at once ephemeral and ambiguous, that persons can lie with words in a way they cannot with feelings. I encourage my patients to explore what they know *based on what they feel* is between us so that words become unnecessary, even thin compared to the depth of attachment between us. It is as if the treatment is designed to hone their radar or antennae, directed at their own feelingful experience of the relationship, including and especially, what they sense I feel about them.

Earlier in my career, I put how I felt about a patient into words and I regret it. This was a male patient referred to me during my internship year. He spent the first year or two letting me know directly and vociferously that he had no use for me, that I was not helping him, and that he was intellectually (and in all other ways) superior to me. I hung in there through this grueling year and did not let on that I actually (silently) agreed with him. He made me feel incompetent, unhelpful, and painfully inexperienced as well as doubtful that I had any natural talent for this line of work. At the same time, he never missed a session. And he got better, progressing in his career, social relations, and becoming more personally appealing. He had a sharp sense of humor and endeared himself to me despite himself. He also paid me an unreasonably low fee and I colluded with this arrangement beyond his financial need for fear of unleashing a torrent of abuse about how I did not deserve a penny higher.

After a few years, I mustered the confidence to broach the subject of raising his fee. Through a discussion with a trusted supervisor, we speculated that there was a strong, mutual attachment despite all this angry tension on the surface that needed to be explicitly acknowledged. I said to my patient, "Because of the love that there is there between us (or some such awkward phrasing), I've neglected to raise your fee and I think we should talk about it". Well, the fee became a side issue very quickly, because all he heard was that four letter word. He came in the next day dressed in a suit and high with expectations that we would begin dating. It was painful for both of us to come to terms with that.

It is tempting to think that making statements, directly answering a question, will quiet inner doubts. Why not just tell the patient I like him? Or love him, especially since I do? But as one patient often put it, "*Acta non verba*": Latin for "Action, not words" (or so he tells me). Words can have an excruciatingly short lifespan. (In effect, you just said you love me, but what about now?) The only lasting truths are the ones we feel, the ones that are informed by our guts, our ability to intuit, feel, and recognize as real what is already in the atmosphere between us. These are the skills I try to help my patients hone; to pay attention to what they know because they can *feel* it. Knowing from that level is more reliable compared to what anyone might say. After all, words hold power only as they resonate with a recognized felt inner state.

I do not mean to resurrect the prudery or wooden anonymity of the blank screen caricature, but to encourage a profound appreciation for the complexity of the analytic relationship, including the multitude of meanings and modes of relating emergent at any one time. While the mutuality of our participation in the analytic relationship is inescapable, unwitting, and undisclaimable, the asymmetry is our promise, our commitment to our patients and our discipline. Though it is equally rife with unconscious factors, it is more of a choice at each moment. Thereby, the promise of asymmetry is a tempting playground for self-deceptive rationalizations, deriving from our own needs that can seduce us away from our promise of disciplined self-restraint.

Notes

1 For a selection of readings on this controversial subject, see Davies, 1994, 1998b, 2001; Gabbard, 1994, 1996, 1998; Barrett, 2003; Cooper, 1998; de Peyer, 2002; Elise, 2002; Hoffman, 1998, 2009; Knoblauch, 1995; Rabin, 2003; Sherman, 2002, Ehrenberg, 1992; Maroda, 2012; Renn, 2013; Renik, 1993; Hirsch, 2008; Kuchuck, 2013; Atlas, 2013; Wells, 2013.
2 It is always a risk to present clinical material out of context. For the serious reader, I encourage a full acquaintance with this material and its context by reading the entire articles cited herein.
3 Personal communication, October, 2013.
4 Samuels (1985) speaks of the alchemical metaphor used by Jung in describing personality, dialogical 'fluids' and the analytical 'container'.
5 In Atlas' case, the phrase referred to a third person. How much more saturated with meaning the phrase would be if it were uttered in relation to the two of them.
6 A testament, no doubt, to mutual right-hemisphere unconscious communications accounting for their unverbalized 'knowing' of each other (Schore, 2011).
7 As Slavin (2013) has succinctly put it, "The moment of truth [is] speaking the truth, *not* disclosing it" (p. 145, italics in original). Similarly, Bollas (1983) cautions that direct expression of countertransference, "must be experienced by the patient as a legitimate and natural part of the analytic process. If it comes as a shock then the analyst has failed in his technique" (p. 12).
8 See Celenza (2011) for a related discussion on touch in the analytic setting.

References

2018-year-in-review#2018. Retrieved December 23, 2018, from https://pornhub.com/ insights: 2018-year-in-review#2018.

Abraham, K. (1913). Restrictions and transformations of scopophilia in psychoneurotics with remarks on analogous phenomena in folk-psychology. In: *Selected Papers on Psychoanalysis*, ed., K. Abraham, pp. 161–172. New York: Brunner/Mazel.

Abramova, O., Baumann, A., Krasnova, H., and Buxmann, P. (2016). Gender differences in online dating: What do we know so far? A systematic literature review. *Conference paper presented at the 49th Hawaii International Conference on System Sciences*, January 5–8, 2016.

Adair, M.J. (1993). A speculation on perversion and hallucination. *International Journal of Psychoanalysis* 74: 81–92.

Akhtar, S. (2000). The shy narcissist. In: *Changing Ideas in a Changing World: Essays in Honor of Arnold Cooper*, eds. J. Sandler, R. Michels, and P. Fonagy, pp. 111–119. London: Karnac Books.

Akhtar, S. (2009). *Comprehensive Dictionary of Psychoanalysis*. London: Karnac Books.

Akhtar, S. (2017). Open-mouthed and wide-eyed: Psychoanalytic reflections on curiosity. *Journal of the American Psychoanalytic Association* 65: 285–304.

Allen, D.W. (1974). *The Fear of Looking*. Charlottesville, VA: University Press of Virginia.

Almansi, R. (1979). Scopophilia and object loss. *Psychoanalytic Quarterly* 48: 601–619.

Als, H. (2016). Maggie Nelson's many selves. *The New Yorker*. Retrieved from: www. newyorker.com/magazine/2016/04/18/maggie-nelsons-many-selves, accessed January 13, 2019.

Altman, N. (1995). *The Analyst in the Inner city: Race, Class, and Culture through a Psycho-analytic Lens*. Hillsdale, NJ: Analytic Press.

Andrews, W.G. and Kalpakli, M. (2005). *The Age of the Beloveds: Love and the Beloved in Early-Modern Ottoman and European Culture and Society*. Durham, NC: Duke University Press.

Anisimowicz, Y. and O'Sullivan, L.F. (2017). Men's and women's use and creation of online sexually explicit materials including fandom-related works. *Archives of Sexual Behavior* 46: 823–833.

Arango, A. (1989). *Dirty Words: Psychoanalytic Insights*. Northvale, NJ: Jason Aronson.

Arlow, J.A. (1969a). Unconscious fantasy and disturbances of conscious experience. *Psychoanalytic Quarterly* 38: 1–27.

Arlow, J.A. (1969b). Fantasy, memory, and reality testing. *Psychoanalytic Quarterly* 38: 28–51.

Arlow, J.A. (1980). The revenge motive in the primal scene. *Journal of the American Psychoanalytic Association* 28: 519–541.

Armstrong, E.A., Enland, P., and Fogarty, A.C. (2010). Orgasm in college hookups and relationships. In: *Families as They Really Are*, ed. B. Risman, pp. 362–377. New York: W.W. Norton.

Armstrong, E.A., Enland, P., and Fogarty, A.C. (2012). Accounting for women's orgasm and sexual environment in college hookups and relationships. *American Sociological Review* 77: 435–462.

Aron, L. (1996). *A Meeting of Minds: Mutuality in Psychoanalysis*. Northvale, NJ: Analytic Press.

Atlas, G. (2013). What's love got to do with it? Sexuality, shame, and the use of the other. *Studies in Gender and Sexuality* 14: 51–58.

Atlas, G. (2015). Touch me, know me: The enigma of erotic longing. *Psychoanalytic Psychology* 32: 123–139.

Atlis, G. (2012). Sex in the kitchen: Thoughts on culture and hidden desire. *Psychoanalytic Perspectives* 9: 1–12.

Aulagnier, P. (1975). *The Violence of Interpretation: From Pictogram to Statement*, London: Brunner-Routledge.

Aulagnier, P. (1986). Demande et identification. In: *Un Interprète en Quête de Sens*, ed. P. Aulagnier, pp. 161–198. Paris: Ramsay.

Bagnol, B. and Esmeralda M. (2012). *Gender, Sexuality and Vaginal Practices,* Maputo, Mozambique: Universidade Eduardo Mondlane.

Bailey, J.M., Gaulin, S., Agyei, Y., and Gladue, B. (1994). Effects of gender and sexual orientation on evolutionary relevant aspects of human mating psychology, *Journal of Personality and Social Psychology* 66: 1081–1093.

Bak, R.C. and Stewart, W.A. (1975). Fetishism, transvestism, and voyeurism: A psychoanalytic approach. In: *American Handbook of Psychiatry, Second Edition, Volume 3*, eds. S. Arieti and E.B. Brody, pp. 352–365. New York: Basic Books.

Balsam, R.H. (2003). The vanished pregnant body in psychoanalytic female development theory. *Journal of the American Psychoanalytic Association* 51: 1153–1179.

Barrett, M.M. (2003). Desire and the couch: Perspectives from both sides of the analytic encounter. *Psychoanalytic Psychology* 20: 167–169.

Basch, M.F. (1983). The perception of reality and the disavowal of meaning. *Annual of Psychoanalysis* 11: 125–153. New York: International Universities Press.

Baselice, K. and Thomson, J.A. (2018). Evolutionary psychology. In: *Textbook of Applied Psychoanalysis*, eds. S. Akhtar and S. Twemlow, pp. 81–97. London: Routledge.

Bass, A. (1997). The problem of concreteness. *Psychoanalytic Quarterly* 66: 642–682.

Bass, A. (2000). *Difference and Disavowal: The Trauma of Eros*. Stanford: Stanford University Press.

Bataille, G. (1985). *Visions of Excess: Selected Writings 1927–1939*, ed. A. Stoekl. Minneapolis, MN: University of Minnesota Press.

Baumeister, R.F. (2000). Gender differences in erotic plasticity: The female sex drive as socially flexible and responsive. *Psychological Bulletin* 126: 347–374.

Bell, A.P. and Weinberg, M.S. (1978). *Homosexualities: A Study of Diversity Among Men and Women*. New York: Simon and Schuster.

Benjamin, J. (1988). *The Bonds of Love: Psychoanalysis, Feminism, and the Problem of Domination*. New York: Pantheon Books.

Benjamin, J. (1991). Father and daughter: Identification with difference – a contribution to gender heterodoxy. *Psychoanalytic Dialogues* 1: 277–299.

Benjamin, J. (1994). Commentary on papers by Tansey, Davies, and Hirsch. *Psychoanalytic Dialogues* 4: 193–201.

Benjamin, J. (1997). Psychoanalysis as a vocation. *Psychoanalytic Dialogues* 7: 781–802.

Benjamin, J. (2018). *Beyond Doer and Done To: Recognition Theory, Intersubjectivity and the Third*. New York: Routledge.

Bergler, E. (1944). Eight prerequisites for the psychoanalytic treatment of homosexuality. *Psychoanalytic Review* 31: 253–286.

Bergler, E. (1957). Voyeurism. *Archives of Criminal Psychodynamics* 2: 211–225.

Bettleheim, B. (1983). *Freud and Man's Soul*. New York: Alfred Knopf.

Beymer, M.R., Weiss, R.E., Bolan, R.K., Rudy, E.T., Bourque, L.B., Rodriguez, J.P., and Morisky, D.E. (2014). Sex on demand: Geosocial networking phone apps and risk of sexually transmitted infections among a cross-sectional sample of men who have sex with men in Los Angeles County. *Sex Transmitted Infection* 90: 567–572.

Bick, E. (1964). Notes on infant observation in analytic training. *International Journal of Psycho-Analysis* 45: 558–566.

Bion, F. (1981). Memorial meeting for Dr. Wilfred Bion. *International Review of Psycho-Analysis* 8: 3–14.

Bion, F (1994). The days of our lives. In: *The Complete Works of W.R. Bion, Volume XV*, eds. C. Mawson and F. Bion. London: Karnac Books, 2014.

Bion, W.R. (1970). *Attention and Interpretation*. London: Maresfield.

Bion, W.R. (1991). *Learning from Experience*. London: Karnac Books.

Bion, W.R. (1994). *Cogitations: New Extended Edition*, ed. F. Bion. London: Karnac Books.

Bion, W.R. (2015). *War Memoirs: 1917–1919*, 2nd edition, ed. F. Bion. London: Karnac Books.

Bivona, J. and Critelli, J. (2009). The nature of women's rape fantasies: An analysis of prevalence, frequency and contents. *Journal of Sex Research* 46: 33–45.

Blatt, S. (2008). *Polarities of Experience: Relatedness and Self-Definition in Personality Development, Psychopathology, and the Therapeutic Process*. Washington, DC: American Psychological Association.

Blechner, M. (2015). Bigenderism and bisexuality. *Contemporary Psychoanalysis* 51: 503–522.

Bloom, K. (2006). *The Embodied Self: Movement and Psychoanalysis*. London: Karnac.

Blum, H.P. (1973). The concept of erotized transference. *Journal of the American Psychoanalytic Association* 21: 61–76.

Blum, H.P. (1977). Masochism, the ego ideal, and the psychology of women. In: *Female Psychology: Contemporary Psychoanalytic Views*, ed. H.P. Blum, pp. 157–191. Oxford, England: International Universities Press.

Blum, H.P. (1990). Freud, Fliess, and the parenthood of psychoanalysis. *Psychoanalytic Quarterly* 59: 21–40.

Bollas, C. (1983). Expressive uses of the countertransference: Notes to the patient from oneself. *Contemporary Psychoanalysis* 19: 1–33.

Bollas, C. (1987). *The Shadow of the Object: Psychoanalysis of the Unthought Known*. New York: Columbia University Press.

Bollas, C. (1992). Cruising in the homosexual arena. In: *Being a Character*, pp. 144–164. New York: Hill and Wang.

Bolognini, S. (1994). Transference: Erotised, erotic, loving, affectionate. *International Journal of Psychoanalysis* 75: 73–86.

Bonomi, C. (2015). *The Cut and the Building of Psychoanalysis, Vol 1: Sigmund Freud and Emma Eckstein*. London: Routledge.

Bonomi, C. (2018). *The Cut and the Building of Psychoanalysis, Vol II: Sigmund Freud and Sandor Ferenczi*. London: Routledge.

Bowlby, J. (1969). *Attachment and Loss*. New York: Basic Books.

Boyer, L.B. (1967). Office treatment of schizophrenic patients: The use of psychoanalytic therapy with few parameters. In: *Psychoanalytic Treatment of Characterological and Schizophrenic Disorders*, eds. L.B. Boyer and P.L. Giovacchini, pp. 143–188. New York: Science House.

Brady, M.T. (2011). Sometimes we are prejudiced against ourselves: Internalized and external homophobia in the treatment of an adolescent boy. *Contemporary Psychoanalysis* 47: 458–479.

Bridges, A.J., Bergner, R.M., and Hesson-McInnis, M. (2003). Romantic partners' use of pornography: Its significance for women. *Journal of Sex and Marital Therapy* 29: 1–14.

Brodman, J. (2017). *Sex Rules!: Astonishing Sexual Practices and Gender Roles Around The World*. Coral Gables, FL: Mango Publishing Group.

Bromberg, P.M. (1998). *Standing in the Spaces: Essays on Clinical Process, Trauma, and Dissociation*. Hillsdale, NJ: The Analytic Press.

Brown, L.J. (2012). Bion's discovery of alpha function: Thinking under fire on the battlefield and in the consulting room. *International Journal of Psycho-Analysis* 93: 1191–1214.

Brown, N.O. (1991). *Apocalypse and/or Metamorphosis*. Berkeley, CA: University of California Press.

Buss, D. (1988). The evolution of human intrasexual competition: Tactics of mate attraction. *Journal of Personality and Social Psychology* 54: 616–628.

Buss, D. (1989). Sex differences in human mate preferences: Evolutionary hypothesis testing in 37 cultures. *Behavioral and Brain Sciences* 12: 1–49.

Buss, D. (2004). *Evolutionary Psychology: The New Science of the Mind*, 2nd ed. Boston, MA: Pearson Education, Inc.

Butler, J. (1990). *Gender Trouble: Feminism and the Subversion of Identity*. New York: Routledge.

Calef, V. and Weinshel, E. (1984). Anxiety and the restitutional function of homosexual cruising. *International Journal of Psychoanalysis* 45: 45–53.

Campbell, D. (2018). Alienating identifications and sexuality. In *Psychic Bisexuality: A British-French Dialogue*, ed. R. Perelberg, pp. 227–242. London: Routledge.

Caplan, P. (1984). The myth of women's masochism. *American Psychologist* 39: 130–139.

Carvalho, J., Gomes, A.Q., Laja, P., Oliveria, C., Vilarinho, S., Janssen, E., and Nobre, P. (2013). Gender differences in sexual arousal and affective responses to erotica: The effects of type of film and fantasy instructions. *Archives of Sexual Behavior* 42: 1011–1019.

Celenza, A. (2006). The threat of male-to-female erotic transference. *Journal of the American Psychoanalytic Association* 54: 1207–1231.

Celenza, A. (2010). The guilty pleasure of erotic countertransference: Searching for radial true. *Studies in Gender and Sexuality* 11: 175–183.

Celenza, A. (2011). Touching the patient. In: *Unusual Interventions: Alternations of the Frame, Method, and Relationship in Psychotherapy and Psychoanalysis*, ed. S. Akhtar, pp. 165–176. London: Karnac Books.

Celenza, A. (2014). *Erotic Revelations: Clinical Applications and Perverse Scenarios*. New York: Routledge.

Chivers, M., Rieger, G., Latty, E., and Bailey, J.M. (2004). A sex difference in the specificity of sexual arousal. *Psychological Science* 15: 736–744.

Chivers, M., Seto, M.D., and Blanchard, R. (2007). Gender and sexual orientation differences in sexual response to sexual activities versus gender in actors in sexual films. *Journal of Personality and Social Psychology* 93: 1108–1121.

Chivers, M., Seto, M., LaLumiere, M.L., Laan, E., and Grimbos, T. (2010). Agreement of self-reported and genital measures of sexual arousal in men and women: A meta-analysis. *Archives of Sexual Behavior* 39: 5–56.

Chodorow, N.J. (1992). Heterosexuality as a compromise formation: Reflections on the psychoanalytic theory of sexual development. *Psychoanalysis and Contemporary Thought* 15: 267–304.

Chrystal, P. (2016). *In Bed with the Romans*. Gloucestershire: Amberley Publishing.

Cleland, J. (1748). *Memoirs of a Woman of Pleasure*. New York: CreateSpace Independent Publishing Platform, 2018.

Coehlo, P. (2014) The Alchemist: 25th Anniversary Edition, P. 58, New York, Harper Collins Publisher Inc.

Coen, S.J. (1981). Sexualization as a predominate mode of defense. *Journal of the American Psychoanalytic Association* 4: 893–920.

Cohler, B.J. and Galatzer-levy, R.M. (2008). Freud, Anna, and the problem of female sexuality. *Psychoanalytic Inquiry*, 28: 3–26.

Cooper, S.H. (1998). Flirting, post-Oedipus, and mutual protectiveness in the analytic dyad: Commentary on paper by Jody Messler Davies. *Psychoanalytic Dialogues* 8: 767–779.

Corbett, K. (1996). Homosexual boyhood: Notes on girlyboys. *Gender and Psychoanalysis* 1: 429–461.

Corbett, K (2009a). Boyhood femininity, gender identity disorder, masculine presuppositions, and the anxiety of regulation. *Psychoanalytic Dialogues* 19: 353–370.

Corbett, K. (2009b). *Boyhoods: Rethinking Masculinities*. New Haven, CT: Yale University Press.

Corbett, K. (2011). Gender regulation. *Psychoanalytic Quarterly* 80: 441–459.

Corbett, K. (2013). Shifting sexual cultures, the potential space of online relations, and the promise of psychoanalytic listening. *Journal of the American Psychoanalytic Association* 61: 25–44.

Cornell, W.F. (2009). Stranger to desire: Entering the erotic field. *Studies in Gender and Sexuality* 10: 75–92.

Cosmides, L. and Tooby, J. (1992). Cognitive adaptations for social exchanges. In: *The Adapted Mind*, eds. J. Barklow, L. Cosmides, and J. Tooby, pp. 601–624. New York: Oxford University Press.

Cosmides, L. and Tooby, J. (2013). Evolutionary psychology: New perspectives on cognition and motivation. *Annual Review of Psychology* 64: 201–229.

Crespi, L. (1995). Some thoughts on the role of mourning in the development of a positive lesbian identity. In *Disorienting Sexuality: Psychoanalytic Reappraisals of Sexual Identities*, eds. T. Domenici and R.C. Lesser, pp. 19–32. New York: Routledge.

Cunningham, M., Druen, P., and Barbee, A. (1997). Angels, mentors, and friends: Trade-offs among evolutionary, social, and individual variables in physical appearance. In: *Evolutionary Social Psychology*, eds. A. Simpson and D.T. Kenrick, pp. 109–140. Hillsdale, NJ: Lawrence Erlbaum Associates, Inc.

Darieussecq, M. (2002). *Le Bébé*. Paris: Paul Otchakovsky Laurens.

Davies, J.M. (1994). Love in the afternoon: A relational reconsideration of desire and dread in the countertransference. *Psychoanalytic Dialogues* 4: 153–170.

Davies, J.M. (1998a). Between the disclosure and foreclosure of erotic transference-countertransference: Can psychoanalysis find a place for adult sexuality? *Psychoanalytic Dialogues* 8: 747–766.

Davies, J.M. (1998b). Thoughts on the nature of desires: The ambiguous, the transitional, and the poetic. Reply to commentaries. *Psychoanalytic Dialogues* 8: 805–823.

Davies, J.M. (2001). Erotic overstimulation and the co-construction of sexual meanings in transference-countertransference experience. *Psychoanalytic Quarterly* 70: 757–788.

Davoine, F. and Gaudilliere, J.M. (2004). *History beyond Trauma*. New York: Other Press.

Darwin, C. (2004). *On the Origin of Species*, 1859. Abingdon: Routledge.

de Kuyper, E. (1993). The Freudian construction of sexuality: The gay foundations of heterosexuality and straight homophobia. In: *If You Seduce a Straight Person, Can You Make Them Gay?*, eds. J.P. De Cecco and J.P. Elia, pp. 137–144. New York: Harrington Park Press.

De Mijolla, A. (ed.) (2005). *International Dictionary of Psychoanalysis*. Farmington Hills, MI: Thomson Gale.

de Peyer, J. (2002). Private terrors: Sexualized aggression and a psychoanalyst's fear of her patient. *Psychoanalytic Dialogues* 12: 509–530.

Deutsch, H. (1944). *The Psychology of Women: A Psychoanalytic interpretation, Vol. 2. Motherhood*. New York: Grune and Stratton.

Diamond, L. (2005). A new view of lesbian subtypes: Stable versus fluid identity trajectories over an 8-year period. *Psychology of Women Quarterly* 29: 119–128.

Diamond, L., Dickenson, J., and Blair, K. (2017). Stability of sexual attractions across different timescales: The roles of bisexuality and gender. *Archives of Sexual Behavior* 46: 193–204.

Diamond, M. (2017). The missing father function in psychoanalytic theory and technique: The analyst's internal couple and maturing intimacy. *Psychoanalytic Quarterly* 86: 861–887.

Dimen, M. (2000). The body as Rorschach. *Studies in Gender and Sexuality* 1: 9–39.

Dimen, M. (2005). Sexuality and suffering, or the eew! factor. *Studies in Gender and Sexuality* 6: 1–18.

Dimen, M. and Goldner, V. (2004). *Gender in Psychoanalytic Space: Between Clinic and Culture*. New York: Other Press.

Draper, P. and Harpending, H. (1988). A sociobiological perspective on the development of human reproductive strategies. In: *Sociobiological Perspectives on Human Development*, ed. K.B. MacDonald, pp. 340–372. New York: Springer-Verlag.

Drescher, J. (2008). A history of homosexuality and organized psychoanalysis. *Journal of the American Academy of Psychoanalysis and Dynamic Psychiatry* 36: 443–460.

Ducat, S. (2004). *The Wimp Factor: Gender Gaps, Holy Wars, and the Politics of Anxious Masculinity*. Boston, MA: Beacon Press.

Ducat, S., Metzl, M., and Rothschild, L. (2008). Male fantasies/fantasies of maleness: Psychoanalytic readings of anxious masculinity. *Panel presentation at the Division 39 Spring Meeting*, April 2008, New York, NY.

Ehrenberg, D.B. (1992). *The Intimate Edge: Extending the Reach of Psychoanalytic Interaction*. New York: W.W. Norton.

Ehrensaft, D. (2007). Raising girlyboys: A parent's perspective. *Studies in Gender and Sexuality* 8: 269–302.

Ehrensaft, D. (2009). One pill makes you boy, one pill makes you girl. *International Journal of Applied Psychoanalytic Studies* 6: 12–24.

Eidelberg, L. (1945). A contribution to the study of the masturbation phantasy. *International Journal of Psychoanalysis* 26: 127–137.

Eidelberg, L. (ed.) (1968). *The Encyclopedia of Psychoanalysis*. New York: Free Press.

Eigen, M. (1993/2004). Ideal images, creativity, and the Freudian drama. In: *The Electrified Tightrope*, ed. A. Phillips, pp. 95–108. London: Karnac Books.

Eigen, M. (1998). One reality. In: *The Couch and the Tree: Dialogues in Psychoanalysis and Buddhism*, ed. A. Molino, pp. 217–230. New York: North Point Press.

Eigen, M. (1999). The area of faith in Winnicott, Lacan, and Bion. In: *Relational Psychoanalysis: The Emergence of a Tradition*, eds. S. Mitchell and L. Aron, pp. 1–38. Hillsdale, NJ: Analytic Press.

Eigen, M. (2001). *Ecstasy*. Middletown, CT: Wesleyan University Press.

Eigen, M. (2004). *The Sensitive Self*. Middletown, CT: Wesleyan University Press.

Eigen, M. (2006). *Lust*. Middletown, CT: Wesleyan University Press.

Eigen, M. (2007). *Feeling Matters: From the Yosemite God to the Annihilated Self*. London: Karnac Books.

Eigen, M. (2009). *Flames from the Unconscious: Trauma, Madness, and Faith*. London: Karnac Books.

Eigen, M. (2010). *Eigen in Seoul: Volume One, Madness and Murder*. London: Karnac Books.

Eigen, M. (2011). *Contact with the Depths*. London: Karnac Books.

Eigen, M. (2012). *Kabbalah and Psychoanalysis*. London: Karnac Books.

Ellenberger, H.F. (1970). *The Discovery of the Unconscious: The History and Evolution of Dynamic Psychiatry*. New York: Basic Books.

Elise, D. (2002). Blocked creativity and inhibited erotic transference. *Studies in Gender and Sexuality* 3: 161–195.

Elman, R.A. (1997). Disability pornography: The fetishization of women's vulnerabilities. *Violence Against Women* 3: 257–270.

Erikson, E. (1950). *Childhood and Society*. New York: W.W. Norton.

Escoffier, J. (2011). Imagining the she/male: Pornography and the transsexualization of the heterosexual male. *Studies in Gender and Sexuality* 12: 268–281.

Essig, T. (2015). The gains and losses of screen relations: A clinical approach to simulation entrapment and simulation avoidance in a case of excessive Internet pornography use. *Contemporary Psychoanalysis* 51: 680–703.

Fain, M. (1954). Contribution à l'étude du voyeurism. *Revue Française de Psychanalyse* 18: 177–192.

Fairfield, S. (2002). Analyzing multiplicity: A postmodern perspective on some current psychoanalytic theories of subjectivity. In: *Bringing the Plague: Toward a Postmodern Psychoanalysis*, eds. S. Fairfield, L. Layton, and C. Stack, pp. 69–102. New York: Other Press.

Fairfield, S., Layton, L., and Stack, C. (eds.) (2002). *Bringing the Plague: Toward a Postmodern Psychoanalysis*. New York: Other Press.

Fajardo, B. (2001). The therapeutic alliance: Coupled oscillators in biological synchrony. *Paper presented at the Chicago Psychoanalytic Society*, September 25, 2001.

Feingold, A. (1992). Gender differences in mate selection preferences: A test of the parental investment model. *Psychological Bulletin* 112: 125–139.

Fenichel, O. (1935). The scoptophilic instinct and identification. In: *The Collected Papers, First Series*, eds. H. Fenichel and D. Rapaport, pp. 373–397. New York: W.W. Norton, 1953.

Fenichel, O. (1945). *The Psychoanalytic Theory of Neurosis*. New York: W.W. Norton.

Ferenczi, S. (1911). On obscene words. In: *First Contributions to Psycho-Analysis*, pp. 132–153. New York: Bruno/Mazel, 1955.

Ferenczi, S. (1916). Pollution without dream orgasm and dream orgasm without pollution. In: *Further Contributions to the Theory and Technique of Psychoanalysis*, pp. 297–304. New York: Boni and Liveright, 1927.

Ferenczi, S. (1921). A contribution to the understanding of the psychoneuroses of the age of involution. In: *Final Contributions to the Problems and Methods of Psychoanalysis*, pp. 205–211. New York: Bruno/Mazel, 1955.

Ferenczi, S. (1922). Psychoanalysis and the mental disorders of general paralysis of the insane. In: *Final Contributions to the Problems and Methods of Psychoanalysis*, ed. S. Ferenczi, pp. 351–370. New York: Bruno/Mazel, 1955.

Ferenczi, S. (1933). On the confusion of tongues between adults and the child. In: *Final Contributions to the Problems and Methods of Psychoanalysis*, ed. S. Ferenczi, pp. 155–167. New York, NY: Basic Books, 1955.

Fetting, M. (2015). *Michael Eigen: Rich Impacts. In: Living Moments: On the Work of Michael Eigen*, eds. S. Bloch and L. Daws, pp. 177–196. London: Karnac.

Fisher, H.E. (1989). Evolution of human serial pair-bonding. *American Journal of Physical Anthropology* 78: 331–354.

Fisher, T.D., Moore, Z.T., and Pittenger, M-J. (2012). Sex on the brain? An examination of frequency of sexual cognitions as a function of gender, erotophilia, and social desirability. *Journal of Sex Research* 49: 69–77.

Fleischman, D. (2016). An evolutionary behaviorist perspective on orgasm. *Socioaffective Neuroscience and Psychology* 6: 32130–32140.

Fonagy, P. and Allison, E. (2015). A scientific theory of homosexuality for psychoanalysis. In: *Sexualities: Contemporary Psychoanalytic Perspectives*, eds. A. Lemma and P. Lynch, pp. 125–137. New York: Routledge.

Ford, J. and England, P. (2014). Hookups, sex and relationships at college. *Online Article*. Retrieved from: https://contexts.org/blog/hookups-sex-and-relationships-at-college/, accessed January 16, 2019.

Foucault, M. (1977a). What is an author? In: *Language, Counter-Memory, Practice: Selected Essays and Interviews*, ed. D.F. Bouchard, pp. 113–138. Ithaca, NY: Cornell University Press.

Freud, A. (1923). The relation of beating-phantasies to a day-dream. *International Journal of Psychoanalysis* 4: 89–102.

Freud, A. (1936). *The Ego and the Mechanisms of Defense*. New York: International Universities Press, 1966.

Freud, S. (1895a). Project for a scientific psychology. *Standard Edition* 1: 281–391.

Freud, S. (1895b). Studies on hysteria. *Standard Edition* 2: 1–323.

Freud, S. (1896). Heredity and the aetiology of the neuroses. *Standard Edition* 3: 141–156.

Freud, S. (1899). Screen memories. *Standard Edition* 3: 299–322.

Freud, S. (1900). The interpretation of dreams (second part). *Standard Edition* 5: 339–627.

Freud, S. (1905a). Three essays on the theory of sexuality. *Standard Edition* 7: 135–243.

Freud, S. (1905b). Fragment of an analysis of a case of hysteria. *Standard Edition* 7: 1–122.

Freud, S. (1908a). Hysterical phantasies and their relation to bisexuality. *Standard Edition* 9: 155–166.

Freud, S. (1908b). Creative writers and day-dreaming. *Standard Edition* 9: 141–154.

Freud, S. (1910). Five lectures on psycho-analysis, Leonardo da Vinci, and other works. *Standard Edition* 11: 209–218.

Freud, S. (1911). Formulations on the two principles of mental functioning. *Standard Edition* 12: 213–226.

Freud, S. (1912a). Contributions to a discussion on masturbation. *Standard Edition* 12: 239–254.

Freud, S. (1912b). On the universal tendency to debasement in the sphere of love (Contributions to the Psychology of Love II). *Standard Edition* 11: 177–190.

Freud, S. (1912c). Types of onset of neurosis. *Standard Edition* 12: 227–238.

Freud, S. (1912d). The dynamics of transference. *Standard Edition* 12: 97–108.

Freud, S. (1914). On narcissism: An introduction. *Standard Edition* 14: 69–102.

Freud, S. (1915a). Instincts and their vicissitudes. *Standard Edition* 14: 117–140.

Freud, S. (1915b). The unconscious. *Standard Edition* 14: 159–216.

Freud, S. (1915c). Observations on transference love. *Standard Edition* 12: 157–171.

Freud, S. (1915d). Our attitude towards death. *Standard Edition* 14: 289–300.

Freud, S. (1916–17). Introductory lectures on psychoanalysis. *Standard Edition* 15: 15–173.

Freud, S. (1917). Introductory lectures on psycho-analysis. *Standard Edition* 16: 241–463.

Freud, S. (1919). 'A child is being beaten': A contribution to the study of the sexual origin of perversions. *Standard Edition* 17: 175–204.

Freud, S. (1920a). The psychogenesis of a case of homosexuality in a woman. *Standard Edition* 18: 145–174.

Freud, S. (1920b). Beyond the pleasure principle. *Standard Edition* 18: 7–64.

Freud, S. (1923). The ego and the id. *Standard Edition* 19: 1–66.

Freud, S. (1924a). Dissolution of the Oedipus complex. *Standard Edition* 19: 171–188.

Freud, S. (1924b). The economic problem of masochism. *Standard Edition* 19: 155–170.

Freud, S. (1925). Some psychical consequences of the anatomic distinction between the sexes. *Standard Edition* 19: 241–258.

Freud, S. (1926). The question of lay analysis: Conversations with an impartial person. *Standard Edition* 20: 177–250.

Freud, S. (1927). Fetishism. *Standard Edition* 21: 147–158.

Freud, S. (1930). Civilization and its discontents. *Standard Edition* 21: 59–145.

Freud, S. (1933). New introductory lectures to psychoanalysis. *Standard Edition* 22: 7–182.

Freud, S. (1937). Analysis terminable and interminable. *Standard Edition* 23: 209–255.

Freud, S. (1938). An outline of psychoanalysis. *Standard Edition* 23: 139–207.

Freud, S. (1939). Moses and monotheism. *Standard Edition* 23: 7–137.

Furnham, A., Swami, V., and Shah, K. (2006). Body weight, waist-to-hip ratio and breast size correlates of ratings of attractiveness and health. *Personality and Individual Differences* 41: 443–454.

Gabbard, G.O. (1994). Commentary on papers by Tansey, Hirsch, and Davies. *Psychoanalytic Dialogues* 4: 203–213.

Gabbard, G.O. (1996). The analyst's contribution to the erotic transference. *Contemporary Psychoanalysis* 32: 249.

Gabbard, G.O. (1998). Commentary on paper by Jody Messler Davies. *Psychoanalytic Dialogues* 8: 781–789.

Gagnon, J.H. and Simon, W. (1973). *Sexual Conduct: The Social Sources of Human Sexuality*. Livingston, NJ: Aldine.

Gallup, G., Ampel, B., Wedberg, N., and Pogosjan, A. (2014). Do orgasms give women feedback about mate choice? *Evolutionary Psychology* 12: 958–978.

Gallup, G., Towne, J.P., and Stolz, J. (2018). An evolutionary perspective on orgasm. *Evolutionary Behavioral Sciences* 12: 52–69.

Garza, E. (2007). *Getting Off: One Woman's Journey Through Sex and Porn Addiction*. New York: Simon and Schuster.

Gediman, H.K. (2017). *Stalker, Hacker, Voyeur, Spy: A Psychoanalytic Study of Erotomania, Voyeurism, Surveillance, and Invasions of Privacy*. London: Karnac Books.

Gentile, J. (2013). From "Truth or Dare" to "Show and Tell": Reflections on childhood ritual, play and the evolution of symbolic life. *Psychoanalytic Dialogues* 23: 150–169.

Gerard, L. (2017). Take a stand on your Grindr profile. Retrieved from: www.advocate.com/race/2017/5/09/take-stand-your-grindr-profile, accessed October 18, 2018.

Gerson, S. (2009). When the third is dead: Memory, mourning, and witnessing in the aftermath of the holocaust. *International Journal of Psycho-Analysis* 90: 1341–1357.

Ghalib, A.U.K. (1841). *Divan-e-Ghalib*, p. 72. New Delhi, India: Maktaba Jamia Ltd, 1969.

Gherovici, P. (2017). *Transgender Psychoanalysis*. New York: Routledge.

Glick, S.N., Morris, M., Foxman, B., Aral, S.O., Manhart, L.E., Holmes, K.K., and Golden, M. (2012). A comparison of sexual behavior patterns among men who have sex with men and heterosexual men and women. *Journal of Acquired Immune Deficiency Syndromes* 60: 83–90.

Goldberg, A. (1995). *The Problem of Perversion: The View from Self Psychology*. New Haven, CT: Yale University Press.

Goldberg, A. (2008). Personal communication.

Goldsmith, S. (1995). Oedipus or Orestes? Aspects of gender identity in homosexual men. *Psychoanalytic Inquiry* 15: 112.

Grant, M. and Mulas, A. (1997). *Eros in Pompeii: The Erotic Art Collection of the Museum of Naples*. New York: Stewart, Tabori and Chang.

Graziano, W., Jensen-Campbell, L., Todd, M., and Finch, J. (1997). Interpersonal attraction from an evolutionary psychology perspective: Women's reactions to dominant and prosocial men. In: *Evolutionary Social Psychology*, eds. A. Simpson and D.T. Kenrick, pp. 141–167. Hillsdale, NJ: Lawrence Erlbaum Associates, Inc.

Great Balls of Fire. (1957). Written by O. Blackwell and J. Hammer, recorded by Jerry Lee Lewis. Sheet music. New York: Hill and Range Songs.

Grebowicz, M. (2015). When species meat: Confronting bestiality pornography. In: *New Views on Pornography: Sexuality, Politics, and the Law*, eds. L. Comella, and S. Tarrant, pp. 217–232. Santa Barbara, CA: Praeger/ABC-CLIO.

Green, A. (1996). *On Private Madness*. London: Karnac.

Green, A. (1999). *The Work of the Negative*, transl. A. Weller. London, UK: Free Association Books.

Green, A. (2005). *Play and Reflection in Donald Winnicott's Writings: The Donald Winnicott Memorial Lecture*, given by Andre Green. London: Karnac Books.

Green, A. (2009). The construction of the lost father. In *The Dead Father: A Psychoanalytic Inquiry*, eds. L. Kalinich and S. Taylor. London: Routledge.

Green, A. (2018). The neuter gender. In: *Psychic Bisexuality: A British-French Dialogue*, ed. R. Perelberg, pp. 243–257. London: Routledge.

Greenacre, P. (1953). Certain relationship between fetishism and faulty development of the body image. *Psychoanalytic Study of the Child* 8: 79–98.

Greenberg, J.R. and Mitchell, S.A. (1983). *Object Relations in Psychoanalytic Theory*. Cambridge, MA: Harvard University Press.

Gregersen, E. (1994). *The World of Human Sexuality: Behaviors, Customs, and Beliefs.* New York: Irvington Publishers.

Gorry, A.M. (1999). Leaving home for romance: Tourist women's adventures abroad. *Unpublished doctoral dissertation,* Department of Psychology, University of California, Santa Barbara. UMI Number 9958930.

Grossman, W.I. and Kaplan, D.M. (1988). Three commentaries on gender in Freud's thought: A prologue to the psychoanalytic theory of sexuality. In: *Fantasy, Myth, and Reality: Essays in Honor of Jacob A. Arlow, M.D,* eds. H.P. Blum, Y. Kramer, A.K. Richards, and A.D. Richards, pp. 339–370. Madison, CT: International Universities Press.

Grotjahn, M. (1951). Historical notes: A letter from Freud. *International Journal of Psycho-Analysis* 32: 331.

Guntrip, H. (1975). My experience of analysis with Fairbairn and Winnicott. *International Review of Psychoanalysis* 2: 145–156.

Hansbury, G. (2017). The masculine vaginal. *Journal of the American Psychoanalytic Association* 65: 1009–1031.

Harlow, H.E. (1958). The nature of love. *American Psychologist* 13: 673–685.

Harlow, H.E. (1971). *Learning to Love.* San Francisco, CA: Albion.

Harris, A. (2000). Gender as a soft assembly: Tomboys' stories. *Studies in Gender & Sexuality* 1: 223–250.

Harris, A. (2005). *Gender as a Soft Assembly.* Hillsdale, NJ: Analytic Press.

Harris, A. (2008). "Fathers' and 'daughters.' *Psychoanalytic Inquiry* 28: 39–59.

Harris, A. (2010). Dread is just memory in the future tense. In: *First Do No Harm: The Paradoxical Encounters of Psychoanalysis, Warmaking, and Resistance,* eds. A. Harris and S. Botticelli, pp. 349–358. New York: Routledge.

Harris, A. and Botticelli, S. (2010). eds. *First Do No Harm: The Paradoxical Encounters of Psychoanalysis, Warmaking, and Resistance.* New York: Routledge.

Hartmann, H. (1939). *Ego Psychology and the Problem of Adaptation,* transl. D. Rapaport. New York: International Universities Press, 1958.

Hartmann, H., Kris, E., and Loewenstein, R.M. (1949). Notes on the theory of aggression. *Psychoanalytic Study of the Child* 3: 9–36.

Haslam, N. and Rothschild, L. (1998). Pleasure. In: *Encyclopedia of Human Emotions, Vol 2,* eds. D. Levinson, J. Ponzetti and P. Jorgenson, pp. 515–523. New York: Macmillan.

Herdt, G. (ed.) (1994). *Third Sex, Third Gender: Beyond Diamorphism in Culture and History.* New York: Zone Books.

Hirsch, I. (1994). Countertransference love and theoretical model. *Psychoanalytic Dialogues* 4: 171–192.

Hirsch, I. (2008). *Coasting in the Countertransference: Conflicts of Self-Interest Between Analyst and Patient.* New York: Routledge.

Hirschfeld, M. (2000). *The Homosexuality of Men and Women,* transl. M. Lombardi-Nash. Amherst, NY: Prometheus Books.

Hirschfeld, M. (2017). *Berlin's Third Sex,* transl. J.L. Conway. Berlin, Germany: Rixdorf Editions.

Hoffer, A. (1985). Towards a definition of psychoanalytic neutrality. *Journal of the American Psychoanalytic Association* 33: 771–795.

Hoffer, A. (1996). Asymmetry and mutuality in the analytic relationship: Contemporary lessons from the Freud-Ferenczi dialogue. In: *Ferenczi's Turn in Psychoanalysis,* eds. P.L. Rudnytsky, A. Bokay, and P. Giampieri-Deutsch, pp. 107–119. New York: New York University Press.

Hoffman, I.Z. (1998). Poetic transformations of erotic experience: Commentary on paper by Jody Messler Davies. *Psychoanalytic Dialogues* 8: 791–804.

Hoffman, I.Z. (2009). Therapeutic passion in the countertransference. *Psychoanalytic Dialogues* 19: 617–637.

Hoffman, I.Z. (2013). Therapeutic passion in the countertransference. Discussion on IARPP list-serve, May.

Holvoet, L., Huys, W., Coppens, V., Seeuws, J., Goethals, K., and Morrens, M. (2017). Fifty shades of Belgian Gray: The prevalence of BDSM-related fantasies and activities in the general population. *Journal of Sexual Medicine* 14: 1152–1159.

Hooks, B. (2004). Understanding patriarchy. In: *The Will to Change: Men, Masculinity, and Love*, pp. 17–34. New York: Washington Square Press.

Horney, K. (1967). *Feminine Psychology*. New York: W.W. Norton.

Hull, J.W. and Lane, R.C. (1996). Repetitive dreams and the central masturbation fantasy. *Psychoanalytic Review* 83: 673–684.

ISAPS 2017 International Study Cosmetic Procedures.pdf. Retrieved from: www.isaps.org/wp-content/uploads/2018/, accessed December 23, 2018.

Isay, R. (1989). *Homosexual Men and Their Development*. New York: Farrar, Straus, and Giroux.

James, E.L. (2011). *Fifty Shades of Grey*. New York: Vintage Books/Random House.

Jensen-Campbell, L., Graziano, W., and West, S. (1995). Dominance, prosocial orientation, and female preference: Do nice guys really finish last. *Journal of Personality and Social Psychology* 68: 427–440.

Joannadis, P. (2004). *Sex in Cyber Space: From Sputnik to Eatmypussy.com*. Waldport, OR: Goofy Foot Press.

Jones, E. (1936). Review of the 'Dictionary of Psychology' by H.C. Warren. *International Journal of Psychoanalysis* 17: 247–248.

Jong, E. (1973). *Fear of Flying*. New York: Holt, Rhineheart, and Winston.

Joseph, P.N., Sharma, R., Agarwal, A., and Sirot, L. (2015). Men ejaculate larger volumes of semen, more motile sperm and more quickly when exposed to images of novel women. *Evolutionary Psychological Science* 1: 195–200.

Jozifkova, E. and Kolackova, M. (2017). Sexual arousal by dominance and submission in relation to increased reproductive success in the general population. *Neuroendocrinology Letter* 38: 381–387.

Julian, K. (2018). Why are young people having so little sex? *The Atlantic*, Retrieved December 23, 2018, from www.theatlantic.com/magazine/.

Kamal, M. and Newman, W.J. (2016). Revenge pornography: Mental health implications and related legislation. *Journal of the American Academy of Psychiatry and the Law* 44: 359–367.

Karlan, S., Feder, J.L., and Rial, M. (2017). Here are the world's most popular dating apps for gay dudes. Retrieved from: www.buzzfeed.com/skarlan/here-are-the-worlds-most-popular-hook-up-apps-for-gay-dudes, accessed November 1, 2018.

Kaufmann, W. (ed.) (1967). Editor's introduction to "Ecce Homo". In: *Ecce Homo*, ed. F. Nietzsche, pp. vii–xvii. New York: Vintage Books.

Kenny, E. and Nichols, E. (2017). *Beauty Around the World: A Cultural Encyclopedia*. Santa Barbara, CA: ABC-CLIO, LLC.

Kernberg, O. (1980). *Internal World and External Reality: Object Relations Theory Applied*. New York, NY: Jason Aronson.

Kernberg, O. (1991). Sadomasochism, sexual excitement, and perversion. *Journal of the American Psychoanalytic Association* 39: 333–362.

Kernberg, O. (1994). Love in the analytic setting. *Journal of the American Psychoanalytic Association* 42: 1137–1157.

Khan, M.M. (1972). Dread of surrender to resourceless dependence in the analytic situation. *International Journal of Psycho-Analysis* 53: 225–230.

Khan, M.M. (1983). *Hidden Selves: Between Theory and Practice in Psychoanalysis*. New York: International University Press.

Kieffer, C. (2014). *Mutuality, Recognition, and the Self: Psychoanalytic Reflections*. London: Karnac Books.

Kiersky, S. (1996). Exiled desire: The problem of reality in psychoanalysis and lesbian experience. *Psychoanalysis & Psychotherapy* 13: 130–141.

Kinsey, A.C. and Institute for Sex Research. (1953). *Sexual Behavior in the Human Female*. Philadelphia, PA: Saunders.

Kinsey, A.C., Pomeroy, W.B., and Martin, C.E. (1948). *Sexual Behavior in the Human Male*. Philadelphia, PA: Saunders.

Klein, M. (1925). A contribution to the psychogenesis of tics. In: *Love, Guilt and Reparation: And Other Works 1921–1945*, eds. M. Klein and J. Riviere, pp. 106–127. New York: The Free Press, 1975.

Klein, M. (1958). On the development of mental functioning. In: *Envy and Gratitude and Other Works – 1946–1963*, ed. M. Klein, pp. 236–246. New York: Free Press, 1975.

Knafo, D. and Lo Bosco, R. (2017). *The Age of Perversion: Desire and Technology in Psychoanalysis and Culture*. New York: Routledge.

Knightley, P. and Kennedy, C. (1987). *An Affair of State: Profumo Case and the Framing of Stephen Ward*. London: Jonathan Cape Ltd.

Knoblauch, S.H. (1995). To speak or not to speak? How and when is that the question?: Commentary on Papers by Davies and Gabbard. *Psychoanalytic Dialogues* 5: 151–155.

Kohon, G. (2018). Bye-bye, sexuality. In: *Psychic Bisexuality: A British-French Dialogue*, ed. R. Perelberg, pp. 258–276. London: Routledge.

Kohut, H. (1977). *Restoration of the Self*. Madison, CT: International Universities Press.

Kohut, H. (1996). *The Chicago Institute Lectures*, eds. P. Tolpin and M. Tolpin. Hillsdale, NJ: Analytic Press.

Koukounas, E. and Over, R. (1993). Habituation and dishabituation of male sexual arousal, *Behavioral Research and Therapy* 31: 575–585.

Kris, E. (1954). Introduction: Wilhelm Fliess's scientific interests. In: *The Origins of Psychoanalysis: Letters to Wilhelm Fliess, Drafts and Notes, 1887–1902*, eds. A. Freud and M. Bonaparte. New York: Basic Books.

Kristeva, J. (1982). *The Powers of Horror: An Essay on Abjection*. New York: Columbia University Press, 1982.

Kristeva, J. (2014). Reliance or maternal eroticism. *Journal of the American Psychoanalytic Association* 62: 87–100.

Kuchuck, S. (2013). Please (don't) want me: The therapeutic action of male sexual desire in the treatment of heterosexual men. *Contemporary Psychoanalysis* 48: 544–562.

Kupers, T.A. (1993). *Revisioning Men's Lives: Gender, Intimacy, and Power*. New York: Guilford Press.

Lacan, J. (1966). *Ecrits: A Selection*, transl. B. Fink. New York: W.W. Norton, 2002.

Lacan, J. (1997). *The Ethics of Psychoanalysis (1959–1960), Book VII*. New York: W.W. Norton, 1997.

Lacan, J. (2006). The mirror stage. In: *Ecrits*, transl. B. Fink. New York: W.W. Norton.

Laplanche, J. (1970). *Life and Death in Psychoanalysis*, transl. J. Mehlman. Baltimore, MD: Johns Hopkins University Press, 1976.

Laplanche, J. (1989). *New Foundations for Psychoanalysis*. Oxford: Basil Blackwell Ltd.

Laplanche, J. (1992). *La Révolution Copernicienne Inachevée*. Paris: Aubier.

Laplanche, J. (1999). *Essays on Otherness*. New York: Routledge.

Laplanche, J. and Pontalis, J.B. (1967). *The Language of Psychoanalysis*, transl. D. Nicholson-Smith. New York: W.W. Norton, 1973.

Laufer, M. (1968). The body image, the function of masturbation, and adolescence – problems of the ownership of the body. *Psychoanalytic Study of the Child* 23: 114–137.

Laufer, M. (1976). The central masturbation fantasy, the final sexual organization, and adolescence. *Psychoanalytic Study of the Child* 31: 297–316.

Laufer, M.E. (1982). Female masturbation in adolescence and the development of the relationship to the body. *International Journal of Psychoanalysis* 63: 295–302.

Lax, R.F. (1992). A variation on Freud's theme in "A child is being beaten" – mother's role: Some implications for superego development in women. *Journal of the American Psychoanalytic Association* 40: 455–473.

Layton, L. (2000). The psychopolitics of bisexuality. *Studies in Gender and Sexuality* 1: 41–60.

Layton, L. (2004a). Working nine to nine: The new women of prime time. *Studies in Gender and Sexuality* 5: 351–369.

Layton, L. (2004b). Relational no more: Defensive autonomy in middle-class women. In: *Annual of Psychoanalysis, Vol. 32: Psychoanalysis and Women*, ed. J. Winer, pp. 29–57. Hillsdale, NJ: Analytic Press.

Lemma, A. and Lynch, P. (eds.) (2015). *Sexualities: Contemporary Psychoanalytic Perspectives*. New York: Routledge.

Li, N.P., Yong, J.C., Tov, W., Sng, O., Fletcher, G.J., Valentine, K., Jiang, Y.F., and Balliet, D. (2013). Mate preferences do predict attraction and choices in the early stages of mate selection. *Journal of Personality and Social Psychology* 105: 757–776.

Lippa, J. (2006). Is high sex drive associated with increased sexual attraction to bother sexes? It depends on whether you are male or female. *Psychological Science* 17: 46–52.

Lippa, J. (2009). Sex differences in sex drive, sociosexuality, and height across 53 nations: Testing evolutionary and social structural theories. *Archives of Sexual Behavior* 38: 631–651.

Lijtmaer, R.M. (2004). The place of erotic transference and countertransference in clinical practice. *Journal American Academy Psychoanalysis* 32: 483–498.

Loewald, H.W. (1971). On motivation, and instinct theory. In: *Papers on Psychoanalysis*, ed. H.W. Loewald, pp. 102–137. New Haven, CT: Yale University Press, 1980.

Loewald, H.W. (1980). *Papers on Psychoanalysis*. New Haven, CT: Yale University Press.

Lorand, S. (1933). The psychology of nudism. *Psychoanalytic Review* 20: 197–207.

Lorde, A. (1984a). The master's tools will never dismantle the master's house. In: *Sister Outsider: Essays and Speeches*, ed. A. Lorde, pp. 110–113. Freedom, CA: Crossing Press.

Lorde, A. (1984b). Uses of the erotic: The erotic as power. In: *Sister Outsider: Essays and Speeches*, ed. A. Lorde, pp. 53–59. Freedom, CA: Crossing Press.

Mahler, M.S. (1974). Symbiosis and individuation: The psychological birth of the human infant. In: *The Selected Papers of Margaret S. Mahler, Vol. 2*. pp. 149–165. New York: Jason Aronson.

Mahony, P. (1989). Aspects of non-perverse scopophilia within an analysis. *Journal of the American Psychoanalytic Association* 37: 365–399.

Mancini, E. (2010). *Magnus Hirschfeld and the Quest for Sexual Freedom*. New York: Palgrave Macmillan.

Mann, D. (1994). The psychotherapist's erotic subjectivity. *British Journal Psychotherapy* 10: 344–354.

Maroda, K.J. (2012). *Psychodynamic Techniques: Working with Emotion in the Therapeutic Relationship.* New York: Guilford.

Masson, J. (ed.) (1985). *The Complete Letters of Sigmund Freud to Wilhelm Fliess.* Cambridge, MA: Harvard University Press.

Matchett, C. (2017, May 20). 5 creepy guy types you'll meet on Tinder. Retrieved from: www.huffingtonpost.com/2017/5/20/entry/5-creepy-guy-*types-youll-meet-on-tinder_ us*, accessed October 18, 2018.

Max, T. and Miller, G. (2016). *What Women Want.* New York: Little, Brown and Company.

McAfee, S. and Schwing, D. (2012). Borderline personality disorder: Keeping the system stable. In: *The LGBT Casebook,* eds. P. Levounic, J., Drescher, and M. Barber, pp. 205–213. Washington, DC: American Psychiatric Publishing Inc.

McLaren, A. (1979). Contraception and its discontents: Sigmund Freud and birth control. *Journal of Social History* 12: 513–529.

McLaughlin, J.T. (1991). Clinical and theoretical aspects of enactment. *Journal of the American Psychoanalytic Association* 39: 595–614.

Metzl, J.M. (2004). Voyeur nation? Changing definition of voyeurism. *Harvard Review of Psychiatry* 12: 127–131.

Mikshe, M. (2016). Grindr, Tinder, Scruff: A recipe for loneliness. Retrieved from: www.advocate.com/current-issue/2016/5/05/grindr-tinder-scruff-recipe-loneliness, accessed November 1, 2018.

Miller, L.C. and Fishkin, S. (1997). 'On the dynamics of human bonding and reproductive success: Seeking a 'windows' on the 'adapted for' human-environmental interface. In: *Evolutionary Social Psychology,* eds. J.A. Simpson and T.D. Kenrick, pp. 197–236. Hillsdale, NJ: Lawrence Erlbaum Associates, Inc.

Minarcik, J., Wetterneck, C.T., and Short, M.B. (2016). The effects of sexually explicit material use on romantic relationship dynamics. *Journal of Behavioral Addictions* 5: 700–707.

Mitchell, J. (2018). Foreword. In: *Psychic Bisexuality: A British-French Dialogue,* ed. R. Perelberg, pp. xvi–xxiii. London: Routledge.

Mitchell, J. and Rose, J. (1982). *Feminine Sexuality: Jacques Lacan and the école freudienne.* New York: W.W. Norton.

Mitchell, S.A. (1978). Psychodynamics, homosexuality, and the question of pathology. *Psychiatry* 41: 254–263.

Mitchell, S.A. (1988). *Relational Concepts in Psychoanalysis: An Integration.* Cambridge, MA: Harvard University Press.

Modell, A. (1991). Resistance to the exposure of the private self. *Contemporary Psychoanalysis* 27: 731–736.

Moore, B. and Fine, B. (eds.) (1990). *Psychoanalytic Terms and Concepts.* New Haven, CT: Yale University Press.

Morgan, E.M. (2011). Associations between young adults' use of sexually explicit materials and their sexual preferences, behaviors and satisfaction, *Journal of Sex Research* 48: 520–530.

Moss, D. (2010). War stories. In: *First Do No Harm: The Paradoxical Encounters of Psychoanalysis, Warmaking, and Resistance,* eds. A. Harris and S. Botticelli, pp. 243–250. New York: Routledge.

Muller, J. (1932). A contribution to the problem of libidinal development of the genital phase in girls. *International Journal of Psycho-Analysis* 13: 361–368.

Müller-Eckhard, H. (1955). Analyse eines jugendlichen Voyeurs Praxis. *Kinderpsychologie* 4: 285–289.

Narayan, A. (ed.) (2017). *The Parrots of Desire: 3,000 Years of Indian Erotica*. New Delhi, India: Aleph Book Company.

Nelson, M. (2015). *The Argonauts*. Minneapolis, MN: Graywolf Press.

Nevandomsky, J., and Ekhaguosa A. (1995). The clothing of political identity: Costume and scarification in the Benin Kingdom. *African Arts* 28(1): 62–73.

Nierenberg, H. (1950). A case of voyeurism. *Samiksa* 4: 140–166.

Novick, J. and Novick, A. (1973). Beating fantasies in children. *International Journal of Psychoanalysis* 53: 237–242.

Nuttall, J. (1968). *Bomb Culture*. London: Paladin.

Ogas, O. and Gaddman, S. (2011). *A Billion Wicked Thoughts: What the Internet Tells Us About Sexual Relationships*. New York: Dutton/Penguin Books.

Olner, M. (1988). *Cultivating Freud's Garden in France*. Northvale, NJ: Jason Aronson.

Orgel, S. (1996). Freud and the repudiation of the feminine. *Journal of the American Psychoanalytic Association* 44S: 45–67.

Ornston, D. (1985). The invention of 'cathexis' and Strachey's strategy. *International Review of Psychoanalysis* 12: 401–410.

Orwell, G. (1953). *Such, Such Were the Joys*. New York: Harcourt Brace Jovanovich.

Palace, E. and Gorzalka, B.B. (1990). The enhancing effects of anxiety on arousal in sexually dysfunctional and functional women. *Journal of Abnormal Psychology* 99: 403–411.

Paras, E. (2006). *Foucault 2.0: Beyond Power and Knowledge*. New York: Other Press.

Parsons, J., Kelly, B., Bimbu, D., DiMaria, L., Wainberg, M., and Morgenstern, J. (2008). Explanations for the origins of sexual compulsivity among gay and bisexual men. *Archives of Sexual Behavior* 37: 817–827.

Paul, R. (2016). Is the nature of psychoanalytic thinking and practice (e.g., in regard to sexuality) determined by extra-analytic, social and cultural developments?: Sexuality: Biological fact or cultural construction? The view from dual inheritance theory. *International Journal of Psychoanalysis* 97: 823–837.

Pauley, D. (2018a). The negative transitional object: Theoretical elaboration and clinical illustration. *Psychoanalytic Dialogues* 28: 131–143.

Pauley, D. (2018b). Response to discussants Lesley Caldwell and Van Dyke DeGolia. *Psychoanalytic Dialogues* 28: 157–163.

Paz, O. (1996). *The Double Flame*. New York: Harcourt Brace and Company.

Pelaccio, J. (1996). Masturbation fantasies in a prelatency girl: Early female body fantasy conflicts as a major determinant in the experience of primary femininity. *Journal of the American Psychoanalytic Association* 44S: 333–350.

Perelberg, R. (ed.) (2018). *Psychic Bisexuality: A British-French Dialogue*. London: Routledge.

Perry, S.L. (2017). Does viewing pornography reduce marital quality over time? Evidence from longitudinal data. *Archives of Sexual Behavior* 46: 549–559.

Person, E.S. (1985). The erotic transference in women and in men: Differences and consequences. *Journal of the American Academy of Psychoanalysis* 13: 159–180.

Peterson, C.A. (1991). Pornography and the primal scene: A report on the voyage to Brobdingnag. *Psychoanalytic Review* 78: 411–424.

Peterson, Z.D., Janssen, E., and Laan, E. (2010). Women's sexual responses to heterosexual and lesbian erotica: The role of stimulus intensity, affective reaction, and sexual history. *Archives of Sexual Behavior* 39: 880–897.

Philips, S. (2001). The overstimulation of everyday life: I. New aspects of male homosexuality. *Journal of the American Psychoanalytic Association* 49: 1235–1267.

Phillips, A. (1993). *On Kissing, Tickling, and Being Bored: Psychoanalytic Essays on the Unexamined Life*. Cambridge, MA: Harvard University Press.

Phillips, A. (1988). *Winnicott*. Cambridge, MA: Harvard University Press.

Pine, F. (1988). The four psychologies of psychoanalysis and their place in clinical work. *Journal of the American Psychoanalytic Association* 36: 571–596.

Plato (c 360BC) (2008). *Timaeus and Critias*. London: Penguin Classics.

Rabin, H.M. (2003). Love in the countertransference: Controversies and questions. *Psychoanalytic Psychology* 20: 677–690.

Racker, H. (1968). Transference and countertransference. *International Psycho-Analysis Library* 73: 1–196.

Reddy, G. (2005). *With Respect to Sex: Negotiating Hijra Identity in South Asia*. Chicago, IL: University of Chicago Press.

Reich, A. (1951). The discussion of 1912 on masturbation and our present-day views. *Psychoanalytic Study of the Child* 6: 80–94.

Reik, T. (1941). *Masochism in Modern Man*. New York: Farrar, Straus & Co.

Renik, O. (1993). Analytic interaction: Conceptualizing technique in the light of the analyst's irreducible subjectivity. *Psychoanalytic Quarterly* 62: 553–571.

Renik, O. (1999). Playing one's cards face up analysis: An approach to the problem of self-disclosure. *Psychoanalytic Quarterly* 68: 521–539.

Renn, P. (2013). Moments of meeting: The relational challenges of sexuality in the consulting room. *British Journal Psychotherapy* 29: 135–153.

Resch, M.N. and Alderson, K.B. (2014). Female partners of men who use pornography: Are honesty and mutual use associated with relationship satisfaction. *Journal of Sex and Marital Therapy* 40: 410–424.

Riviere, J. (1929). Womanliness as a masquerade. *International Journal of Psycho-Analysis* 10: 303–313.

Roheim, G. (1932). Psycho-analysis of primitive cultural types. *International Journal of Psycho-Analysis* 13: 1–221.

Rosen, I. (1964). *The Pathology and Treatment of Sexual Deviation*. London: Oxford University Press.

Rothschild, L. (2003). Penis. In: *Men and Masculinities: A Social, Cultural, and Historical Encyclopedia*, eds. M. Kimmel and A. Aronson. New York: ABC-Clio.

Rothschild, L. and Haslam, N. (2003). Thirsty for H2O? Multiple essences and psychological essentialism. *New Ideas in Psychology* 21: 31–41.

Roudinesco, E. (1990). *Jacques Lacan & Co.: A History of Psychoanalysis in France, 1925–1985*, transl. J. Mehlman. Chicago, IL: University of Chicago Press.

Roudinesco, E. (1997). *Jacques Lacan*, transl. B. Bray. New York: Columbia University Press.

Roudinesco, E. (2002). Homosexualities today: A challenge for psychoanalysis? Transl. M. Lieberman. *European Journal of Psychoanalysis/ Psychomedia*. www.psychomedia.it/jep/number15/roudinesco.htm.

Roudinesco, E. (2014). *Lacan: In Spite of Everything*, transl. G. Elliot. London: Verso.

Roudinesco, E. (2016). *Freud: In His Time and Ours*, transl. C. Porter. Cambridge, MA: Harvard University Press.

Roughgarden, J. (2009). *Evolution's Rainbow: Diversity, Gender, and Sexuality in Nature and People*. Berkeley, CA: University of California Press.

Rozmarin, E. (2011). The place of the radical in the cure: Reply to commentaries. *Psychoanalytic Dialogues* 21: 359–370.

Rubin, G. (1975). The traffic in women: Notes on the 'political economy' of sex. In: *Women, Class, and the Feminist Imagination*, eds. K. Hansen and I. Philipson, pp. 74–113. Philadelphia, PA: Temple University Press.

Sabbadini, A. (2000). Watching voyeurs: Michael Powell's *Peeping Tom* (1960). *International Journal of Psychoanalysis* 81: 809–813.

Sadalla, E.K., Kenrick, D.T., and Vershure, B. (1987). Dominance and heterosexual attraction, *Journal of Personality and Social Psychology* 52: 730–738.

Sadowski, M. (2013). *In a Queer Voice: Journeys of Resilience from Adolescence to Adulthood*. Philadelphia, PA: Temple University Press.

Safron, A., Klimaj, V., Sylvia, D., Rosenthal, A.M., Meng, L., Walter, M., and Bailey, J.M. (2018). Neural correlates of sexual orientation in heterosexual, bisexual, and homosexual women. *Scientific Reports* 8: 1–14.

Saketopoulou, A. (2014). Mourning the body as bedrock: Developmental considerations in treating transsexual patients analytically. *Journal of the American Psychoanalytic Association* 62: 773–806.

Saketopoulou, A. (2017). Between Freud's second and third essays on sexuality: Commentary on Hansbury. *Journal of the American Psychoanalytic Association* 65: 1033–1048.

Salmon, C. (2004). The pornography debate: What sex differences in erotica can tell about human sexuality. In: *Evolutionary Psychology, Public Policy and Personal Decisions*, eds. C. Crawford and C. Salmon, pp. 217–230. Mahwah, NJ: Lawrence Erlbaum Associates.

Salmon, C. and Symons, D. (2003). *Warrior Lovers: Erotic Fiction, Evolution and Female Sexuality*. New Haven, CT: Yale University Press.

Samuels, A. (1985). Symbolic dimensions of Eros in transference-counter transference: Some clinical uses of Jung's alchemical metaphor. *International Review of Psychoanalysis* 12: 199–214.

Sandler, J. (1976). Countertransference and role-responsiveness. *International Review of Psychoanalysis* 3: 43–47.

Sarason, S.B. (1981). An asocial psychology and a misdirected clinical psychology. *American Psychologist* 36: 827–836.

Satoshi, K. (2017). Possible evolutionary origins of human female sexual fluidity. *Biological Reviews* 92: 1251–1274.

Saul, L.J. (1962). The erotic transference. *Psychoanalytic Quarterly* 31: 54–61.

Savacool, J. (2009). *The World Has Curves: The Global Quest for the Perfect Body*. New York: Rodale.

Scarfone, D. (2012). Winnicott: Early libido and the deep sexual. *Canadian Journal of Psychoanalysis* 20: 3–16.

Schachtel, E.G. (1959). *Metamorphosis: On the Conflict of Human Development and the Psychology of Creativity*. Hillsdale, NJ: Analytic Press, 2001.

Schachtel, E.G. (1966). *Experiential Foundations of Rorschach's Test*. Hillsdale, NJ: Analytic Press, 2001.

Schafer, R. (2002). On male nonnormative sexuality and perversion in psychoanalytic discourse. *Annual of Psychoanalysis* 30: 23–35.

Schneider, J.P. (2007). A qualitative study of cybersex participants: Gender difference, recovery issues and implications for therapists. *Sexual Addiction and Compulsivity* 7: 249–278.

Schore, A.N. (2011). The right brain implicit self lies at the core of psychoanalysis. *Psychoanalytic Dialogues* 21: 75–100.

Shapiro, D. (1965). *Neurotic Styles*. New York: Basic Books.

Shapiro, D. (1981). *Autonomy and Rigid Character*. New York: Basic Books.

Shapiro, T. (2008). Masturbation, sexuality, and adaptation: Normalization in adolescence. *Journal of the American Psychoanalytic Association* 56: 123–146.

Sharpe, E.F. (1940). Psychophysical problems revealed in language: An examination of metaphor. *International Journal of Psychoanalysis* 41: 201–220.

Shaws, I. (1939). Girls in their summer dresses. *The New Yorker*. Retrieved from: https://www.newyorker.com/magazine/1939/02/04/girls-in-their-summer-dresses

Shelby, R.D. (2000). About cruising and being cruised. *Annual of Psychoanalysis* 30: 191–208.

Sherman, E. (2002). Homoerotic countertransference: The love that dare not speak its name? *Psychoanalytic Dialogues* 12: 649–666.

Silberer, H. (1914). *Problem der Mystik und ihrer Symbolik*. Leipzig: Hugo Heller.

Silver, S. (2018). After 10 years, here's why I'm over online dating. Retrieved from: www.huffingtonpost.com/2018/02/20/entry/personal-silver-online-dating_us, accessed November 8, 2018.

Singh, D. (1993). Adaptive significance of female physical attractiveness: Role of waist-to-hip ratio. *Journal of Personality and Social Psychology* 65: 293–307.

Singh, D., Dixson, B.J., Jessop, T.S., Morgan, B., and Dixson, A.F. 2010. Cross-cultural consensus for waist–hip ratio and women's attractiveness. *Evolution and Human Behavior* 31(3): 176–181.

Singh, D. and Young, R. (1995). Body weight, waist-to-hip ratio, breasts, and hips: Role in judgments of female attractiveness and desirability for relationships. *Ethology and Sociobiology* 16: 483–507.

Smith, A. and Anderson, M. (2016). 5 Facts about online dating. Retrieved from: www.pewresearch.org/fact-tank/2016/02/29/5-facts-about-online-dating, accessed November 1, 2018.

Slavin, J.H. (2013). Moments of truth and perverse scenarios in psychoanalysis: Revisiting Davies' "Love in the afternoon." *Psychoanalytic Dialogues* 23: 139–149.

Slavin, J.H., Rahmani, M., and Pollock, L. (1998). Reality and danger in psychoanalytic treatment. *Psychoanalytic Quarterly* 67: 191–217.

Smith, S. (1977). The Golden Fantasy: A regressive reaction to separation anxiety. *International Journal Psychoanalysis* 58: 311–324.

Socarides, C.W. (1968). A provisional theory of aetiology in male homosexuality – a case of preoedipal origin. *International Journal of Psychoanalysis* 49: 27–37.

Socarides, C.W. (1978). *Homosexuality*. New York: Jason Aronson.

Speilrein, S. (1923). A voyeur type. *International Journal of Psychoanalysis* 9: 201–211.

Spitz, R. (1965). *The First Year of Life*. New York: International Universities Press.

Stark, M. (2017a). Relentless hope: The refusal to grieve (International Psychotherapy Institute eBook). Retrieved from: www. FreePsychotherapyBooks.org, accessed February 19, 2019.

Stark, M. (2017b). The schizoid defense of relentless despair: A heart shattered and the private self. *Paper presented at the Fall Conference of the Rhode Island Association for Psychoanalytic Psychologies*, November 4, 2017.

Stern, D.B. (2010). *Partners in Thought: Working with Unformulated Experience, Dissociation, and Enactment*. New York: Routledge.

Stoller, R.J. (1964). A contribution to the study of gender identity. *International Journal of Psycho-Analysis* 45: 220–226.

Stoller, R.J. (1970). Pornography and perversion. *Archives of General Psychiatry* 22: 490–499.

Stoller, R.J. (1975). *The Erotic Form of Hatred*. New York: Pantheon Books.

Stoller, R.J. (1976). Sexual excitement. *Archives of General Psychiatry* 33: 899–909.

Stoller, R.J. (1979a). *Sexual Excitement: Dynamics of Erotic Life*. New York: Pantheon.

Stoller, R.J. (1979b). Centerfold: An essay on excitement. *Archives of General Psychiatry* 36: 1019–1024.

Stoller, R.J. (1985). *Presentations of Gender*. New Haven, CT: Yale University Press.

Stoller, R.J. (1987). Pornography: Daydreams to cure humiliation. In: *The Many Faces of Shame*, ed. D.L. Nathanson, pp. 292–307. New York: Guilford Press.

Strachey, J. (1963). Obituary of Joan Riviere, 1838–1962. *International Journal of Psychoanalysis* 44: 228–230.

Strager, S. (2003). What men watch when they watch pornography. *Sexuality and Culture: An Interdisciplinary Quarterly* 7: 50–61.

Survey (2017). Shocking number of gay men admit to sending dic pics on dating apps. Retrieved from: https://grabhim.net/2015/03/17/read-the-results-of-our-survey-on-gay-dating-apps, accessed November 8, 2018.

Symons, D. (1979). *The Evolution of Human Sexuality*. Oxford: Oxford University Press.

Tannahill, R. (1980). *Sex in History*. Briarcliff Manor, NY: Stein and Day.

Target, M. (2015). A developmental model of sexual excitement, desire and alienation. In: *Sexualities: Contemporary Psychoanalytic Perspectives*, eds. A. Lemma and P. Lynch, pp. 43–62. London: Routledge.

Tausk, V. (1912). On masturbation. *Psychoanalytic Study of the Child* 6: 61–79, transl. W.G. Niederland, 1951.

Thornhill, R. and Gangestad, S. (1994). Human fluctuating asymmetry and sexual behavior. *Psychological Science* 5: 297–302.

Thurber, J. and White, E.B. (1929). *Is Sex Necessary? Or Why You Feel the Way You Do*. New York: Harper Perennial, 2004.

Tolpin, M. (1997). The development of sexuality and the self. *Annual of Psychoanalysis* 25: 173–188.

Tolpin, M. (2000). Personal communication.

Trilling, L. (1950). The Kinsey report. In: *Lionel Trilling, The Liberal Imagination: Essays on Literature and Society*, ed. L. Trilling, pp. 223–242. New York: New York Review of Books Classics, 2008.

Trivers, R. (1971). The evolution of reciprocal altruism. *The Quarterly Review of Biology* 46: 35–57.

Trivers, R. (1972). Parental investment and sexual selection. In: *Sexual Selection and the Descent of Man, 1871–1971*, ed. B. Campbell, pp. 136–179. Chicago, IL: Aldine Press.

Tylim, I. (2011). Dining with Anna Freud. *Buenos Aires Herald*. Retrieved from: www.buenosairesherald.com/articles, accessed February 11, 2019.

Tyson, G., Perta, V.C., Haddadi, H., and Seto, M.D. (2016). A first look at user activity on Tinder. Retrieved from www.researchgate.net/publication/305007166, accessed February 15, 2019.

Ulrichs, K. (1864). *The Riddle of "Man-Manly" Love*, transl. M. Lombardi-Nash. Buffalo, NY: Prometheus Books, 1994.

Van der Kolk, B. (2014). *The Body Keeps the Score*. New York: Viking Press.

Van Haute, P. and Westerink, H. (2016). Sexuality and its object in Freud's 1905 edition of "Three Essays on the Theory of Sexuality". *International Journal of Psychoanalysis* 97: 563–589.

Vannier, S.A., Currie, A.B., and O'Sullivan, L.F. (2014). Schoolgirls and soccer moms: A content analysis of free 'teen' and 'MILF' online pornography. *Journal of Sex Research* 51: 253–264.

Vilarinho, S., Laja, P., Carvalho, J., Quinta-Gomes, A.L., Oliveira, C., Janssen, E., and Norbe, P.J. (2014). Affective and cognitive determinants of women's sexual response to erotica. *The Journal of Sexual Medicine* 11(11): 2671–2678.

Volkan, V. (1976). *Primitive Internalized Object Relations*. New York: International Universities Press.

Volkan, V. (1987). *Six Steps in the Treatment of Borderline Personality Organization*. Northvale, NJ: Jason Aronson.

Voracek, M. and Fisher, M.L. (2002). Shapely centrefolds? Temporal change in body measures: Trend analysis. *BMJ* 325: 21–28.

Voracek, M. and Fisher, M.L. (2006). Success is all in the measures: Androgenousness, curvaceousness, and starring frequencies in adult media actresses. *Archives of Sexual Behavior* 35: 297–304.

Vuong, O. (2016). *Night Sky with Exit Wounds*. Port Townsend, WA: Copper Canyon Press.

Waddell, M. (2006). Infant observation in Britain: The Tavistock approach. *International Journal of Psychoanalysis* 87: 1103–1120.

Waelder, R. (1936). The principle of multiple function: Observations on multiple determination. *Psychoanalytic Quarterly* 41: 283–290.

Walter, C. (2013). *Last Ape Standing: The Seven-Million-Year Story of How and Why We Survived*. New York: Walker and Company.

Ward, D. (2014). A Kentucky of mothers. *PEN America*. Retrieved from: https://pen.org/a-kentucky-of-mothers, accessed January 19, 2019.

Weissman, P. (1960). Psychopathological characters in current drama: A study of a trio of heroines. *American Imago* 17: 271–288.

Wells, H. (2013). Client's perspectives on therapist's self-disclosure. *Unpublished doctoral dissertation*, Massachusetts School for Professional Psychology (MSPP), Newton, MA.

What Men Think is Attractive in Different Parts of the World. (2019). Retrieved January 3, 2019, from The List: www.thelist.com/.

Wheeler Vega, J.A. (2001). Naturalism and feminism: Conflicting explanations of rape in a wider context. *Psychology, Evolution, and Gender* 3: 47–85.

Wiegman, R. and Wilson, E.A. (2015). Introduction: Antinormativity's queer conventions. *Differences: A Journal of Feminist Cultural Studies* 26: 1–25.

Wikipedia. Buck Angel. Retrieved from: https://en.wikipedia.org/wiki/Buck_Angel, accessed November 20, 2018.

Willard, C. (1934). Internationale Zeitschrift fiir Psychoanalyse. *Psychoanalytic Review* 21: 208–220.

Williams, M.H. (2010). *Bion's Dream: A Reading of the Autobiographies*. London: Karnac Books.

Willick, M. (1988). Dynamics of homosexual cruising. In: *Fantasy, Myth and Reality: Essays in Honor of Jacob A. Arlow, M.D.*, ed. H.P. Blum, pp. 441–449. Madison, CT: International Universities Press.

Willoughby, B.C., Carroll, J.S., Busby, D.M., and Brown, C.C. (2016). Differences in pornography use among couples: Associations with satisfaction, stability, and relationship process. *Archives of Sexual Behavior* 45: 145–158.

Winnicott, D.W. (1947). Hate in the countertransference. In: *Through Paediatrics to Psychoanalysis: Collected Papers*, pp. 194–203. New York: Brunner/Mazel, 1992.

Winnicott, D.W. (1953). Transitional objects and transitional phenomena. *International Journal of Psycho-Analysis* 34: 89–97.

Winnicott, D.W. (1956). Primary maternal preoccupation. In: *Collected Papers*: *Through Paediatrics to Psychoanalysis*, ed. D.W. Winnicott, pp. 300–305. New York: Basic Books, 1958.

Winnicott, D.W. (1961). Letter to Masud Khan, 26 June 1961. In: *The Spontaneous Gesture: Selected Letters of D.W. Winnicott*, ed. F.R. Rodman, p. 132. Cambridge, MA: Harvard University Press, 1987.

Winnicott, D.W. (1963). Communicating and not communicating leading to a study of certain opposites. In: *The Maturational Processes and the Facilitating Environment*, pp. 179–192. New York: International Universities Press, 1965.

Winnicott, D.W. (1971). *Playing and Reality*. London: Routledge.

Wong, K. (2018). I give up on trying to explain why the fetishization of Asian women is bad. Retrieved from: www.huffingtonpost.com/2018/02/05/entry/i-give-up-on-trying-to-explain-*why-the-fetishization-of-asian-women-is-bad*, accessed November 8, 2018.

Wright, K. (1991). *Vision and Separation*. Northvale, NJ: Jason Aronson.

Yates, C. (2015). *The Play of Political Culture, Emotion and Identity*. London: Palgrave Macmillan.

Young-Breuhl, E. (1998). *Anna Freud: A Biography*. New York: Summit Books.

Young-Breuhl, E. (2001). Are human beings 'by nature' bisexual? *Studies in Gender and Sexuality 2*: 179–213.

Young-Breuhl, E. (2008). *Anna Freud: A Biography by Elisabeth Young-Bruehl*. Second Edition. New Haven and London: Yale University Press.

Zeal, P. (2008). Staying close to the subject. In: *Object Relations and Social Relations: The Implications of the Relational Turn in Psychoanalysis*, eds. S. Clarke, H. Hahn, and P. Hoggett, pp. 45–64. London: Karnac Books.

Zeavin, L. (2011). Imagining the she/male: Pornography and the transsexualization of the heterosexual male: Psychoanalytic reflections. *Studies in Gender and Sexuality* 12: 282–287.

Zhou, Y. and Paul, B. (2016). Lotus blossom or dragon lady: A content analysis of 'Asian Women' online pornography. *Sexuality and Culture: An Interdisciplinary Quarterly* 20: 1083–1100.

Index

Note: Page numbers in *italic* indicate a figure on the corresponding page.